023

Happy Birthday
Love

D1644128

LAWYERLY LIBATIONS

LAWYERLY LIBATIONS, CONCOCTIONS FOR THE COUNSELOR, APÉRITIFS FOR THE ATTORNEY, ELIXIRS FOR THE ESQUIRE, AND ADDITIONAL ALCOHOLIC ANECDOTES:

A COCKTAIL COMPILATION FOR THE BURGEONING BARRISTER'S BAR

MICHAEL J. MCCORMICK

Lawyerly Libations, Concoctions for the Counselor,
Apéritifs for the Attorney, Elixirs for the Esquire,
and Additional Alcoholic Anecdotes:
A Cocktail Compilation for the Burgeoning Barrister's Bar

Copyright © 2022 Michael J. McCormick
Published in Houston, Texas
lawyerlylibations@gmail.com

This publication is not a substitute for the advice of an attorney.
If you require legal or other expert advice, you should seek the
services of a competent attorney or other professional.

Hardcover ISBN: 978-1-7376047-0-9
Paperback ISBN: 978-1-7376047-1-6

Library of Congress Control Number: 2021914379

Cover Design by Morgane Leoni

Pour one out for all the law students meticulously
verifying citations and editing law review articles.

Hey Ya!
Words and Music by Andre Benjamin
Copyright © 2003 BMG Monarch and Gnat Booty Music
All Rights Administered by BMG Rights Management (US) LLC.
All Rights Reserved. Used by Permission.
Reprinted by Permission of Hal Leonard LLC.

Bali Ha'i
from SOUTH PACIFIC
Lyrics by Oscar Hammerstein II
Music by Richard Rogers
Copyright © 1949 by Williamson Music Company
c/o Concord Music Publishing
Copyright Renewed.
International Copyright Secured. All Rights Reserved.
Reprinted by Permission of Hal Leonard LLC.

FOR CAROLYN—THE GREATEST BIBLIOPHILE,
ATTORNEY, WIFE, AND PARTNER I COULD
EVER ASK FOR IN LIFE

Hablot K. "Phiz" Browne, *Legal Functionaries* (etching)
in CHARLES J. LEVER, NUTS AND NUTCRACKERS pl. 3
(London, Bradbury & Evans 1845).

Disclaimer

This book is for entertainment purposes only and does not constitute, or purport to provide, legal advice or guidance of any kind. Many of the court cases and laws discussed herein are either superseded, outdated, or pertain to jurisdictions that may differ from your own. If you require legal advice, you should retain the services of an attorney—especially if you consider reading *this* book to be a fair substitute for receiving such guidance.

Please drink responsibly and never drink and drive.

A Note About the Illustrations

Many of the humorous illustrations in this book are by the Victorian illustrator Hablot Knight "Phiz" Browne (1815–1882). Phiz is probably best known for illustrating books for Charles Dickens, but he also did work for William Harrison Ainsworth and Charles James Lever. He adopted the pseudonym "Phiz" because it paired well with Dickens's early pen name, "Boz."

Rather than referencing a page number, Phiz's larger etchings are cited sequentially based on the order in which they appeared in a book. This is because large illustrations were customarily printed on a heavier, unnumbered paper called a plate (abbreviated "pl.") that was then sewn into the signatures of the book—sometimes in the wrong order. Small illustrations, on the other hand, were frequently placed on a numbered page and are cited accordingly.

Most of the remaining illustrations come from a long-running periodical called *Harper's Weekly* (1857–1916). While best characterized as a political journal, it also served as a pictorial of current events. At one time, it was the most widely read publication in the United States.

Preface

One of the fun parts of being an attorney is having occasion to stumble upon court cases and laws that almost seem unbelievable by today's standards. As I have always enjoyed history and a well-made cocktail, combining some of that interesting law, history, and the recipes for my favorite cocktails seemed like too much fun *not* to do.

I once had the honor of serving as the Chief Articles Editor (Editorial Board No. 55) of the *Houston Law Review*, and the folly that follows is written in the style of a very unusual law review article. Old habits die hard, but I have mostly dispensed with the rigid issue, rule, application/analysis, and conclusion ("IRAC") structure. In any case, I encourage you to read the footnotes at your leisure. After all, sometimes half of the fun is contained in the sidebars of a conversation.

As a field, cocktail history is notoriously imprecise. The story of how a particular cocktail came to be often ends up consisting of *several*—or sometimes zero—plausible histories. This can make any armchair historian uncomfortable. However, judges, attorneys, and potential jurors alike should feel right at home when tasked with reconciling such factual inconsistencies.

Each chapter begins with the history of its namesake cocktail and a recipe for the tipple. I do not profess these recipes represent the best variant of their respective cocktails, but these are the libations I enjoy sharing with my family and friends. Feel free to take a red pen to each formulation to make modifications as you please.

Then, the real fun begins: Following the recipe, each cocktail, or an ingredient thereof, is lovingly paired with a law-related story. Admittedly, some of the highlighted legal points are only tangentially (even tenuously) related to the cocktail they are paired with, but I hope you will forgive any awkward segues in favor of the entertainment value the anecdotes provide.

Finally, there are a few things I will point out for readers who are obsessed with details. First, die-hard fans of appellate briefing will notice the font used in this book is within the Century family (Century Schoolbook, to be precise). If that rings any bells, it is probably because the Supreme Court of the United States requires all documents filed with the Court to use a Century font.[1] Second, you had better believe the artisanal, fair trade, and bespoke citations contained herein were hand crafted using *The Bluebook*.[2] Finally, from the preceding sentence, this sentence, and throughout this entire book, you will notice I am a proponent of the Oxford comma.

"May neither precedent nor antiquity be
a sanction to errors pernicious to mankind."[3]

Michael J. McCormick
July 4, 2022

---

1. SUP. CT. R. 33.1(b). Century Schoolbook was mainly selected because I favor serif typefaces, but this is an interesting bit of trivia nevertheless.

2. THE BLUEBOOK: A UNIFORM SYSTEM OF CITATION (Columbia L. Rev. Ass'n et al. eds., 21st ed. 2020). International citations and other conventions I favor were also adapted from the 19th edition of the Bluebook and my own opinions.

3. THE UNIVERSAL TOAST MASTER, OR, TREASURY OF SENTIMENT; COMPRISING A COLLECTION OF UPWARDS OF TWO THOUSAND TOASTS AND SENTIMENTS 9 (London, J. Limbird ed., 1840).

Table of Contents

§1

The Corpse Reviver No. 2 and . . . Zombies

An entire class of cocktails known as "Corpse Revivers" originated as hangover cures during the second half of the 19th century.[4] The treatment was premised on consuming some of the "hair of the dog that bit you," but a Corpse Reviver was some elegant medicine for the time nonetheless. In fact, cocktail historian David Wondrich posits that much of the advancement of the cocktail as a medium of culinary expression was "intimately connected to the search for a better hangover cure" in a time before the advent of aspirin and ibuprofen.[5] Necessity is truly the mother of invention!

Evidently, in the late 19th century Europeans thought of Corpse Revivers as a stereotypical American cocktail, but most American bartenders had never heard of such a libation before 1900. The likely culprit for this misconception appears to have been an American-themed bar (not an uncommon novelty at the time) located in

---

4. DAVID WONDRICH, IMBIBE! UPDATED AND REVISED EDITION: FROM ABSINTHE COCKTAIL TO WHISKEY SMASH, A SALUTE IN STORIES AND DRINKS TO "PROFESSOR" JERRY THOMAS, PIONEER OF THE AMERICAN BAR 311–12 (Perigee Books 2015).
5. *Id.* at 311.

Piccadilly, London, during the late 1850s that popularized the cocktail.[6] Still, Americans eventually welcomed Corpse Revivers to their country with open arms (once someone was kind enough to acquaint them with the decidedly European innovation).

Bartender Harry Craddock included a note with his recipe for the Corpse Reviver No. 2 in *The Savoy Cocktail Book* (1930), warning that "[f]our of these taken in swift succession will unrevive the corpse again."[7] Try one—you will see why. This cocktail packs a real punch yet remains remarkably smooth—so long as you incorporate the ingredients in equal measures. If you would like to experiment with this recipe, try varying the brand of each ingredient rather than its relative proportion.[8]

Aside from sounding really, really cool, the "No. 2" in the cocktail's name indicates it is the gin variant of the drink; the "No. 1" is its brandy-based cousin. Both are worth trying but, in my opinion, the No. 2 is in a league of its own.

---

6.   THE OXFORD COMPANION TO SPIRITS AND COCKTAILS 199–200 (David Wondrich et al. eds., Oxford Univ. Press 2021) [hereinafter OXFORD COMPANION].

7.   HARRY CRADDOCK, THE SAVOY COCKTAIL BOOK 52 (Richard R. Smith 1930). As an aside, this book is beautifully designed and is full of Art Deco motifs (and cocktails). If you enjoy an old book, I encourage you to track down an original copy . . . to borrow. Originals in good condition sell for thousands of dollars. *See* Richard Davies, *The Coolest Book in the World*, ABE BOOKS (July 28, 2021), https://lexspirit.link/JNPW.

8.   *See* Robert Simonson, *In Search of the Ultimate Corpse Reviver No. 2*, PUNCH (Jan. 17, 2019), https://lexspirit.link/VLSG.

Corpse Reviver No. 2[9]

1. Combine the following ingredients in a cocktail shaker with ice:
   a. 1 oz. gin
   b. 1 oz. *fresh-squeezed*[10] lemon juice
   c. 1 oz. Cointreau® Orange Liqueur
   d. 1 oz. Lillet® Blanc Apéritif[11]
2. Cap the cocktail shaker and shake vigorously for 20–30 seconds.[12]
3. Rinse a coupe glass with about 1/8 oz. of absinthe and then discard any remainder.[13]
4. Double strain[14] the contents of the shaker into the coupe glass and serve "up"[15] with a lemon peel twist for garnish.
5. Imbibe![16]

---

9. CRADDOCK, *supra* note 7, at 52.
10. One of the easiest ways to improve any cocktail is to use freshly squeezed juice. Citrus juices oxidize fairly quickly and are best used within 12 hours of juicing.
11. Lillet Blanc is a French fortified white wine *apéritif* (like an appetizer, but a drink). OXFORD COMPANION, *supra* note 6, at 26.
12. For a master class on shaking, see OUTKAST, *Hey Ya!*, on SPEAKERBOXXX/THE LOVE BELOW, at 2:43–3:04 (LaFace Records 2003) ("Lend me some sugar, I am your neighbor! Ah! Here we go now, shake it, shake it, shake it, shake it, shake it, shake it, shake it, shake it, shake it, shake it like a Polaroid picture!"). In all seriousness, shake vigorously because melted ice cubes are an intentional ingredient of many cocktails—including this one.
13. This is optional but serves as a liquid aromatic garnish.
14. This involves using both a Hawthorne strainer and a fine sieve to "double strain" the fine bits of ice and pulp out of the mixture prior to serving.
15. Serving something "up" means to serve it chilled in a coupe glass without any ice.
16. A hospitable command to drink. *Imbibe*, MERRIAM-WEBSTER'S COLLEGIATE DICTIONARY 620 (11th ed. 2003).

Zombies

It is difficult to avoid associating a cocktail called the "Corpse Reviver" with something that goes bump in the night—namely, zombies. The term "zombie" has West African roots, as that is the origin of the enslaved people the French brought to Saint-Domingue (modern-day Haiti) during the 17th and 18th centuries.[17] Haitian slaves routinely endured torture, and slave owners worked them to death on tobacco and sugar plantations.[18] The heartbreaking and macabre truth of the matter is suicide was not an uncommon response to those conditions. As a result, slave owners and overseers either hijacked existing West African folklore, or propagated a new myth, that an enslaved person who took their own life would not go to a heavenly place. Instead, they would become a zombie doomed to eternally work in their owner's fields.[19] A fate worse than death.

After the Haitian Revolution (1791–1804) brought about the abolition of slavery and the end of French colonial rule, the concept of a zombie was incorporated into the lore of Haitian *Vodou*/Voodoo, where it came to refer to reanimated corpses under the control of a powerful sorcerer called a *bokor*.[20] In Vodou, anyone who dies an unnatural death, whether by suicide or sorcery, can be

---

17. Amy Wilentz, *A Zombie Is a Slave Forever*, N.Y. TIMES (Oct. 30, 2012), https://lexspirit.link/CMO8.
18. WADE DAVIS, PASSAGE OF DARKNESS: THE ETHNOBIOLOGY OF THE HAITIAN ZOMBIE 17, 215 (Univ. N.C. Press 1988). Conditions were so wretched for enslaved persons that the *annual* mortality rate has been estimated to be 8%. *Id.* at 25. While keeping workers healthy would seem to be in a slave owner's best interest, importing replacement labor was apparently so cheap the extraordinary cruelty taking place was considered economical. *Id.*
19. *Id.* at 3, 216.
20. *Id.* at 18, 213.

claimed by a bokor as a zombie: an empty vessel devoid of free will.

Zombification is said to occur under the combined influence of a bokor's magic and the effects of a potion. Crucially, Haitians are more afraid of *becoming* a zombie (i.e., losing their free will) than being harmed by an unruly horde of the undead.[21] This explains why for 150 years the Haitian Penal Code prohibited the use of poison (thought to consist of tetrodotoxin extracted from a pufferfish) that, while not killing a victim, "will cause a more-or-less prolonged state of lethargy" (i.e., appearing to be dead, despite technically being alive).[22] Making "zombification by poisoning" a crime seems a bit superfluous in retrospect because poisoning someone was already a crime under Haitian law, but they clearly had strong feelings on this point.

What popular culture now regards as a zombie—a flesh eating, necrotic corpse wearing tattered clothing that wanders about aimlessly in a trance-like state—is loosely based on (and some would say is a whitewashed version of)

---

21. *Id.* at 8–9.

22. This provision appears to have been enacted in 1864 and was only recently eliminated with the 2020 overhaul of the Haitian Penal Code.

> Est aussi qualifié attentat à la vie d'une personne, par empoisonnement, l'emploi qui sera fait contre elle de substances *qui sans donner la mort, auront produit un état léthargique plus ou moins prolongé*, de quelque manière que ces substances aient été employées et quelles qu'en aient été les suites.

CODE PÉNAL HAÏTIEN art. 246 (1883) (emphasis added); *Id.* art. 246 (2011); Anne Guha, *Does the Haitian Criminal Code Outlaw Making Zombies?*, LIBR. CONG.: IN CUSTODIA LEGIS (Oct. 31, 2014), https://lexspirit.link/DLNG (exploring the history of this provision and providing a translation).

the Haitian concept of the term.[23] This popular depiction represents the culmination of decades of pulp fiction, horror movies, and a certain music video featuring Michael Jackson, but many of the characteristics embodied in the popular incarnation of the term are directly traceable to the "Father of the Zombie Film," George A. Romero. His *Night of the Living Dead* (1968) and *Dawn of the Dead* (1978) are widely viewed as having laid the foundation for today's popular perception of zombies.[24] However, while brain-hungry, reanimated corpses are now a permanent fixture of our collective nightmares, perhaps the circumstances surrounding the etymology of the term "zombie" are more horrific than the modern fiction associated with the word.

Given that they are a creature of fiction, encountering the walking dead might seem to be an unlikely scenario, but—just in case—the Centers for Disease Control and Prevention (the "CDC"), a forward-thinking United States governmental agency, published some official guidance on zombie apocalypse preparedness in 2011.[25] While the information was not immediately useful, the public's attention was captured by the subject matter. As a result of the CDC website's newfound popularity, the agency's

---

23.   DAVIS, *supra* note 18, at 56.
24.   *See* Mike Mariani, *The Tragic, Forgotten History of Zombies*, THE ATLANTIC (Oct. 28, 2015), https://lexspirit.link/YZPB; *see also* NIGHT OF THE LIVING DEAD (Image Ten 1968); DAWN OF THE DEAD (Laurel Group 1978). The word "ghoul" was used to refer to the flesh-devouring monsters in the 1968 movie's script, but Romero's 1978 follow-up to the film (and subsequent entries in the series) called the undead antagonists "zombies."
25.   Ali S. Khan, *Preparedness 101: Zombie Apocalypse*, CDC (May 16, 2011, 11:48 AM), https://lexspirit.link/EASH. This article was not written by some rogue government intern. His friends might call him "Al," but it's Rear Admiral Ali S. Khan, MD, MPH, to you and me.

servers crashed within mere hours of the article's publication.

That said, with the possible exception of the CDC, the remainder of the federal government remains woefully unprepared to handle a zombie apocalypse. Most people would imagine that scenario might entail fighting off hordes of brain-hungry zombies, but perhaps the scarier reality would be peaceful zombies seeking to coexist with the living. For instance, there is a colorable argument our legal system would not accommodate the undead because laws presumably apply *only* to the living.[26]

Fortunately, Professor Adam Chodorow of the Arizona State University Sandra Day O'Connor College of Law has selflessly taken it upon himself to explore the implications of taxing the undead. He wrote a journal article that adroitly considers *not only* the taxation of zombies, but of vampires and ghosts too![27] Chodorow makes the interesting point that, while "[o]ne does not typically think of zombies as earning income . . . zombies have been known to return to places where they used to work."[28] That observation is tagged with a footnote citing Big Law associates as being a prime example of this phenomenon, which is a pretty brutal (and not necessarily incorrect) comparison to make. And you thought tax attorneys were drab![29]

---

26. Entire fields of law, such as probate, could also become anachronistic.
27. *See generally* Adam S. Chodorow, *Death and Taxes and Zombies*, 98 IOWA L. REV. 1207 (2013).
28. *Id.* at 1219.
29. "Characterized by dullness and monotony." *Drab*, MERRIAM-WEBSTER'S COLLEGIATE DICTIONARY 377. Interestingly, the official color of the hood bestowed upon someone receiving an advanced degree in accounting is also called "drab." Why do I get the feeling this color choice was not sheer coincidence?

Notwithstanding issues involving taxation, if you have not stumbled across a zombie contingency clause while performing contract diligence, you may not have been reading closely enough. For example, while software developers utilizing Amazon Lumberyard® (the Amazon Web Services® game engine) are not permitted to use it for medical, transportation, or military applications, that restriction *does not* apply if the undead begin devastating the earth's population. As a general business practice, planning for contingencies (however remote) is an effective way to mitigate risk. Hopefully such provisions never become relevant in practice!

---

§ 42.10 Acceptable Use; Safety-Critical Systems.

Your use of the Lumberyard Materials must comply with the AWS Acceptable Use Policy. The Lumberyard Materials are not intended for use with life-critical or safety-critical systems . . . . However, this restriction will not apply in the event of the occurrence (certified by the United States Centers for Disease Control or successor body) of a *widespread viral infection transmitted via bites or contact with bodily fluids that causes human corpses to reanimate and seek to consume living human flesh, blood, brain or nerve tissue and is likely to result in the fall of organized civilization.*[30]

---

30. Amazon, AWS Service Terms § 42.10 (July 9, 2021), https://lexspirit.link/VCDH (emphasis added but reanimated, flesh-eating corpses found in original).

§ 2

A Tart Margarita and the Tequila War

In the 1870s, some bars in New York City's financial district began adding seltzer water to their Brandy and Whiskey Sours.[31] They called the resulting concoction a "Daisy." Daisies became an entire class of cocktails in their own right, but most fell out of favor after several decades. One type of Daisy, however, went on to become the stuff of legend.

In the early 20th century, Tequila[32] was not a commonly encountered spirit in the United States. But

---

31. <u>Whiskey Sour</u>: 1-½ oz. Bourbon, 1 oz. simple syrup, and ¾ oz. fresh-squeezed lemon juice. Combine those ingredients with ice in a cocktail shaker, shake well, and serve "on the rocks." Garnish with a Luxardo® Cocktail Cherry and an orange slice. Optionally, you can also add ¼ oz. of egg white to the shaker and serve "up." DALE DEGROFF, THE ESSENTIAL COCKTAIL: THE ART OF MIXING PERFECT DRINKS 138 (Clarkson Potter 2008). The Whiskey Sour was my grandmother's favorite cocktail. Her name was Hazel, and she was an extraordinary person. So extraordinary, in fact, that my wife and I named our first daughter after her.

32. THE CHAMPS, *Tequila, on* GO, CHAMPS, GO! (Challenge Records 1958) ("Tequila . . . Tequila . . . Te-quiiiii-laaaaahhh!"). If you cannot sing but find yourself cornered at a karaoke bar, this Grammy® Award winning ditty is the song for you! It only has three words. (Actually, it is one word repeated three times.) As an added bonus, it is impossible to sing a wrong note.

sometime during the 1930s, a bartender in Mexico (or maybe it was in California or Texas—it is not quite clear) concocted a Tequila Daisy. If that does not ring any bells, you might be interested to know the Spanish word for "daisy" is *margarita*.[33] The Spanish name stuck with the beverage through the years, but the seltzer water did not.

Confusingly, another distinct possibility is the Margarita started as a Tequila-based variant of the Sidecar (which, itself, is another variation on the Whiskey Sour) and never involved seltzer water at all![34] Even if there is significant uncertainty about the precise origin of the Margarita, we know exactly who created the first dedicated frozen Margarita machine: Mariano Martinez.

By the early 1970s, people had been using blenders to produce frozen Margaritas for several decades, but the bartenders at Mariano's® Mexican Cuisine in Dallas, Texas, found themselves inundated with frozen Margarita orders. To save time, the bartenders stopped diligently measuring out ingredients before pouring them into the blender, and the resulting cocktails were inconsistent—at best.[35] Martinez was not pleased.

Fortunately, a proverbial apple struck Martinez on the head when he stopped in a 7-Eleven® one day and saw customers serving themselves frozen beverages from the

---

33. WONDRICH, *supra* note 4, at 127–29. Some accounts indicate the Margarita was named for someone's customer or spouse named "Margaret," but it seems more plausible that it was named for its precursor cocktail: the Daisy. Simon Difford, *Margarita Cocktail: Origins & History*, DIFFORD'S GUIDE, https://lexspirit.link/QBG4.

34. OXFORD COMPANION, *supra* note 6, at 438–40.

Sidecar: 2 oz. Cognac, ¾ oz. Cointreau® Orange Liqueur, and ¾ oz. fresh-squeezed lemon juice. Combine those ingredients with ice in a cocktail shaker, shake well, and serve "up." DEGROFF, *supra* note 31, at 134.

35. Franz Lidz, *The Uniquely Texan Origins of the Frozen Margarita*, SMITHSONIAN MAG., July/Aug. 2018, at 22, 22–24, https://lexspirit.link/FXTZ.

Slurpee® slush machines. He realized that using a frozen drink dispenser would ensure his customers consistently received high-quality frozen Margaritas, provided he could determine how to modify the recipe to account for the fact that alcohol does not freeze.[36] When 7-Eleven flat-out refused to sell Martinez a Slurpee machine to tinker with, he was forced to improvise.

On May 11, 1971, Martinez plugged in a modified soft-serve ice cream machine and (a few hours later) took a sip of the world's first prefabricated frozen Margarita.[37] He never patented his invention (assuming it was even eligible to be patented), and he donated the original machine to the National Museum of American History in 2005.[38] The machine's retirement came after 34 years of daily use, and it was a worthy addition to the museum's collection.

The Margarita recipe that follows is unconventional, but the tart and sour flavor strikes an interesting balance with the Tequila that many people enjoy. It may seem a bit light on the Tequila,[39] but I encourage you to give it a whirl before adjusting the proportions. I would not salt the rim of the glass for this Margarita because of its inherent tartness, but it's also a free country.

---

36. *Id.* at 23–24.

37. *See id.*; *see also* Erik M. Jensen, *The Unwritten Article*, 17 NOVA L. REV. 785 (1993), https://lexspirit.link/W5A9 (falling somewhere in between eloquence and madness, this article has positively nothing to do with the text above).

38. *Press Release: National Museum of American History Acquires Frozen Margarita Machine*, NAT'L MUSEUM AM. HIST. (Sept. 27, 2005), https://lexspirit.link/MZRP. After reading the title of this press release, employees of the museum must have been crestfallen to learn the machine was not acquired for their use in the break room.

39. Admittedly, this is a fair criticism. A more traditional Margarita recipe would look something like this: 2 oz. Tequila, 1 oz. fresh-squeezed lime juice, ½ oz. agave syrup (*see* recipe *infra* p. 12), and ½ oz. Cointreau Orange Liqueur.

Tart Margarita[40]

1. Combine the following ingredients in a cocktail shaker with ice:
   a. 2 oz. fresh-squeezed lime juice
   b. 1-1/2 oz. reposado Tequila[41]
   c. 1/2 oz. Cointreau® Orange Liqueur
   d. 1/2 oz. Grand Marnier® Cordon Rouge Orange Liqueur
   e. 1/4 oz. agave syrup (recipe follows)
2. Cap the cocktail shaker and shake vigorously for 20–30 seconds.
3. Garnish an old fashioned glass with a lime wheel and add several large pieces of ice.
4. Strain the contents of the shaker into the glass and serve "on the rocks."[42]

Agave Syrup

Agave nectar[43] is a thick syrup you can find at the grocery store near the granulated sugar. But before mixing agave nectar into a cocktail, it needs to be diluted. This is easily accomplished by combining it with an equal amount of water over low heat. Stir until combined and then bottle the mixture. If refrigerated, it keeps for several weeks.

---

40. A toast to John Laue at Proof Productions for contributing this recipe.
41. I find *reposado* Tequila ("rested," aged in barrels for 2–12 months) works better than *blanco* ("white," unaged) or *añejo* ("old," aged in barrels for up to 3 years) for this recipe.
42. "On the rocks" denotes the presence of ice cubes in a cocktail when it is served. Rather than using the pulverized ice cubes from the cocktail shaker, I suggest using fresh ice cubes. Presentation matters!
43. Tequila is derived from Blue Agave, so using a sweetener derived from the plant in a Margarita is a no-brainer.

The Tequila War

A Margarita made without Tequila seems like a bit of an oxymoron, does it not? Well, in the early 1990s, Seagram & Co. and E. & J. Gallo Winery each introduced "Margarita-flavored" coolers made with fermented malt (i.e., beer) and wine, respectively.[44] In other words, neither beverage contained any Tequila, making them much cheaper to produce. A four-pack of premixed Margaritas (made with Tequila) retailed for $4.99, while an equal quantity of the Margarita-flavored product (made without Tequila) sold for about half as much. As an added bonus, the liquor-free product benefitted from wider distribution because it could be sold at convenience stores.[45] Americans apparently had no qualms about purchasing and consuming the imitation Margaritas, and Tequila distillers claimed the lower-priced knockoffs were responsible for a 30% drop in premixed Margarita sales in 1994.[46]

Mexican distillers panicked and orchestrated a three-pronged counterattack on this intrusion into their market. First, Heublein, Inc. (the United States importer of Jose Cuervo® Tequila at the time) petitioned the Bureau of Alcohol, Tobacco, Firearms and Explosives (the "ATF") to amend its regulations to forbid labels from including the word "Margarita" unless the product in question contained

---

44. Linda E. Prudhomme, *The Margarita Wars: Does the Popular Mixed Drink Margarita Qualify as Intellectual Property?*, 4 Sw. J.L. & Trade Ams. 109, 111–12 (1997). By the way, no country other than Mexico can produce Tequila. "Tequila" made anywhere else is just "agave-derived liquor."
45. *Id.* at 119. In most states, liquor cannot be sold at convenience stores.
46. Chris Kraul, *Cocktail Quarrel: Tequila Distillers Take On Wineries Over Just What Makes a Margarita*, L.A. Times, Oct. 23, 1995, at Dl.

Tequila.[47] Second, the distillers persuaded the government of Mexico to lodge trade complaints with the Office of the United States Trade Representative, the Treasury Department, and the White House.[48] Finally, Heublein filed lawsuits against Seagram and E. & J. Gallo alleging a violation of federal law through "false and misleading commercial advertising and promotion and unfair competition."[49] Collectively, these actions represented the opening salvo of the Tequila War of the 1990s—perhaps the coldest (and saltiest) conflict on this side of the Cold War.

Battling with the ATF

In 1994, federal regulations specifically forbade wine labels from containing any "statement . . . which tends to create the impression that a wine contains distilled spirits."[50] Heublein argued E. & J. Gallo's Margarita-flavored wine coolers ran afoul of this regulation because including the word "Margarita" on the label implied the presence of a distilled spirit: Tequila. The ATF considered the matter but ultimately determined labeling a wine-based product as being "Margarita-*flavored*" did not create an impression that it contained distilled spirits—even if the qualification appeared in smaller print.[51]

---

47.   Prudhomme, *supra* note 44, at 119.

48.   *Id.* at 130.

49.   *Id.* at 118; Heublein, Inc. v. E. & J. Gallo Winery, No. 1:94-cv-08155 (S.D.N.Y. Nov. 10, 1994); Heublein, Inc. v. Joseph E. Seagram, No. 1:94-cv-08153 (S.D.N.Y. Nov. 10, 1994). There was a typo in the original filing for the Seagram case and the party sued was actually listed as "Jospeh [*sic*] E. Seagram." This Author speculates Tequila may not have been responsible for the mistake.

50.   Prudhomme, *supra* note 44, at 127; Prohibited Practices (Wine), 27 C.F.R. § 4.39(a)(7)(i) (1994).

51.   Prudhomme, *supra* note 44, at 121, 127.

Interestingly, the regulations concerning malt beverage labels at the time did not contain an analogous restriction on implying the presence of liquor. Heublein suggested the ATF adopt a similar labeling rule for malt beverages; specifically, one that would outlaw describing a malt beverage as a Margarita. Once again, the ATF saw no issue with labeling a beverage as being "Margarita-flavored," but they *did* eventually fix the inconsistency between the wine and malt beverage regulations that Heublein was kind enough to point out. Unfortunately, this was not helpful to Tequila distillers because the amended rules specifically permitted a malt beverage label to reference the name of a cocktail (e.g., a Margarita) to describe a flavor profile.[52]

Trade Diplomacy

On the diplomatic front, the Mexican government structured its complaints to the United States around Annex 313 of the North American Free Trade Agreement ("NAFTA"), which went into effect only a few months earlier in January 1994. In Annex 313 Canada and the United States committed to recognize Tequila and Mezcal (Tequila's smoky cousin) as "distinctive products of Mexico" and to not allow the sale of a product by either name unless the liquor in question was manufactured in Mexico according to Mexican regulations.[53] In return,

---

52. "This paragraph does not prohibit . . . the use of a cocktail name as a brand name or fanciful name of a malt beverage, provided that the overall label does not present a misleading impression about the identity of the product." Flavored Malt Beverage and Related Regulatory Amendments, 70 Fed. Reg. 194, 235 (Jan. 3, 2005) (codified as amended at 27 C.F.R. § 7.128(b)(3) (2022)).

53. *See* North American Free Trade Agreement (NAFTA), Dec. 17, 1992, 32 I.L.M. 289, 319 ("Canada and the United States shall recognize Tequila and Mezcal as distinctive products of Mexico.

Bourbon, Tennessee Whiskey, and Canadian Whisky each received similar protections in Mexico. Mexico's core argument under NAFTA was that a Margarita made without Tequila was both ridiculous and impossible.[54] Accordingly, calling a beverage "Margarita-flavored" was akin to saying it contained Tequila, which violated Annex 313 of NAFTA if the beverage was neither agave-based nor produced in Mexico.[55]

It was a creative argument, but Margaritas did not receive protection under NAFTA—Tequila did. Additionally, like the arguments presented to the ATF, the "flavored" qualifier on the label proved fatal for the distillers because it implied that the beverage, itself, was *not* a Margarita. Mexico's diplomatic intercession on behalf of the Tequila distillers failed to alter the status quo. That was strike two.

Waging War in the Courtroom

The Tequila distillers' final hope for success lay in Heublein's cases against Seagram and E. & J. Gallo. Both cases made identical claims of false and misleading advertising, promotion, and unfair competition under section 43(a) of the Lanham Act. At first blush, the foundation for these claims may seem odd because the Lanham Act forms the statutory basis for federal

---

Accordingly, Canada and the United States shall not permit the sale of any product as Tequila or Mezcal, unless it has been manufactured in Mexico . . . ."); *see also* OFF. U.S. TRADE REP., EXEC. OFF. PRESIDENT, AGREEMENT BETWEEN THE UNITED STATES OF AMERICA, THE UNITED MEXICAN STATES, AND CANADA (USMCA) Annex 3-C, art. 3.C.2 (Oct. 1, 2018) (illustrating the successor treaty to NAFTA continues to offer those same protections today); Prudhomme, *supra* note 44, at 132–33.

54. Actually, that *is* a pretty great argument.

55. Prudhomme, *supra* note 44, at 130.

trademark law, and nobody had registered a trademark for the Margarita cocktail.[56] But a 1988 revision to the Lanham Act codified judicial interpretations of section 43(a) that permitted a plaintiff to make a claim of false advertising, false designation of origin, unfair competition, or all of the above against a party for infringing on a yet-to-be-registered trademark, which (arguably) could include the Margarita.[57]

If Heublein could prove the term "Margarita" referred to a cocktail that was *exclusively* made with Tequila (and never any other type of alcohol), then it might be able to prove the term functioned as a trademark and was entitled to protection under the Lanham Act.[58] But even if they were able to accomplish that feat, Heublein still would not prevail unless they also showed that the term "Margarita-flavored" had a high likelihood of misleading consumers as to the origin or contents of a beverage.[59] It was an ambitious strategy.

Fortunately for Seagram and E. & J. Gallo, Heublein's cases had a major flaw that likely precluded it from ever receiving the injunctive relief they sought: the Clean Hands Doctrine.[60] Heublein introduced a wine-based

---

56. *See* Lanham Act, ch. 540, 60 Stat. 427 (1946) (codified as amended at 15 U.S.C. § 1051 *et seq.*). For further information on intellectual property rights in cocktails, see discussion *infra* p. 142.

57. Prudhomme, *supra* note 44, at 124–25; Trademark Law Revision Act of 1988, Pub. L. No. 100-667, § 132, 102 Stat. 3935, 3946 (codified as amended at 15 U.S.C. § 1125(a)).

58. Prudhomme, *supra* note 44, at 137. A term can function as a trademark if it is "used by a source of a product to identify itself to the public as the source of its product and to create in the public consciousness an awareness of the uniqueness of the source and of its products." Sands, Taylor & Wood Co. v. Quaker Oats Co., 978 F.2d 947, 953 (7th Cir. 1992) (quoting M.B.H. Enter. v. Woky, Inc., 633 F.2d 50, 54 (7th Cir. 1980)).

59. Prudhomme, *supra* note 44, at 142–55.

60. "The principle that a party cannot seek equitable relief or assert an equitable defense if that party has violated an equitable

Margarita-flavored product called the "Club 'Garita" in 1989 and a similar vodka-based product called the "Moscow Margarita" in 1993—both of which were remarkably similar to the Tequila-free products they now sought to enjoin Seagram and E. & J. Gallo from selling.[61] Heublein abruptly stopped producing those beverages only a few months before filing the lawsuits, and the sudden cancellation of those product lines looked suspicious— almost as if it was done in anticipation of litigating this very issue. That gave a sour flavor to the lawsuits (Margarita flavored, if you like), and it appeared as if Heublein was unfairly attempting to use the court system to obtain a monopoly on a particular flavor profile.

The Clean Hands Doctrine states, "He who comes into equity must come with clean hands," and the concept will usually convince a court to deny equitable relief (such as an injunction) to a party when granting such relief would be against good conscience.[62] Heublein stood a fair chance of falling squarely within the policy of the doctrine because of its recently retired product lines, and Seagram and E. & J. Gallo almost certainly pointed that out to the plaintiff.

Probably in large part because they came to court with unclean hands, Heublein settled both cases in early 1996 on the condition that each company redesign their packaging in a mutually acceptable manner.[63] You can still purchase a non-Tequila, Margarita-flavored cooler at the store today. Fortunately, Tequila distillers do not appear to have been driven into bankruptcy as a result.

---

principle, such as good faith." *Clean Hands Doctrine*, BLACK'S LAW DICTIONARY 317.
   61.   Prudhomme, *supra* note 44, at 121–22, 159.
   62.   Shaver v. Heller & Merz Co., 108 F. 821, 834 (8th Cir. 1901).
   63.   Prudhomme, *supra* note 44, at 161.

§3

A Mildly Modified Manhattan and Poor Pigg

On November 5 (or perhaps it was December 29), 1874, the ballroom of the Manhattan Club was packed with men and women of high society sporting black jackets with coattails and elaborate ball gowns.[64] Jennie Jerome (a Brooklyn heiress colloquially remembered as Sir Winston Churchill's mother) was the hostess of the *soirée*, a banquet in honor of Samuel J. Tilden, the newly elected governor of the State of New York. While the attendees ate, drank, and gossiped to their hearts' content, a swarm of frantic bartenders worked tirelessly to churn out droves of a brand-new cocktail making its debut at the banquet: the Manhattan.

What a fantastic story that is! While the pervasive and oft-repeated tale features the correct city and a believable time period for the Manhattan's creation, there is

---

64. The Manhattan Club hosted large parties on both of those evenings, and either may have served as the backdrop for this story. PHILIP J. GREENE, THE MANHATTAN: THE STORY OF THE FIRST MODERN COCKTAIL 38 (Sterling Epicure 2016).

substantial doubt about the rest of it.[65] Ms. Jerome could not have been drinking Manhattans or hosting a gala in New York City on either of those dates because she was on the other side of the Atlantic Ocean. She gave birth to Winston Churchill on November 30, 1874, in Oxfordshire, England.[66]

But Jennie Jerome's connection to the Manhattan Club is not entirely unfounded. In 1899, decades after the Manhattan cocktail made its grand entrance, the social club found itself short of funds and relocated to lower rent accommodations at the southeast corner of Madison Avenue and East 26th Street.[67] Despite the more economical price tag, the new location was a lavish six-story mansion that had served as the clubhouse for several venerable organizations through the years, most recently the University Club. Even though it had changed hands several times, the building was commonly referred to as the "Leonard Jerome Mansion." It was Jennie's childhood home.

But if the Manhattan was not created by a bartender at the Manhattan Club, who invented it? Writing in 1922, William F. Mulhall provided an answer that has garnered credence but is profoundly vague: "The Manhattan cocktail was invented by a man named Black, who kept a place ten doors below Houston Street on Broadway in the [eighteen-]sixties . . . ."[68] Mulhall was a bartender at the

---

65. *Id.* at 34–39.

66. WONDRICH, *supra* note 4, at 253–55.

67. HENRY WATTERSON, HISTORY OF THE MANHATTAN CLUB: A NARRATIVE OF THE ACTIVITIES OF HALF A CENTURY 83–84 (Manhattan Club 1916); *Manhattan Club at Home*, N.Y. TIMES, July 18, 1899, at 12, https://lexspirit.link/KQXN; *Manhattan Club Will Move Up Town*, N.Y. TIMES, June 10, 1911, at 5, https://lexspirit.link/CHIE.

68. William M. Mulhall, *The Golden Age of Booze*, *in* VALENTINE'S MANUAL OF OLD NEW YORK, No. 7, NEW SERIES 1923, at 126, 134 (Henry Collins Brown ed., 1922).

elegant and reputable Hoffman House for several decades and probably knew what he was talking about.[69] When cocktail historian David Wondrich dug into Mulhall's claim, he found an 1881 notice advertising the sale of a bar "formerly owned and conducted by George Black, known as the Manhattan Inn, No. 493 Broadway, near the corner Broome St."[70]

A Mister Black? Check.

Establishment has a similar name to the cocktail? Interesting.

Located on Broadway? Check.

Ten doors down from Houston Street? More like three blocks, but Mulhall was writing about the subject several decades after the fact. In other words, the story holds water and might be true!

Vivacious Vermouth

The Manhattan (along with the Martini[71]) was revolutionary because it featured a new-ish ingredient called vermouth. Vermouth reached the United States around 1840 but remained relatively obscure and underutilized until the 1870s. But once people discovered what they had been missing, the fortified wine quickly became the "bartender's ketchup" of the late 19th century.[72] Vermouth introduced new flavors (both sweet

---

69. OXFORD COMPANION, *supra* note 6, at 435; GREENE, *supra* note 64, at 42–43.

70. *For Sale—The Popular Lunch and Sample Room,* N.Y. HERALD, June 9, 1881, at 2, https://lexspirit.link/J97A.

71. Dry Martini: 2-½ oz. dry gin or vodka and 4 dashes of dry vermouth. Combine those ingredients in a stirring glass with ice, stir well, and strain into a chilled cocktail glass. Garnish with a pitted olive and a lemon twist. DEGROFF, *supra* note 31, at 104.

72. GREENE, *supra* note 64, at 7–10; WONDRICH, *supra* note 4, at 250. Modern-day "bartender's ketchup" is St~Germain® Elderflower Liqueur. It can go in just about everything—maybe even ketchup.

and dry) that made the established cocktail formula of "spirit, sugar, water, and bitters" seem "Old Fashioned" (*see* cocktail *infra* p. 49).[73]

Ever since the first Manhattan was poured into a glass people have debated what the "proper" ratio of whiskey to vermouth is. During the first half century of the cocktail's existence, publications featured recipes ranging from a 1:1 whiskey-to-vermouth ratio to an especially spirited 3:1 ratio.[74] Ratios continued to climb throughout the 20th century (meaning less and less vermouth was used) before settling into more reasonable territory during the cocktail revival of the 1990s.[75]

The version of the Manhattan that follows features a fairly standard 2:1 ratio, but it is also unconventional because it uses ruby Port in place of one-half of the vermouth. I think the ruby Port complements the other flavors and adds depth and complexity to the cocktail. If you prefer a more traditional Manhattan, simply use a full ounce of vermouth. But remember: There is no wrong way to prefer your Manhattan—just so long as you will have one!

---

73. GREENE, *supra* note 64, at 2. Italian vermouth is usually sweet; French vermouth is typically dry. However, there are many exceptions to this general rule—and a whole spectrum of flavors. *Id.* at 8.

74. *Id.* at 218–25.

75. *Id.* at 100–11.

Mildly Modified Manhattan[76]

1. Combine the following ingredients in a stirring glass with ice:
   a. 2 oz. rye whiskey[77]
   b. 1/2 oz. sweet vermouth
   c. 1/2 oz. ruby Port[78]
   d. 2 dashes of Angostura® Bitters[79]
2. Stir[80] the contents of the stirring glass with a bar spoon for about 1 minute.
3. Garnish a chilled coupe glass with a Luxardo® Cocktail Cherry.[81]
4. Strain the contents of the stirring glass into the coupe glass and serve "up."

---

76. A tip of the hat to Conner Donovan for this modification to the Manhattan. CONNER DONOVAN, KILLER COCKTAILS: 14 COCKTAIL RECIPES TO ASSIST YOU IN YOUR HOMICIDE INVESTIGATION 13 (Hunt a Killer 2019).

77. Michter's® Rye Whiskey is an excellent choice here, but if you want to go premium, try Angel's Envy® Finished Rye Whiskey (aged in rum casks). This footnote is not sponsored by either distiller, but I am open to such a prospect!

78. I recommend using Fonseca® Ruby Porto.

79. Or 3 or 4—I am particularly heavy-handed when it comes to bitters.

80. I recommend you avoid shaking this libation. Aerating and overdiluting a spirit-forward cocktail will not enhance your experience. Am I suggesting James Bond is committing sacrilege by ordering his Vesper Martini "shaken, not stirred"? IAN FLEMING, CASINO ROYALE 45 (Penguin Books 2002) (1953). Kind of. Shaking a cocktail will *always* get it far colder than stirring it, and perhaps Bond cares more about the temperature of his Martini than anything else. Such sacrilege has even spawned a new phrase: "Bonding it," meaning to shake a cocktail when you normally would not.

81. Luxardo cherries are NOT cheap, but they will change your life. Most other cocktail cherries, such as the ones at the grocery store that are a radioactive shade of bright red, are a poor substitute—at best.

Poor Pigg

Appellate courts are not typically inclined to consider factual issues when reviewing a case because findings of fact are within the purview of trial courts. (The credibility and demeanor of witnesses are difficult to capture in a transcript.) As such, factual determinations made by a jury will be upheld on appeal unless a fact is not supported by "substantial evidence," which is a sufficient amount of proof that a "reasonable mind might accept as adequate to support a conclusion."[82] If a judge served as the fact finder at trial (meaning there was no jury), their factual findings will be respected so long as they are not "clearly erroneous."[83] However, if an essential question of fact was not addressed *at all* during trial, an appellate court will often reverse the lower court's decision and remand for further proceedings. Enter the concept of judicial notice.

Sometimes a fact is so notorious and obvious that a court takes judicial notice[84] of its existence without requiring evidence on the matter. For instance, a court might take judicial notice of the fact that December 7, 1941, was a Sunday because the fact is both readily apparent and well-known. However, much like adverbs and Everclear®, this powerful tool is best used sparingly.[85]

---

82. Consol. Edison Co. v. NLRB, 305 U.S. 197, 229 (1938). This amount of evidence is often described as being "more than a mere scintilla," which is a rather specific word for an amorphous quantity.

83. FED. R. CIV. P. 52(a)(6); Maine v. Taylor, 477 U.S. 131, 145 (1986) (holding Federal Rule of Civil Procedure 52's "clearly erroneous" standard applies in criminal cases tried without a jury).

84. "A court's acceptance, for purposes of convenience and without requiring a party's proof, of a well-known and indisputable fact." *Judicial Notice*, BLACK'S LAW DICTIONARY 1012. This concept is also codified in the Federal Rules of Evidence. *See* FED. R. EVID. 201.

85. "I believe the road to hell is paved with adverbs, and I will shout it from the rooftops." STEPHEN KING, ON WRITING: A MEMOIR OF THE CRAFT 125 (Scribner 2020) (2000). I suppose we all have our vices.

In 1908, the Supreme Court of Kansas heard the appeal of a criminal case in which the defendant, Pigg, was convicted of violating a statute prohibiting the sale of intoxicating liquor.[86] It seemed like an open-and-shut case, but in an apparent twist the prosecution failed to offer any evidence at trial to establish the Manhattan cocktail Pigg served a patron qualified as an intoxicating beverage. Because every element of a crime must be proven beyond a reasonable doubt to secure a conviction in a criminal case, that would certainly seem to negate a required element of the crime.[87] Reversed and remanded, right? Well, as it turned out, Pigg's argument that it was reversible error to convict him without requiring evidence as to whether a Manhattan is an intoxicating beverage was almost as clever as it was audacious—almost. The appellate court had little hesitation in taking judicial notice of the fact that a Manhattan is an intoxicating beverage, and Pigg's conviction was upheld as a result.[88]

A learned practitioner reviewing the case made some observations about judges that bear repeating: "[W]hile it is generally admitted that judges are underpaid and so presumably have little money to spend on vacation travels, they have been known to travel, and it is quite possible that a western judge may have visited the eastern island metropolis and there learned to distinguish 'sky-scrapers' from 'corncribs' and 'oyster cocktails' from 'Manhattan

---

86. State v. Pigg, 78 Kan. 618, 620–21 (1908).
87. *In re* Winship, 397 U.S. 358, 361–64 (1970) (exploring the "guilty beyond a reasonable doubt" requirement in a historical and constitutional context).
88. "The particular kind of cocktail under discussion is popularly understood to have taken its name from the island whose inhabitants first became addicted to its use. While its characteristics are not so widely known as those of whiskey, brandy, or gin, it is our understanding that a Manhattan cocktail is generally and popularly known to be intoxicating." *Pigg*, 78 Kan. at 620–21.

cocktails.'"[89] Those remarks were likely fueled by public skepticism that a rural Kansas judge was intimately familiar with something as modern and urban as the Manhattan cocktail, but the point the practitioner was attempting to make is the range of topics a court is willing to take judicial notice of tends to vary by geographic location and the judge's familiarity with the relevant issues. For example, while a Kansas court's lack of proximity to the ocean means they might not consider taking judicial notice of elementary maritime principles without hearing evidence on the matter, a judge in New Orleans might do so—but they would never be required to.

Speaking of regional traditions—that point dovetails nicely with a similar Texas case concerning judicial notice: *Potts v. State.* Two years before *State v. Pigg* was decided, the Texas Court of Criminal Appeals reviewed a case with a nearly identical law and fact pattern, but refused to take judicial notice that "lager beer" is intoxicating![90] There has been a large German population in Texas since the 1830s, and that particular ruling might have been made under the influence . . . of that tradition. Either way, an enterprising prosecutor could surely devise a method to introduce evidence on the intoxicating characteristics of beer![91]

---

89.   James H. Brewster, *The Kansas "Manhattan Cocktail Case" and Some Others Concerning Judicial Notice*, 7 MICH. L. REV. 336, 337 (1909).

90.   *Id.* at 336–37; Potts v. State, 97 S.W. 477, 479 (Tex. Crim. App. 1906).

91.   I would never suggest an attorney appear in court after consuming several large steins of beer. But, hypothetically, if someone *did* do that, it could qualify as a demonstrative exhibit, malpractice, or ineffective assistance of counsel. Then again, I suppose none of those outcomes are mutually exclusive!

§4

Signature Lemonade Sangria and Virginian Vino

Sangria[92] is a beverage closely associated with Spain and typically consists of a mixture of sweet wine, spirits, sugar, chopped fruit, and spices. The punch's precursor may have come from the Spanish West Indies (the Greater Antilles) during the 18th century in the form of a similar beverage called "sangaree" or "sangre."[93] That said, accurately tracing the history of Sangria is difficult because mixing wine with spices and fruit is hardly a novel venture. In fact, a similar beverage called Hippocras was enjoyed by the Romans over 2,000 years ago![94] In recognition of the fact that punches like Sangria are so timeless, I hope you will forgive my reluctance to recount several millennia of tradition. Instead, I will explore the beverage's more recent history in the United States.

---

92. Literal translation: "bleeding" or "bloodletting," which is a reference to the sanguine color of the punch.

93. *See* WONDRICH, *supra* note 4, at 201–02.

94. Nick Hines, *The History of Sangria*, VINEPAIR (June 30, 2017), https://lexspirit.link/B60A.

Sangria became popular in the United States after the Spanish Pavilion at the 1964 New York World's Fair featured the beverage and introduced it to tens of thousands of guests.[95] I am certain many attendees enjoyed a Sangria and tapas before walking eastward to experience some of Walt Disney's famous attractions at the fair: *It's a Small World* (UNICEF® Pavilion sponsored by Pepsi-Cola®) and the *Carousel of Progress* (General Electric® Pavilion).[96]

Alberto Heras, the restaurateur manager of two of the four restaurants at the Spanish Pavilion, is credited with formulating the Sangria recipe that became so popular with visitors.[97] His version of the beverage was served at both of his restaurants and helped to make the culinary showcase at the Spanish Pavilion one of the highlights of the fair. Heras planned to capitalize upon the success of the more popular of his two restaurant concepts, Marisquería Taberna Madrid, by replicating the seafood restaurant at a permanent venue after the fair ended in 1965. To that end, Heras registered the trademark "La Marisquería" with the New York Secretary of State on October 26, 1964, as a placeholder for the venture.

Unfortunately for Heras, a man named Jose Mena had a similar (i.e., identical) idea. Mena purchased Marisquería's kitchen equipment when the fair ended and opened El Toro Marisquería, which was also a Spanish seafood restaurant. When Heras heard about Mena's restaurant, he promptly sued to enjoin Mena's use of the

---

95. Ted Haigh, *History Lesson: The Sangaree*, IMBIBE (Sept. 17, 2009), https://lexspirit.link/DKTR.

96. *See* *It's a Small World*, DISNEYLAND, https://lexspirit.link/9SWY; *Walt Disney's Carousel of Progress*, WALT DISNEY WORLD, https://lexspirit.link/OKMG.

97. JOHN F. MARIANI, THE ENCYCLOPEDIA OF AMERICAN FOOD AND DRINK 447 (Bloomsbury 2013).

word Marisquería in the establishment's name.[98] It did not go well. Translated from Spanish, *Marisquería* simply means "seafood restaurant," which is far too generic to be successfully trademarked.[99] Interestingly, the court denied Heras's motion for temporary injunction on other grounds by ruling that Heras—despite planning to use the mark in the near future—had abandoned the mark by not using it since the World's Fair ended.[100] But don't fret! Heras eventually opened his Spanish seafood restaurant in New York City in 1966. He creatively named it "The Spanish Pavilion," and it was known for its Sangria.[101] Unfortunately, the food was only so-so, and it was quite expensive. It is unclear how long the restaurant remained open, but it was not for very long. Even so, Heras's lasting legacy is his role in popularizing Sangria in the United States.

The Sangria recipe that follows was served as the signature cocktail at my wedding reception. I would not classify it as a traditional Sangria, but it has the advantage of producing a single serving of the beverage. This obviates the necessity of whipping up an entire pitcher's worth of the punch.

---

98.   Heras v. Mena, 52 Misc. 2d 396, 397 (Sup. Ct. N.Y. Cnty. 1966).

99.   If a business ceases to use a trademark for long enough that the public no longer regards the mark as being distinctive of the holder's business, the rights to the mark are lost—regardless of the mark's registration status or the holder's future plans. *See* Lanham Act §§ 14(c), 45, 60 Stat. at 433, 444 (codified as amended at 15 U.S.C. §§ 1064(3), 1127); *see also* discussion *infra* p. 143. Federal trademark principles are often analogous to applicable state laws.

100.   *Heras*, 52 Misc. 2d at 397–98.

101.   "[A] favorite drink at the restaurant appears to be the Sangria. It is made there with red Spanish wine, ice, fruits, Spanish brandy, a touch of Cointreau and a small bottle of club soda." Craig Clairborne, *The Spanish Pavilion: A Restaurant Among the Most Beautiful in Manhattan*, N.Y. TIMES, Dec. 13, 1966, at 77, https://lexspirit.link/N2VE.

Signature Lemonade Sangria[102]

1. Combine the following ingredients in a cocktail shaker with ice:
   a. 1 oz. vodka
   b. 1 oz. simple syrup
   c. 1 oz. fresh-squeezed lemon juice
   d. 1/2 oz. Grand Marnier® Cordon Rouge Orange Liqueur
2. Cap the cocktail shaker and shake vigorously for 20–30 seconds.
3. Pour 1/2 oz. of merlot into the cocktail shaker and stir in gently.[103]
4. Garnish a wine glass with a lemon wheel and add a few pieces of ice.[104]
5. Strain the contents of the cocktail shaker into the wine glass.
6. *¡Salud!*

---

102. This particular recipe was "discovered" on a cocktail napkin at McCormick (no relation) & Schmick's®.

103. Pinot noir would also work well in place of merlot. Feel free to add more wine to suit your taste. Speaking of which, another beverage people seem to enjoy calls for 1 oz. wine (red or white), another ½ oz. of wine, and an additional 2-½ oz. of wine (preferably from the same bottle as the prior two measures). Combine in a wine glass and serve "up." No shaking, stirring, ice, or other sorcery involved!

104. Even though Sangria is wine-based, I promise it is socially acceptable (in this situation) to serve this beverage with ice cubes in the glass to keep the liquid chilled. By the way, my mother, while usually a stickler for etiquette, always enjoys her chardonnay with a few ice cubes. This can be our little secret.

Virginian Vino

Every so often you are liable to hear about some ridiculous "law" in your state that prohibits seemingly innocent or anachronistic conduct. Most of these "laws" have been repealed (if they were ever enacted at all), but occasionally an objectively absurd statute rears its ugly head. For instance, did you know that until late 2008 it was illegal to serve Sangria in the Commonwealth of Virginia? Well, hold on a second; as is the case with most statutes, the devil lurks in the details.

The provision of the 1934 law at issue provided that, "If any person who holds a [liquor] license . . . shall sell wine to which spirits or alcohol, or both, have been added . . . he shall be guilty of a misdemeanor."[105] It was a holdover of sorts from a March 7, 1934 act of the Virginia legislature that was hurriedly passed to regulate alcohol consumption in the wake of Prohibition's repeal in December 1933. Sangria made without an additional spirit is not much more than some wine with chopped fruit floating in it—not Sangria at all! So, even if the statute was not an outright ban on Sangria *per se* (i.e., constituents could still produce their own at home), it certainly prevented commercial sales of the beverage by restaurants and bars in Virginia.

Exactly what harm was the Commonwealth trying to prevent by prohibiting bartenders from mixing wine with another type of alcohol? Your guess is as good as mine! After all, you could still order a plethora of mixed drinks from the bar. Or was serving a patron a Manhattan[106] or Martini[107]—both of which incorporate a fortified wine called vermouth—also outlawed?

---

105. Alcoholic Beverage Control Act, ch. 94, § 41(c), 1934 Va. Acts 100, 125–26 (codified as amended at VA. CODE § 4.1-324.A.3 (2007)).
106. *See* Manhattan recipe *supra* p. 23.
107. *See* Martini recipe *supra* note 71.

The good news is severely outdated and otherwise absurd laws are unlikely to be routinely enforced, which is probably why La Tasca® Spanish Tapas Bar and Restaurant in Alexandria, Virginia, decided to rebel and serve its Sangria the proper way: with brandy added to the wine and fruit mixture. That is, until they were cited by the Virginia Alcoholic Beverage Commission for violating the draconian ban on Sangria in January 2006.[108]

Fortunately, Virginians did not suffer Sangria-less (when visiting a bar or restaurant, anyway) for much longer after La Tasca's martyrdom. The incident drew attention to a law the public no longer favored, and democratic processes took care of the rest. In 2008, Virginia Delegate Adam P. Ebbin (D-Alexandria) introduced a bill to amend the offending statute in such a way that would allow traditional Sangria (artfully defined as consisting of wine mixed with "brandy, triple sec, or other similar spirits") to be served to patrons.[109] The bill was enacted with bipartisan support, thereby allowing Virginians to enjoy spiked wine in peace ever since. Unfortunately, La Tasca was one of the many restaurants and bars that shut their doors permanently during the COVID-19 pandemic, but its legacy will live on in the form of Virginians having the right to enjoy properly made Sangria at establishments throughout the state.[110]

---

108. Anita Kumar, *Virginia's Sangria Ban at Issue in Two Hearings*, WASH. POST (Jan. 24, 2008), https://lexspirit.link/OIV2.
    109. H.R. 1075, 2008 Leg., Reg. Sess. (Va. 2008) (codified as amended at VA. CODE § 4.1-324.A.3 (2020)).
    110. *La Tasca Files for Bankruptcy*, ALEXANDRIA LIVING MAG. (May 31, 2020, 10:13 PM), https://lexspirit.link/7ZAP.

§5

The Bloody Mary and the Mongrel Bill of 1883

The Bloody Mary is a ubiquitous brunch beverage, and its variations are legion. Principally consisting of vodka and tomato juice, the cocktail's origins are no clearer than the cocktail itself. Experts are fairly certain the Bloody Mary was not invented before the end of World War One because there are no widespread reports of people drinking tomato juice before that time. Of course, tomato juice was a common ingredient in many sauces and other culinary expressions before then, but it was not being served as a standalone beverage.[111]

One of the earliest known instances of tomato juice being served as a beverage occurred in 1917 and is attributed to Louis Perrin, a French chef who was on a temporary residency at Indiana's French Lick Springs Hotel®.[112] One morning, Chef Perrin found the kitchen completely devoid of oranges—meaning he could not make the orange juice traditionally served with breakfast. Out

---

111. OXFORD COMPANION, *supra* note 6, at 734.
112. *French Lick Springs Hotel History*, FRENCH LICK RESORT, https://lexspirit.link/XVWF.

of desperation, the chef juiced the only fruit at his disposal (tomatoes), combined it with sugar and a special sauce, and served it to the hotel guests. The beverage was a hit, and (whether or not Chef Perrin served as the sole catalyst) commercial production of tomato juice began soon thereafter. It would become a common breakfast beverage by the late 1920s.[113]

The idea to add vodka to tomato juice (in mainstream fashion, that is) came to fruition in the 1920s as well. Nailing down the culprit responsible for that pairing is another troublesome conundrum of cocktail history, but the blame is often placed with either George Jessel or Fernand "Pete" a/k/a "The Frog" Petiot. As you might expect, each of those men has also been credited with creating the Bloody Mary.

George Jessel was a famous comedic entertainer who was known as the "Toastmaster General of the United States."[114] In his 1975 autobiography, *The World I Lived In*, Jessel claimed he invented the Bloody Mary in 1927 when he needed to nurse a monster hangover after a long night of drinking in Palm Beach, Florida.[115] Despite never having encountered the spirit before, when a bartender produced an unfamiliar bottle of "vodkee," Jessel instinctively requested Worcestershire sauce, tomato juice, and lemon juice to mix with the spirit.[116] As he sipped the rather polished elixir he miraculously managed to compose while in a bottle-ached state, in walks Mary Brown Warburton (of the Wanamaker Department Store family) in an elegant, white evening gown. Mary, when Jessel

---

113. Jeffrey M. Pogash, Bloody Mary 11–12 (Thornwillow Press 2011); Oxford Companion, *supra* note 6, at 734.

114. Pogash, *supra* note 113, at 20–22.

115. George Jessel with John Austin, The World I Lived In 83–84 (Henry Regnery Co. 1975).

116. *Id.* at 84.

offered her a sip of the concoction, promptly spilled it all over her white dress and exclaimed, "Now, you can call me Bloody Mary, George!"[117]

What makes Jessel's story inherently suspect is how neatly laid out everything is. As if the novel idea to combine vodka and tomato juice were not impressive enough, Jessel went whole hog in his account and claimed to formulate a near-final recipe for the Bloody Mary on his first go. Combine that stroke of apparent luck with reports of Parisian establishments serving a vodka and tomato juice cocktail a few years earlier, and the actor's account looks pretty absurd.[118]

Unfortunately, as ridiculous as Jessel's story sounds, Pete Petiot's purported role in combining the two main ingredients for a Bloody Mary ends up being far more dubious. In the 1920s, Petiot tended bar at Harry's New York Bar® (despite the name, that establishment is located in Paris, France), and a vodka and tomato juice cocktail is rumored to have been served during his tenure there.[119] This is problematic because none of the influential French cocktail books of the era includes a tomato juice and vodka-based libation.[120] If such a concoction were being served at Harry's at the time, it is unlikely it would have escaped mention. Crucially, notwithstanding whether or not a proto-Bloody Mary cocktail was served there, even Petiot gave Jessel credit for pairing the major ingredients! In a 1964 interview Petiot remarked, "George Jessel said he created [the Bloody Mary], but it was really nothing but vodka and tomato juice when I took it over."[121]

---

117. *Id.* Seriously?! Was he even *trying* to make this believable?
118. OXFORD COMPANION, *supra* note 6, at 91.
119. POGASH, *supra* note 113, at 12–14.
120. *Id.* at 15–16.
121. *The Talk of the Town—Barman*, NEW YORKER, July 18, 1964, at 19, 20, https://lexspirit.link/YSFC.

Even if Petiot was not responsible for marrying vodka with tomato juice, the consensus is he *was* responsible for adding cayenne pepper, lemon juice, black pepper, and Worcestershire sauce to the humble pairing.[122] Or, in his own words, he "initiated the Bloody Mary of today."[123] In fact, Petiot was probably putting the finishing touches on the cocktail when he moved to the St. Regis® Hotel in New York City in 1933, where he was engaged to tend the King Cole Bar®.[124] The Bloody Mary made its official debut on the menu there in 1934 . . . under the name "Red Snapper." Apparently, hotel management found the name "Bloody Mary" to be too vulgar![125] In modern parlance, a Red Snapper is a Bloody Mary made with gin, but Petiot's 1934 rendition was almost certainly vodka-based.[126]

I will close this venture into the challenging history of the Bloody Mary with an imperfect, but in some ways compelling, story of how the cocktail got its name. While George Jessel's explanation for the origin of the moniker was recounted earlier, it strikes me as too convenient. The following story takes place in Paris during the 1920s, which is a problematic setting for reasons discussed earlier, but I suspect there might be a kernel of truth in it somewhere. The story goes that there was a young patron of Harry's New York Bar named Mary, who frequently sat at the bar, ordered the tomato juice cocktail, and proceeded to wait (in vain) for a gentleman caller.[127] He never showed up. Several repetitions of this scenario prompted the bartenders to liken her to Mary Queen of Scots, a monarch

---

122. *Id.* at 20.
123. *Id.*
124. POGASH, *supra* note 113, at 18–19.
125. *The Original Bloody Mary: The Red Snapper*, ST. REGIS, https://lexspirit.link/OVCT.
126. POGASH, *supra* note 113, at 19–20.
127. *Id.* at 26–27.

who spent several years of her life confined alone in the Tower of London.[128] Someone with a poor recollection of English history probably thought Mary Queen of Scots was the monarch known as "Bloody Mary" (hence, the name of the cocktail), but that macabre title actually belongs to Queen Mary I of England, who earned the moniker during her five-year reign because she had 280 Protestant "heretics" burned at the stake during the English Reformation.[129] Even if it makes historians cringe, this erroneous historical allusion might be a more believable origin for the name than Jessel's tale.

Vodka: It Pays the Bills

Although the Red Snapper quickly became a staple of the King Cole Bar, the Bloody Mary would not enjoy wide popularity until the 1950s. The reason why is surprisingly simple: Vodka was uncommonly encountered in the United States. David A. Embury—incidentally, *not* a bartender, but a tax attorney—commented in *The Fine Art of Mixing Drinks* (1958) that, "[Vodka is] a mysterious liquor from behind the Iron Curtain, and for quite understandable reasons, [Americans] are rather allergic to anything emanating from behind the Iron Curtain."[130] Heublein, Inc. began producing Smirnoff® Vodka domestically beginning in the 1930s, but gin, whiskey, brandy, and rum still ruled the cocktail kingdom as far as Americans were concerned. Vodka was barely a serf tilling the land.

---

128. *Id.* at 26.

129. Meilan Solly, *The Myth of 'Bloody Mary': History Remembers the English Queen as a Murderous Monster, but the Real Story of Mary I Is Far More Nuanced*, SMITHSONIAN MAG. (March 12, 2020, 6:00 AM), https://lexspirit.link/JOP7.

130. DAVID EMBURY, THE FINE ART OF MIXING DRINKS 81 (Doubleday & Co., 3d ed. 1958).

That paradigm changed when Heublein began heavily promoting the Bloody Mary and other vodka-based cocktails in a highly effective 1950s marketing campaign.[131] In 1950, there were less than 1,000,000 gallons of vodka produced annually in the United States, but by 1955 that figure had surged to nearly 7,000,000 gallons![132] While that is an impressive statistic, perhaps no measure of the campaign's success is more flattering than a tableau occurring 24 minutes into the first James Bond movie, *Dr. No* (1962). Shortly after Bond arrives in Jamaica, a scene in his hotel room opens on a conspicuously placed bottle of Smirnoff No. 21 Vodka and then pans out to reveal a butler straining a cocktail into a glass from a shaker. "One medium-dry vodka Martini mixed like you said, sir: not stirred," the butler remarks as he hands the glass to Sean Connery.[133] Even if they paid for the product placement, Heublein executives must have been elated with the exposure.

While vodka is an important component of a Bloody Mary, the other ingredients have a greater bearing on the overall quality of the cocktail. There are many fine mixes to use as a base for a Bloody Mary, but if you want to make your own from scratch, try the recipe that follows. Conveniently, this recipe actually improves after sitting in a refrigerator for several days. You can make it a day or two ahead of time and avoid having to use a noisy blender early in the morning when . . . you know . . . you might have a headache and be wearing sunglasses, or something. Either way, a quiet morning with a low-effort—but high-quality—Bloody Mary? Count me in!

---

131. DEGROFF, *supra* note 31, at 146; OXFORD COMPANION, *supra* note 6, at 758.

132. EMBURY, *supra* note 130, at 81.

133. DR. NO (United Artists 1962). For the wisdom (if any) behind the "shaken, not stirred" instruction, see *supra* note 80.

Bloody Mary[134]

1. In a blender, blend the following ingredients until completely smooth:
   a. 1/4-inch horseradish, chopped
   b. 1-1/2 tsp. Worcestershire sauce
   c. 1/2 of an anchovy[135]
   d. 1 tsp. Sriracha sauce
   e. 1/2 tbsp. Chinese hot mustard
   f. 1 dash of both black pepper and sea salt (feel free to add more pepper to suit your taste)
   g. 1 dash of celery seeds
2. Add the following ingredients to the blender, and blend until completely smooth (again):
   a. 1 qt. tomato juice
   b. 3/4 oz. fresh-squeezed lime juice
   c. 3/4 oz. fresh-squeezed lemon juice
3. Stir in 1 oz. of vodka to prolong freshness.
4. Let the mixture marinate in the refrigerator for *at least* 24 hours, but ideally for 3 days. Certainly, no longer than 5 days.
5. Garnish a highball glass with a stick of celery, olives, ibuprofen, acetaminophen, and some candied bacon.
6. Add ice to the glass, but do not be too surprised if someone prefers theirs without ice (the ol' temperature–dilution tradeoff).
7. Pour 6–8 oz. of the mixture into the highball glass, stir in an additional 2 oz. of vodka, and enjoy!

---

134. Recipe graciously contributed by Dr. Thomas Chilton, and originally attributed to Chase Bracamontes at The Publican® in Chicago.

135. Anchovies are usually sold after being split down the middle, so you do not need to wonder whether this recipe calls for the head or tail of the fish. Instead, the relevant decision is whether to use the starboard or port side.

The Mongrel Bill of 1883

Some people would posit that "America's pastime" is baseball, but I disagree: America's pastime is raising hell over import duties and other forms of taxation.[136] Speaking of taxes, if you had a hankering for a Bloody Mary during the 1880s (ignoring the domestic unavailability of vodka), you had quite a statute to navigate to determine how much tax was owed on the tomatoes, assuming they were imported. Admittedly, this may not be the most plausible scenario, but stick around for the insanity that follows.

The Tariff Act of 1883, affectionately referred to as "The Mongrel Bill of 1883," levied import duties on a broad array of goods.[137] While it was originally drafted to reduce tariffs on foreign goods, it mutated into a partisan behemoth of a bill by the time it passed both houses of Congress. One journalist commented that by the time of its passage, "nobody knew what was in the bill of 1883."[138]

The Mongrel Bill provided for a 10% tariff on imported vegetables (section 2502, schedule G), but levied no general tariff on imported fruits (section 2503).[139] Because tomatoes have seeds (and are therefore a type of fruit), it should have been pretty apparent that tomatoes were exempt from the general import duty.[140] Shockingly, the Supreme Court of the United States had other ideas.

---

136. Recall the Boston Tea Party: A 1773 event where drunken colonists set the world record for brewing the largest quantity of lukewarm, salty tea in Boston Harbor.

137. *See* IDA M. TARBELL, THE TARIFF IN OUR TIMES 109, 113, 129–30 (MacMillan Company 1911).

138. *Id.* at 130.

139. Tariff Act of 1883, ch. 121, §§ 2499, 2502, sched. G, 2503, 22 Stat. 488, 491, 503–04, 514, 519 (imposing a 10% tariff on vegetables, but only levying taxes on certain specifically enumerated fruits). If the vegetables were preserved or processed, a 30% tariff applied.

140. *Sesame Street: The Great Fruit Strike* (PBS television broadcast Jan. 25, 2020) (featuring Alan Muraoka, the current owner of

In *Nix v. Hedden* the Supreme Court faced a "single question[:] . . . whether tomatoes, considered as provisions, [were] to be classed as 'vegetables' or as 'fruit' within the meaning of the Tariff Act of 1883."[141] The Court recognized that, botanically, tomatoes are "a fruit of a vine," and that probably should have been the end of the matter. But it was not.

The Court then rationalized that "in the common language of the people" (huh?!) tomatoes should be considered vegetables for the purposes of the act because they are served with other vegetables at dinner—and not with dessert, as fruits are.[142] This was a unanimous decision. So much for the Court's policy of giving the words of a statute their "ordinary meaning"![143] Although, I suppose "ordinary meanings" are also subject to change through the years.

Even if tomatoes are *culinarily* used as a vegetable, one would think Congress was perfectly capable of specifying the tax applied to imported tomatoes if that was their intent. There is also the matter of tomatoes being juiced and consumed as a beverage (after 1917, anyway)—much like oranges, grapes, and apples. I would hazard a guess that if this case were reconsidered today, there would be a different outcome. Likewise, if the Bloody Mary had been around in the 1880s, the original panel of Justices might have reached the opposite result.[144]

Hooper's Store, singing a country song with the other Muppets® about his favorite *fruit*: tomatoes). Could I have cited an encyclopedia on this point? Probably.

141. Nix v. Hedden, 149 U.S. 304, 306 (1893).

142. *Id.* at 307.

143. *Id.* at 306.

144. For commentary on why the Supreme Court is considered infallible, see *infra* p. 258.

Hablot K. "Phiz" Browne, *Attorney and Client:
Fortitude and Impatience* (etching) *in* CHARLES DICKENS,
BLEAK HOUSE pl. 26 (London, Bradbury & Evans 1853).

§ 6

The Widow's Kiss
and the Farmer

The Widow's Kiss originated from the bar of the Holland House, a hotel once located at Fifth Avenue and Thirtieth Street in New York City.[145] Concocted by bartender George J. Kappeler sometime during the early 1890s, it appeared in his book, *Modern American Drinks* (1895), soon thereafter.[146] Nobody remembers how the cocktail got its name or what widow may have inspired it, but the Widow's Kiss's sweet and herbal notes probably had something to do with it.

If you compare the recipe for the Widow's Kiss with other recipes in this book, you will notice this cocktail looks pretty dangerous on paper. The only ingredient in the libation under 80-proof (40% alcohol by volume, or "ABV") is the ice used to chill the spirits while stirring—and that

---

145. WONDRICH, *supra* note 4, at 298–99.

146. GEORGE J. KAPPELER, MODERN AMERICAN DRINKS: HOW TO MIX AND SERVE ALL KINDS OF CUPS AND DRINKS 110 (Akron, Saalfield Publ'g Co. 1895). The first appearance of a cocktail called the "Widow's Kiss" occurred in 1891, but that cocktail was of William Schmidt's creation and consisted of Yellow Chartreuse® Liqueur, Bénédictine® Liqueur, parfait amour liqueur, and egg white. It does not hold a candle to Kappeler's creation and has largely been forgotten. OXFORD COMPANION, *supra* note 6, at 788.

ends up being strained out! Additionally, apple brandy, Yellow Chartreuse® Liqueur, and Bénédictine® Liqueur are each, individually, *very* potent flavors. However, for some reason, when you combine each of those spirits with Angostura® Bitters you get a complex (albeit boozy) *digestif*.[147] I say "digestif" because you should *never* consume this cocktail on an empty stomach.

Kappeler's book instructs readers to shake the cocktail, but the better practice is to stir it because it is so spirit forward.[148] You might also consider letting the mixture "rest" for a few moments before enjoying it. I find that helps to make the many complex flavors in this cocktail more distinguishable. Finally, I usually opt to use Calvados[149] in a Widow's Kiss, instead of a common apple brandy. It just seems like the "right" thing to do considering Yellow Chartreuse Liqueur and Bénédictine Liqueur are both iconic French liqueurs. Aside from that modification, there really are no substitutes for the other ingredients.

---

147. A *digestif* is a spiritous dram consumed after a meal in order to aid digestion. You will not find much scientific validation for digestifs, but they *are* decidedly posh. *Id.* at 26.
148. KAPPELER, *supra* note 146, at 110. For further information on when stirring is preferable to shaking, see discussion *supra* note 80.
149. Calvados is a brandy made from apples (and sometimes pears, too) in the Normandy region of France that has been aged for a minimum of two years in oak barrels. OXFORD COMPANION, *supra* note 6, at 126.

Hablot K. "Phiz" Browne, *Hyde Park on a Sunday* (etching)
in CHARLES J. LEVER, NUTS AND NUTCRACKERS 81
(London, Bradbury & Evans 1845).

Widow's Kiss[150]

1. Combine the following ingredients in a stirring glass with ice:
    a. 1-1/2 oz. Calvados (or another apple brandy)
    b. 3/4 oz. Yellow Chartreuse® Liqueur
    c. 3/4 oz. Bénédictine® Liqueur
    d. 2 dashes of Angostura® Bitters
2. Stir the contents of the stirring glass with a bar spoon for about 1 minute.
3. Garnish a coupe glass with a Luxardo® Cocktail Cherry.
4. Strain the contents of the stirring glass into the coupe glass and serve "up."

---

150. KAPPELER, *supra* note 146, at 110.

The Farmer

It was inevitable that a cocktail named the "Widow's Kiss" would be paired with a probate case. Call me predictable, but there is an elegance to Occam's Razor—the very antithesis of overthinking.[151] While the story that follows is a bit sad, it illustrates some clever resourcefulness and is a favorite among probate attorneys.

On June 8, 1948, Cecil George Harris, a wheat farmer in Saskatchewan, Canada, was driving a tractor through his fields when a terrible accident transpired that resulted in his left leg becoming pinned underneath the wheel of the tractor.[152] He remained trapped under the heavy machine for an estimated 10–12 hours before he was rescued. Tragically, Harris succumbed to his injuries on June 10th.

Because he had no formal written will, Harris's widow assumed the farmer died intestate[153] until one of the neighbors examined the offending tractor and noticed a message scratched into the red paint on the left fender. It read, "In case I die in this mess I leave all to the wife. Cecil Geo. Harris."[154] It was later deduced that Harris used his pocketknife to scratch his final wishes onto the tractor while trapped underneath it.[155]

---

151. Occam's Razor is a principle of problem solving that favors the simplest solution when choosing among alternatives. It is not so much a scientifically validated preference as it is an aesthetic one. *Occam's Razor*, MERRIAM-WEBSTER'S COLLEGIATE DICTIONARY 857.

152. Geoff Ellwand, *An Analysis of Canada's Most Famous Holograph Will: How a Saskatchewan Farmer Scratched His Way into Legal History*, 77 SASK. L. REV. 1, 3–6 (2014). It is thought that Harris dismounted to adjust some equipment and his tractor rolled backward onto him. *Farmer Pinned Under Tractor*, ROSETOWN EAGLE, June 10, 1948, at 1, https://lexspirit.link/DJAP.

153. "Of, relating to, or involving a person who has died without a valid will." *Intestate*, BLACK'S LAW DICTIONARY 984.

154. Ellwand, *supra* note 152, at 1, 8.

155. *Id.* at 17.

Incidentally, the writing qualified as a "holograph[ic] will" under Saskatchewan law because it was wholly in the handwriting of, and signed by, the deceased farmer—albeit on some pretty unusual stationary.[156] His widow still needed to prove it was her husband's handwriting, but Harris successfully created a valid will without the formalities of a notary or witnesses. Accordingly, the fender was removed from the tractor, dragged into court, and successfully probated. The clerk must have been surprised when an unwieldy, rusted hunk of metal was presented for filing in the public records! Nevertheless, it was dutifully placed on a shelf.

When the courthouse in possession of Harris's tractor fender closed in 1997, the Chief Justice of the Saskatchewan Court of Queen's Bench, Donald K. MacPherson, issued an order for the will to be publicly displayed as a testament to George Harris's ingenuity and resourcefulness in the face of dire circumstances.[157] The tractor fender and Harris's pocketknife were transferred to the University of Saskatchewan Law Library, where the artifacts can be viewed to this day.[158]

While probating a holographic will is not necessarily unusual, the circumstances surrounding (and form of) this will made it rather famous. Despite receiving a fair amount of interest and attention through the years, the probate case was never published in an official reporter— probably because the will was not contested. Even so, you would be hard-pressed to find a textbook on wills that omits the Harris will.

---

156. *In re* Harris Estate, (1948) Kerrobert, SK 1902 (Can. Sask. Surr. Ct.); S.S. 1931, c. 34, § 6(2) (Can.) [1931 Saskatchewan Wills Act].
157. Ellwand, *supra* note 152, at 24.
158. *Id.*

§7

The Old Fashioned and the Whiskey Rebellion

T here is a good reason this cocktail is called the "Old Fashioned": It is likely to be the template for the "original" cocktail.[159] In fact, the recipe for the Old Fashioned can be found in the first recipe book published in the United States devoted entirely to cocktails: *Bar-Tender's Guide, or How to Mix Drinks, or The Bon Vivant's Companion* (1862), by Jeremiah "Jerry" a/k/a "The Professor" Thomas.[160] People had been enjoying cocktails like the Old Fashioned for many decades by that time, but nobody had bothered to publish the recipes for those concoctions en masse—potentially to keep their trade secrets . . . secret. But once Thomas let the cat out of the bag, people began sharing formulas for various elixirs in earnest.

Most of Thomas's recipes followed a deceptively simple formula: combine a strong spirit with sugar, bitters, ice, and (sometimes) a citrus element.[161] No absinthe,

---

159. OXFORD COMPANION, *supra* note 6, at 510.

160. *See* JERRY THOMAS, BAR-TENDER'S GUIDE, OR HOW TO MIX DRINKS, OR THE BON VIVANT'S COMPANION (New York, Dick & Fitzgerald 1862); WONDRICH, *supra* note 4, at 32.

161. *Id.* at 244–47.

vermouth, amari, liquid nitrogen, or other new-fangled ideas were necessary for Thomas to make a name for himself as a mixologist—though, to be sure, part of his fame resulted from his showmanship behind the bar. The Professor called this beverage a "whiskey cocktail," but because it harkens back to a simpler time, we call it the "Old Fashioned" today.[162]

The Old Fashioned quickly goes awry if the proportions are wrong. Use a quality whiskey, and bear in mind that different varieties of sugar and simple syrup impart varying levels of sweetness. Irritatingly, some "bartenders" (particularly those at wedding receptions I have attended) seem to think the bitters or sugar ingredients are interchangeable with club soda. They are not. Similarly, muddling half an orange and several cocktail cherries beyond recognition to create a pulp-laden maelstrom of whiskey and ice is also considered bad form.[163]

With that rant out of the way, please feel free to make your own "New Fashioned" by adding other flavors. A "Fall Fashioned" is one common variation and involves replacing the traditional sugar cube or simple syrup with maple syrup. Add a cinnamon stick for garnish and you have a cocktail reminiscent of fall. No pumpkin spice required!

---

162. THOMAS, *supra* note 160, at 50; JEFFREY MORGENTHALER, MARTHA HOLMBERG & ALANNA HALE, THE BAR BOOK: ELEMENTS OF COCKTAIL TECHNIQUE 81 (Chronicle Books 2014).

163. GREENE, *supra* note 64, at 71. Each of those *faux pas* appear to have been implemented during Prohibition. OXFORD COMPANION, *supra* note 6, at 511. A fine fellow I know in Arkansas managed to convince me that it is possible to craft a respectable Old Fashioned *despite* muddling a slice of orange and some cherries because he made a fine cocktail by doing so. Importantly, he strains most (nearly all) of the pulverized fruit out of the beverage prior to serving.

Old Fashioned[164]

1. Combine the following ingredients in a stirring glass with ice:
   a. 2-1/2 oz. Bourbon or other whiskey
   b. *One* of the following:
      i. A muddled sugar cube mixed with a splash of water; or
      ii. 1 tsp. simple syrup and 1/4 oz. Luxardo® Maraschino Liqueur for a less traditional—but highly effective—way to add sweetness[165]
   c. 3 dashes of Angostura® Bitters
   d. 3 dashes of orange bitters
2. Stir the contents of the stirring glass with a bar spoon for about 1 minute.
3. Place a large ice cube in an old fashioned glass and garnish with a Luxardo® Cocktail Cherry (or three).
4. Express the oils from the exterior of an orange peel into the glass and rub the peel around the rim before placing in the glass.[166]
5. Strain the contents of the stirring glass into the old fashioned glass and serve "on the rocks."

---

164. DeGroff, *supra* note 31, at 40; Donovan, *supra* note 76, at 11.

165. I am a fan of using the tag team of simple syrup and Luxardo Maraschino Liqueur to sweeten an Old Fashioned, but muddled sugar cubes are considered to be more authentic. We are, after all, being old fashioned. Note that the sugar cube may not completely dissolve, but some people enjoy the added character. I say drink whichever version you like better.

166. Some people prefer to use an orange peel with Bourbon and a lemon peel with rye whiskey. Litigators could spend hours debating the wisdom of each of those alternatives, but a clever transactional attorney or mediator would point out what is *really* important—everyone can agree a lime peel would be downright inappropriate.

The Last Hours of Congress (etching) *in* HARPER'S WKLY., Mar. 12, 1859, at 161.

The Whiskey Rebellion

In Lin-Manuel Miranda's *Hamilton: An American Musical* (2015) Thomas Jefferson delivers several choice lines criticizing Alexander Hamilton's plan to fund the payment of the new nation's debt. Most notably, Jefferson lambasts Hamilton's idea to tax domestic whiskey production.[167] It is unfortunate that particular subject was not developed any further in the musical because Hamilton's idea was responsible for spawning an open revolt. Remember how I mentioned raising hell over taxes is America's pastime?[168] Well, as it turns out, politicians with a short memory are not a modern phenomenon.

After the ratification of the Constitution of the United States in 1788, Congress assumed some $25 million of state debt and added it to the towering pile of federal debt from the Revolutionary War. The national debt approached $80 million—a daunting amount for the fledgling nation to bear.[169] Ever the pragmatist, Secretary of the Treasury Alexander Hamilton decided the taxation of domestically produced liquor was an ideal way to fund the payment of the national debt. Because liquor was a luxury good, the idea was the tax would simply be borne by consumers who could afford the extra expense.[170] The plan made sense on paper, and the resulting statute levied the United States' first excise tax on a domestically produced product.[171]

---

167. *See* ORIGINAL BROADWAY CAST, *Cabinet Battle #1*, on HAMILTON: AN AMERICAN MUSICAL, at 0:22–1:19 (Atlantic 2015).

168. *See* discussion *supra* p. 40.

169. WILLIAM HOGELAND, THE WHISKEY REBELLION: GEORGE WASHINGTON, ALEXANDER HAMILTON, AND THE FRONTIER REBELS WHO CHALLENGED AMERICA'S NEWFOUND SOVEREIGNTY 61 (Simon & Schuster 2006).

170. *Id.* at 63.

171. *Id.* at 51, 63.

The Whiskey Tax (as it became known) was levied "upon all spirits which after [June 1791 were] . . . distilled within the United States," but it was calculated in a different manner depending upon whether a distiller was situated in a rural or urban area.[172] Liquor distilled in an urban setting was assessed a tax of 9 to 25 cents per gallon *produced*, depending on the proof of the spirit.[173] On the other hand, stills operated in rural areas were assessed a flat annual tax of 60 cents per gallon of distilling *capacity*.[174] For reference, it took about 100 gallons of wash to produce 12 gallons of spirit.[175] Assuming a farmer owned a 100-gallon still, if they wanted to effectively match the 9 cent per gallon tax applicable to urban distillers (for low proof spirits), they needed to produce 667 gallons of liquor annually to dilute their $60 in fixed costs. Urban distillers, on the other hand, enjoyed the same tax rate per gallon whether they produced 1 gallon of whiskey or 2,000! Unfortunately, rural distillers typically ran small operations that did not produce enough whiskey to offset the flat-rate tax assessed on their still's capacity. As a result, the effective tax they paid per gallon of production was routinely greater than that borne by urban distillers.[176] That paradigm also foreclosed any possibility of rural farmers passing their increased distilling costs to consumers because urban producers would simply undercut their prices.

The egregiously unbalanced rural tax imposed a severe burden on poor farmers—particularly those in western

---

172. Excise Whiskey Tax of 1791, ch. 15, § 15, 1 Stat. 199, 203. "City, town, or village" was the phrase used to describe an urban area in the statute. Everything else was considered to be rural.

173. *Id.*

174. *Id.* § 21, 1 Stat. at 204.

175. HOGELAND, *supra* note 169, at 69.

176. *Id.* at 59.

Pennsylvania. Farmers had become reliant on whiskey production to supplement their income because whiskey was significantly easier and cheaper to transport to market than a corresponding amount of raw grain. It also did not spoil—but was prone to leakage and evaporation.[177] Congress attempted to ameliorate the situation by providing a tax exemption for persons owning only one pot still with a capacity of 50 gallons or less,[178] but anyone remotely serious about distilling would have owned a still with more than 50 gallons of capacity (or multiple smaller stills). Making matters worse, Congress removed this exemption in 1792, meaning no pot still was too small to escape taxation. Another revision to the law also made the failure to register a pot still punishable by a draconian $250 fine per unregistered still.[179] Half of that fine was offered as a bounty to anyone who snitched on their neighbor for owning an unregistered still. Rural farmers were incensed and felt exploited by the federal

---

177. *See* Saul Cornell, *Mobs, Militias, and Magistrates: Popular Constitutionalism and the Whiskey Rebellion*, 81 CHI.-KENT L. REV. 883, 894 (2006).

> To haul twenty-four bushels of milled rye over the Alleghenies to eastern markets would have taken three pack animals. $6 might result from such effort; costs would outrun revenues. Reducing those bushels to two eight-gallon kegs of whiskey reduced transport requirements to a single animal, and while income from such a venture varied . . . [revenues] could approach $16.

HOGELAND, *supra* note 169, at 69.

178. Excise Whiskey Tax of 1791 § 36, 1 Stat. at 208.

179. An Act Concerning the Duties on Spirits Distilled Within the United States, ch. 32, §§ 2, 13, 1 Stat. 267, 268, 270 (1792). This act also slightly lowered the tax rates applicable to urban distillers and made a weak attempt to fairly restructure the regime applicable to rural distillers by offering several alternative bases for taxation. *Id.* § 1, 1 Stat. at 267–68. It was not effective.

government. They made their feelings known just over two months after the Whiskey Tax initially became effective.

On the evening of September 11, 1791, Robert Johnson, a revenue agent in western Pennsylvania, was riding through the woods when he encountered 15 to 20 armed men with blackened faces blocking his path. They were definitely men, but for some reason many wore women's dresses for the occasion. (In all likelihood, they had been drinking.) Johnson was unhorsed by the posse, stripped naked, shaved bare, and brutally tarred and feathered.[180] Johnson survived his ordeal, but it marked the first of many such violent demonstrations against tax collectors in western Pennsylvania.[181]

Never one to be a tyrant, President George Washington (who, incidentally, would venture into commercial whiskey distilling in 1797[182]) tread carefully around the volatile situation. He consulted with his Cabinet and decided to encourage compliance with promises of leniency, much to the chagrin of the hawkish Alexander Hamilton.[183] Hamilton wanted to call out the militia and punish those responsible for this blatant affront to federal authority in the region, but Washington made it clear that federal troops were only to be deployed as a last resort.[184] Unfortunately, things continued to escalate over the following years until that is exactly what happened.

The man in charge of administering the whiskey tax in western Pennsylvania was a veteran of the Revolutionary War named John Neville, and to say he was not well liked

---

180. HOGELAND, *supra* note 169, at 20–23.

181. *Id.* at 137, 143.

182. *Ten Facts About the Distillery*, MOUNT VERNON, https://lexspirit.link/9Y6W. Based on the location of Washington's distillery, he was probably taxed as a rural distiller.

183. Cornell, *supra* note 177, at 894–95.

184. HOGELAND, *supra* note 169, at 124–27.

in the region for having assumed this role would be putting it mildly.[185] On July 15, 1794, Neville and a federal marshal were serving warrants on farmers for having unregistered stills when an angry rabble began taking pot shots at them.[186] Neville prudently retreated to his hilltop mansion and fortified it that evening. The next morning, he awoke to 50 men armed with rifles and muskets demanding he resign his commission, surrender his tax records, and swear to never collect taxes ever again. Neville responded by shooting at the rapscallions. His first shot killed one of the youngest members of the angry mob, snuffing out any hope for a peaceful resolution in an instant.[187]

All hell broke loose for the next half hour as the house was pounded with musket and rifle fire. Neville managed to keep the men at bay by skillfully maintaining a high rate of fire from inside his home. His wife and granddaughter contributed greatly to the defense effort by continuously reloading a series of muskets for Neville to fire. After the attackers suffered four more casualties, they withdrew to a nearby redoubt left over from the French and Indian War called Couch's Fort, where they regrouped and called for reinforcements.[188] Word quickly spread through the region of the skirmish and the ranks of the rebellious farmers soon swelled to nearly 600 men.

On July 17, 1794, the rebels marched back to Neville's home atop Bower Hill to find it defended by Neville's slaves and 10 soldiers under the command of Major Abraham Kirkpatrick. The defenders put up a valiant fight from inside Neville's house, but once the rebels set fire to the

---

185. *Id.* at 97.
186. *Id.* at 143.
187. *Id.* at 147–48.
188. *Id.* at 148–50.

structure, Kirkpatrick was left with no option but to surrender. The farm was ransacked and razed to the ground, and the rebels took several prisoners.[189] Emboldened by their victory, the rebels then decided to march toward Pittsburgh. They called for other aggrieved farmers to join in their demonstrations, and on August 1, 1794, around 7,000 armed rebels assembled on Braddock's Field just outside the city. The citizens of the largely rural region did not feel they were being adequately represented by the federal government, and there were calls for a sovereign territory to be created. A flag was designed, a congress was convened, and debates on how to fairly redistribute the wealth and land of the region were held. Even if poorly organized, it was nothing short of an insurrection.[190]

President Washington and the rest of the federal government in Philadelphia (the capital of the nation at the time) were both infuriated and horrified by the events of July and August 1794, and Washington called out the militia to meet the rebellion head on. Simultaneously, a delegation that included the second Attorney General of the United States, William Bradford, was dispatched to meet with the rebels, but the underlying aim of the negotiations was never to find a solution to the rebels' grievances. Instead, the delegation's primary purpose was to buy time for Washington and Hamilton to mobilize 13,000 militia from New Jersey, (eastern) Pennsylvania, Maryland, and Virginia to put down the rebellion.[191] By

---

189. *Id.* at 152–54.
190. *Id.* at 171–83.
191. *Id.* at 185–202; ROBERT W. COAKLEY, THE ROLE OF FEDERAL MILITARY FORCES IN DOMESTIC DISORDERS, 1789–1878, at 53–58 (Ctr. Mil. Hist. U.S. Army 1988). In his sixth annual message to Congress, Washington claimed he commanded an army of 15,000 soldiers to meet the rebels, but that figure is likely too high. President

early September 1794, the federal troops were assembled and George Washington rode westward with them.[192] To date, it remains the only time a sitting Commander-in-Chief of the armed forces of the United States has donned a uniform and taken personal command of an army in the field. When word of Washington's approach reached the area, the rebels wisely decided to avoid a confrontation with the larger, well-equipped force and promptly dispersed. The rebellion was effectively finished, and most of the noteworthy rebels fled the area. Once it became clear that no rebel force would engage in a battle with the federal forces, Washington departed for Philadelphia and left the army under Hamilton's command.[193] Today, the role of the Secretary of the Treasury is diminutive compared to what it used to entail!

To bring an end to the matter, on the night of November 13, 1794, the cavalry[194] was dispatched to round up suspected rebels in a synchronized raid. In what became known as the "Dreadful Night," some 200 suspected instigators were roused from their beds at the point of a bayonet and arrested. Secretary Hamilton personally interrogated many of the captives.[195]

George Washington, Sixth Annual Message to Congress (Nov. 19, 1794), https://lexspirit.link/P2ED. In any case, Washington *did* command an army larger than any he personally led during the Revolutionary War.

192. HOGELAND, *supra* note 169, at 206.

193. *Id.* at 217.

194. The word "cavalry," referring to soldiers mounted on horseback, is sometimes misspoken as "Calvary," which is one name for the hill Jesus Christ was crucified on (also called Golgotha, which means "Place of a Skull"). The words may look similar, but their meanings certainly are not! *Calvary* & *Cavalry*, MERRIAM-WEBSTER'S COLLEGIATE DICTIONARY 176, 197; *Mark* 15:22.

195. HOGELAND, *supra* note 169, at 220–21.

Of the scores of men arrested, only 20 were marched to Philadelphia to face indictment.[196] But indictments for high treason were difficult to secure against many of those prisoners because of a general lack of evidence, inconclusive and conflicting testimony, and cases of mistaken identity. Also, the local populace in western Pennsylvania was not exactly clamoring to testify against their kith and kin. Ultimately, only 12 rebels were indicted, and their respective trials commenced in May 1795 in the United States Circuit Court for the District of Pennsylvania, with Supreme Court Justice William Paterson presiding.[197]

As with the indictment process, evidentiary issues plagued each of the trials. The Constitution provides that no person can be convicted of treason for levying war against the United States unless at least *two* witnesses to the overt act testify against the accused at trial.[198] The two-witness minimum does not apply if the accused confesses in open court to having committed treason, but prosecutors had no such luck in that department. Finding two witnesses to testify against each of the accused proved more difficult than collecting the Whiskey Tax, and in the

---

196. *Id.* at 235.

197. In the 1790s, there were three circuit courts in the United States, which were each staffed by two Supreme Court Justices and one federal district court judge. While circuit courts often functioned as the appellate courts for federal district courts, they also served as trial courts if the amount of money in controversy or level of punishment were material. In the case of treason (punishable by death), circuit courts had exclusive jurisdiction over those trials because a district court could only hear criminal cases in which the range of punishment did not exceed 30 lashes, a fine not exceeding $100, or a term of imprisonment not exceeding six months. Judiciary Act of 1789, ch. 20, §§ 4, 9, 11, 1 Stat. 73, 74–79.

198. "No person shall be convicted of treason unless on the testimony of two witnesses to the same overt act, or on confession in open court." U.S. CONST. art. III, § 3, cl. 1.

end only two rebels, John Mitchell[199] and Philip Vigol,[200] were convicted of high treason against the United States. Each man was sentenced to be "hanged by the neck till [they] be dead," and their executions were scheduled for June 17, 1795.[201]

Shortly before the men began their walk to the gallows, Washington granted them a reprieve until November 4, 1795.[202] He wanted time to mull over whether to pardon the two men. Separately, on July 10, 1795, Washington issued a general pardon to all those who took part in the rebellion but had not yet been indicted or convicted of an offense.[203] Mitchell and Vigol, however, were excluded from that pardon.

Finally, on November 2, 1795, Washington mercifully issued a pardon to Mitchell and Vigol. In doing so, he commented, "For though I shall always think it a sacred

---

199. John Mitchell was convicted of high treason for his role in attacking and destroying the property of two excise officers, Philip Reagan and Benjamin Wells. United States v. Mitchell, 2 U.S. (2 Dall.) 348 (1795).

200. Philip Vigol was convicted of high treason for having gathered at Couch's Fort, taking part in the attack on General Neville's house at Bower Hill, and assembling at Braddock's Field. United States v. Vigol, 2 U.S. (2 Dall.) 346 (1795).

201. President George Washington, Philip Vigol Stay of Execution (June 16, 1795), https://lexspirit.link/TKD6. There was no lesser sentence available for someone found guilty of treason against the United States, and hanging was the only sanctioned method of execution. Crimes Act of 1790, ch. 9, §§ 1, 33, 1 Stat. 112, 112, 119. If this seems cruel, consider that federally convicted murderers were also eligible to receive a so-called enhancement to their death sentence called "punitive dissection," which entails exactly what you would expect. *Id.* § 4, 1 Stat. at 113.

202. The authority for reprieves and pardons by the President is found in U.S. CONST. art. II, § 2, cl. 1 ("The President . . . shall have power to grant reprieves and pardons for offenses against the United States, except in cases of impeachment.").

203. President George Washington, Proclamation of Pardons in Western Pennsylvania (July 10, 1795), https://lexspirit.link/R3LU.

duty to exercise with firmness and energy the constitutional powers with which I am vested . . . it appears to me no less consistent with the public good . . . to mingle in the operations of government every degree of moderation and tenderness which the national justice, dignity, and safety may permit."[204] These were the first presidential pardons issued in the United States for a criminal conviction.

Aside from the assault on Bower Hill, order was restored without firing a shot. However, it came an estimated cost of nearly $1.2 million—more than the Whiskey Tax brought in during the legislation's entire lifespan.[205] In 1802, Thomas Jefferson put the Whiskey Tax out of its misery when he signed "An Act to Repeal the Internal Taxes" into law, thereby closing a tumultuous chapter in the new nation's history.[206]

---

204. President George Washington, Seventh Annual Message to Congress (Dec. 8, 1795), https://lexspirit.link/FMQK.
205. COAKLEY, *supra* note 191, at 61–63, 65.
206. *See* An Act to Repeal the Internal Taxes, ch. 19, 2 Stat. 148 (1802).

§8

The Paper Plane and
the Process Server

When Toby Maloney opened The Violet Hour® in Chicago in 2007, he asked two of his former colleagues from Milk & Honey®, Sam Ross (of Penicillin[207] fame) and Sasha Petraske, to create an original cocktail for the menu.[208] Petraske and Ross decided to create a whiskey-based cocktail that was a riff on the Last Word[209] (a cocktail featuring equal proportions of four ingredients). After a long night of experimenting, a buzzed—but triumphant—Ross left Maloney a voicemail relaying the name and recipe for the new cocktail. Maloney understood the portion of the voicemail where Ross conveyed the instructions for equal measures of Bourbon, Amaro Nonino Quintessentia® Liqueur, lemon juice, and Campari® Liqueur, but apparently misheard the name of the cocktail as being the "Paper Airplane."[210]

In 2008, the cocktail made its public debut at The Violet Hour under the incorrect name, but it was soon

---

207. *See* Penicillin *infra* p. 93.
208. Robert Simonson, *How the Paper Plane Became a Modern Classic*, PUNCH (Sept. 30, 2020), https://lexspirit.link/CFBC.
209. *See* The Last Word *infra* p. 251.
210. Simonson, *supra* note 208.

revised to reflect the name Ross had given the cocktail: Paper Plane.[211] It was a nod to *Paper Planes*, a single from M.I.A.'s second studio album, *Kala* (2007)—a guilty pleasure of Petraske's at the time.[212]

As it turned out, the name was not the only correction Ross would request. He eventually axed the Campari component of the recipe and replaced it with another bitter spirit—Aperol® Liqueur. To his palate, Campari made the cocktail too bitter and substituting Aperol in its place brought balance to the Paper Plane. Some folks still order the original iteration of the cocktail, but thanks to the Aperol substitution, the Paper Plane quickly became a recognizable—and high-flying—orange-colored cocktail.

Amaro Nonino Quintessentia Liqueur can be a somewhat difficult ingredient to procure, but—thanks in part to the Paper Plane's success—it can generally be found at specialty liquor stores. This cocktail is normally served without a garnish, but folding and affixing a tiny paper plane to the rim of the glass would be considered pretty chic. There are a few empty pages at the end of this book that may be of some assistance in such an endeavor.

---

211. ROBERT SIMONSON, A PROPER DRINK: THE UNTOLD STORY OF HOW A BAND OF BARTENDERS SAVED THE CIVILIZED DRINKING WORLD 288 (Ten Speed Press 2016).

212. SASHA PETRASKE, REGARDING COCKTAILS 125 (Phaidon Press 2016); M.I.A., *Paper Planes, on* KALA (XL Recordings 2007).

Paper Plane[213]

1. Combine the following ingredients in a stirring glass with ice:
   a. 1 oz. Amaro Nonino Quintessentia® Liqueur[214]
   b. 1 oz. Aperol® Liqueur[215]
   c. 1 oz. Bourbon
   d. 1 oz. fresh-squeezed lemon juice
2. Stir the contents of the stirring glass with a bar spoon for about 1 minute.
3. If you wish, garnish a coupe glass with a lemon peel— or a tiny paper plane.
4. Strain the contents of the stirring glass into the coupe glass and serve "up."

---

213. PETRASKE, *supra* note 212, at 125.

214. *Amaro* means "bitter" in Italian, and there are many types of *amari* (the plural form of amaro). Do not make the mistake of thinking any liqueur with the word amaro in its name is a substitute for Amaro Nonino Quintessentia Liqueur. I tried a different amaro once, and the result tasted like ear wax. It was a humbling experience!

215. Yet another variety of amari!

The Process Server

I bet you expected to read about a lawsuit involving a plane crash in this chapter. That would have been a good (but incorrect) guess! Actually, the legal tie-in here involves paper—a physical piece of it. The underlying record is short, and the original wording is too good to forgo, so here it is in its full, unabridged glory:

> ### 12 Feb. 1773, Lord Bathurst
> ### The High Court of Chancery
>
> This was an application without notice, to commit the defendant for a contempt, in making the person, who served him with a subpœna to appear and answer, eat the same, and otherwise ill-treating him; the defendant ordered to stand committed, unless cause; but by reason of his ferocious and terrible disposition, no one being willing to hazard serving him, leaving the order at his house, was to be deemed good service.[216]

Did you catch the part where the defendant made the process server *eat the very paper the subpoena*[217] *was written on?!*[218] The defendant's barbaric antics are now immortalized for all time in the English Reports, and you can chuckle at someone's misfortune nearly 250 years after the fact.

---

216. Williams v. Johns, (1773) 21 Eng. Rep. 355 (Ch) at 355; 2 Dickens 477, 477.

217. "A writ or order commanding a person to appear before a court or other tribunal, subject to a penalty for failing to comply." *Subpoena*, BLACK'S LAW DICTIONARY 1725.

218. I wonder whether the defendant had any help in making the process server eat the subpoena. Perhaps he accomplished that feat of persuasion on his own!

§9

Ranch Water and the Texas Country Club

R anch Water is a West Texas innovation, but nobody seems to know for certain who invented it or when it came about. What we *do* know with some conviction is that the libation was an adaptive response to Texas resembling the surface of the sun during the summer months. Popular wisdom ascribes Ranch Water's origin to the bar at the Gage Hotel® in Marathon, Texas, but the late Kevin Williamson, who opened Ranch 616 in Austin in 1998, claimed the highball originated from his restaurant.[219] In fact, he alleged his staff taught the bartenders at the Gage Hotel how to make the Ranch Water! Williamson even tried to register a trademark for the cocktail in 2017, but the registration was refused because Ranch Water had become so popular by then (and therefore omnipresent) that the United States Patent and Trademark Office considered the mark to be generic.[220]

---

219. M. Carrie Allen, *How to Make Ranch Water, the Tequila-Lime Cocktail That Keeps So Many Texans Cool*, WASH. POST (July 27, 2021, 10:00 AM), https://lexspirit.link/BCDM.

220. *See* U.S. Pat. & Trademark Off., Office Action of August 22, 2018 on U.S. Trademark Application Serial No. 87/399,308 (filed Apr. 5, 2017), https://lexspirit.link/NPZ4. The world of trademarked cocktails is discussed further *infra* p. 143.

Ranch Water has been described as a "crude version of something that seem[s] half Tom Collins and half Margarita."[221] Truthfully, that might be the best description of this highball I have ever heard. It is not much more than Tequila, sparkling mineral water (usually Topo Chico® Agua Mineral), and lime juice, but for all its simplicity, it is incredibly refreshing.

Speaking of which, unlike Ranch Water, Topo Chico Agua Mineral has a well-defined (if not necessarily believable) origin story. In the 1440s, an Aztec princess came down with a mysterious illness. Her father, King Moteuczomatzin Ilhuicamina, asked his priests to find a cure—provided they had some availability after meeting their astronomical daily quota of human sacrifices. The priests suggested the King seek the "strange and hidden waters" to the north, and he immediately organized an expedition. The venturers eventually reached a fertile valley flanked by mountains in what is now Monterrey, Mexico. When they looked east, they saw a little mole-shaped hill (*Cerro del Topo Chico*, in Spanish) with natural springs flowing from it. After the princess bathed in and drank the water from this hill, she was miraculously healed.[222]

That being said, the *verifiable* history of Topo Chico begins in 1895, when a company began carbonating, bottling, and selling the spring water from Cerro del Topo

---

221. *See* Veronica Meewes, *How Ranch Water Became the Unofficial Cocktail of West Texas*, PUNCH (Aug. 30, 2016), https://lexspirit.link/BUQY; *see also* Margarita recipe *supra* p. 12.

Tom Collins: 1-½ oz. gin, 1 oz. simple syrup, and ¾ oz. fresh-squeezed lemon juice. Combine those ingredients with ice in a cocktail shaker, shake well, and strain into a highball glass filled with ice. Top with club soda, gently stir the contents of the glass, and garnish with a cocktail cherry and an orange slice. DEGROFF, *supra* note 31, at 122.

222. *The Legend of the Princess*, TOPO CHICO, https://lexspirit.link/XIWJ.

Chico, from which they derived the name of their product. Topo Chico eventually became a major brand of sparkling water in Mexico and was prevalent in Texas by the 1980s. Thanks in no small part to Ranch Water, it eventually gained a cult following. Coca-Cola® acquired the brand in October 2017, and Topo Chico has only continued to grow in popularity—so much so that there was a national shortage of the product in the United States during the COVID-19 pandemic.[223]

In the recipe that follows I insist you use Topo Chico® Agua Mineral (as opposed to another brand of sparkling mineral water) because it is aggressively effervescent. Seriously—as in, "Would you like some liquid with that carbonation?" levels of bubbly. The carbonation may be the only thing preventing you from downing the glass too quickly!

223. Kate Taylor, *Coca-Cola Is Using a Sparkling-Water Brand with a Cult Following to Take Over a $16 Billion Industry*, BUS. INSIDER (June 15, 2018, 8:40 AM), https://lexspirit.link/YOLX.

Ranch Water[224]

1. Combine the following ingredients in a cocktail shaker with ice:
    a. 3/4 oz. (or more) of fresh-squeezed lime juice
    b. 2 oz. blanco/silver Tequila[225]
2. Cap the cocktail shaker and shake vigorously for 20–30 seconds.
3. Fill about 3/4 of a highball glass with ice and then intersperse several thinly sliced cross sections of a lime throughout the glass to serve as a garnish. If you wish, you can also rim the glass with chili salt.
4. Strain the contents of the shaker into the glass and top with 4 oz. of Topo Chico® Agua Mineral (or enough to fill the glass).
5. Gently stir the contents of the glass with a bar spoon.
6. Keep the rest of the bottle of Topo Chico (and Tequila) nearby in case the drinker would like to top off the glass as they go.

---

224. Formulation courtesy of John Laue at Proof Productions. By the way, nobody would scoff if you haphazardly filled a highball glass with ice, poured in some Topo Chico and Tequila, and then squeezed a lime into the glass. There is nothing wrong with keeping this simple!

225. *See* *for* *no* *particular* *reason* TIM FEDERLE, TEQUILA MOCKINGBIRD: COCKTAILS WITH A LITERARY TWIST (Running Press 2013). This book should not be confused with a similarly named volume by Harper Lee that won the Pulitzer Prize in 1961.

The Texas Country Club

Speaking of West Texas, while the infamous "Compromise of 1850" was largely a series of acts that only served to delay the Civil War by 10 years, one of those statutes fixed Texas's western-most border with the New Mexico Territory.[226] A portion of the border is formed by the Rio Grande as it flows between the latitudes of 31 and 32 degrees north.[227] And yet, in 1906, the El Paso Country Club established itself on the *west* bank (New Mexico's side) of the Rio Grande.[228] What gives? Well, as it turns out, where the Rio Grande chooses to flow is the product of fickle fortune, and the river had meandered around in the preceding decades.[229] Local tradition held the area where the country club was situated was in Texas despite residing on New Mexico's side of the river.

When the New Mexico Territory was admitted as a state in 1912, the New Mexico Constitution reaffirmed that part of the state's border with Texas was defined by the center of the Rio Grande as it existed on September 9, 1850.[230] However, given how precious water and fertile

---

226. Act of Sept. 9, 1850, ch. 49, § 1, 9 Stat. 446, 446. This was one of five acts collectively known as the "Compromise of 1850." The other four acts dealt with (i) establishing a territorial government for Utah (ch. 51, 9 Stat. 453), (ii) admitting California as a state (ch. 50, 9 Stat. 452), (iii) suppressing the slave trade in Washington, D.C. (ch. 63, 9 Stat. 467), and (iv) amending the Fugitive Slave Act of 1793 (ch. 60, 9 Stat. 462).

227. You do not need to be a cartographer to fully appreciate this dispute. Just know the river forms the border.

228. *Club House Dedicated: Country Club Has a Formal Opening*, EL PASO MORNING TIMES, June 8, 1906, at 3, https://lexspirit.link/KHUJ.

229. *See* New Mexico v. Texas, 275 U.S. 279, 282 (1927).

230. N.M. CONST. art. I ("The name of this state is New Mexico, and its boundaries are as follows: . . . thence along said thirty-second parallel to the Rio Grande, also known as the Rio Bravo del Norte, as it existed on the ninth day of September, one thousand eight hundred and

land are in that part of the country, it should come as no surprise that New Mexico had a different recollection as to where exactly the Rio Grande flowed on September 9, 1850. Although, to be fair to New Mexico, the border in that area looks like a heavily caffeinated toddler scribbled it on the map with a crayon during an earthquake. New Mexico sued Texas over this border dispute within a year of becoming a state.[231]

Because it had original jurisdiction[232] in *New Mexico v. Texas*, the Supreme Court appointed a Special Master[233] to conduct fact finding for the case.[234] Both states agreed the Rio Grande had moved since September 9, 1850, so the parties focused on proving where the river had flowed over a half century before.[235] Texas relied on several surveys to support its position, including one conducted in 1859 by a member of the United States and Texas Boundary Commission.[236] While that particular survey occurred nine years *after* the date in question and the original survey

---

fifty [the date fixed by the Compromise of 1850]; thence, following the main channel of said river, as it existed on the ninth day of September, one thousand eight hundred and fifty . . . .").

231. *New Mexico*, 275 U.S. at 281–82.

232. "A court's power to hear and decide a matter before any other court can review the matter." *Original Jurisdiction*, BLACK'S LAW DICTIONARY 1019. Although the Supreme Court of the United States usually functions as the highest appellate court in the land, there are certain situations where it serves as a trial court. One such example of this is when there are "[c]ontroversies between two or more States." U.S. CONST. art. III, § 2, cl. 1.

233. "A parajudicial officer specially appointed to help a court with its proceedings." *Master*, BLACK'S LAW DICTIONARY 1168.

234. William Howard Taft (as President) signed the joint resolution admitting New Mexico as a state on January 6, 1912 (S.J. Res. 57, 62d Cong., 37 Stat. 39 (1911)), and then he (as the Chief Justice of the Supreme Court) presided over New Mexico's case against Texas. He remains the only person to have held both offices.

235. *New Mexico*, 275 U.S. at 281, 283.

236. *Id.* at 290, 295.

monuments[237] had been lost, it was supplemented by the Salazar-Diaz Survey of 1852. The Salazar-Diaz Survey was compiled by a Mexican engineer for the Joint Boundary Commission established at the conclusion of the Mexican–American War (1846–1848), and it was performed much closer to the relevant date.[238] All told, Texas's surveys were very persuasive.

The same could not be said for much of New Mexico's evidence, which relied heavily on eyewitness testimony. In evaluating the quality and credibility of the testimony, the Special Master commented that, "Most of the witnesses were illiterate; they were unable to estimate distances with any degree of accuracy . . . . All . . . were old men, some very old."[239]

Notwithstanding the age of anyone with relevant knowledge of the area, it is not surprising New Mexico faced such difficulty in locating credible witnesses because there were not many people in the area during the 1850s. At that time, the western part of Texas was under the control of the most fearsome light cavalry force the world has ever seen: the Comanche.[240] Because of this, it was

---

237. "Any natural or artificial object that is fixed permanently in land and referred to in a legal description of the land." *Monument*, BLACK'S LAW DICTIONARY 1207.

238. *New Mexico*, 275 U.S. at 295.

239. *Id.* at 287.

240. T.R. FEHRENBACH, LONE STAR: A HISTORY OF TEXAS AND THE TEXANS 58, 469, 535 (1st Da Capo Press 2000) (1968). Even in 1870, Comanche raids (combined with ecological factors, to be fair) held white civilization in Texas largely east of the 98th meridian west. *Id.* at 535. That changed in the 1870s when buffalo, the lifeblood of the Comanche, were hunted to near extinction by white settlers. STEPHEN HARRIGAN, BIG WONDERFUL THING: A HISTORY OF TEXAS 331–33 (Univ. Tex. Press 2019). It was not uncommon for buffalo hunters to carry vials of poison around their necks because retaliatory Comanche raids advanced the field of torture to new frontiers. Neither side had clean hands, but the rest of the frontier was soon "open to settlement" (i.e., no longer "settled" by the roaming Comanche).

several decades before a critical mass of white settlers occupied the area to establish (or recognize) a landmark permanent enough to judge the relative position of the river against.

In short, New Mexico's witness testimony fell flat, Texas won the case, and the Supreme Court admonished the parties to keep track of the boundary in the future.[241] Ironically, by the time the case was adjudicated, the El Paso Country Club had voluntarily relocated to the *east* side of the Rio Grande—where it remains to this day. Even so, this case is still remembered as the "Country Club Dispute."

Hablot K. "Phiz" Browne, *Cheering the Speech of a Comrade* (etching) *in* JAMES GRANT, SKETCHES IN LONDON pl. 8 (London, Wm. Tegg 1838).

241. *New Mexico*, 275 U.S. at 287, 303.

§ 10

Eggnog, the Clerk, and the Archive War

In 1862, Jerry Thomas wrote: "Egg Nogg is a beverage of American origin, but it has a popularity that is cosmopolitan."[242] He might be right about the second part, but Eggnog is only an American innovation insofar as the colonists appear to have replaced the more expensive Sherry in an existing beverage with a cheaper alcohol: rum.

The precursor to Eggnog was a beverage called Posset, which dates back to 13th century Britain and consists of hot ale, curdled milk, and Sherry mixed with eggs and figs.[243] Even though the original concept for the beverage was British, the American formulation soon became distinct from Posset. In addition to swapping the Sherry for rum, the colonists began serving Eggnog cold and dropped the strong ale ("nog") ingredient from the recipe altogether.[244] Eggnog surged in popularity in the colonies partly because eggs and dairy were so much cheaper than in Great Britain, making it a luxury everyone could

---

242. THOMAS, *supra* note 160, at 40.
243. OXFORD COMPANION, *supra* note 6, at 553.
244. Elizabeth Dias, *A Brief History of Eggnog*, TIME (Dec. 21, 2011, 11:27 AM), https://lexspirit.link/XZDO.

afford.[245] As a result, Eggnog soon became a much-beloved holiday favorite in the United States and has remained so for several centuries.[246]

The recipe that follows is best enjoyed after letting the mixture age for several months in the refrigerator. I suggest mixing up a batch in October to enjoy during your Christmas (or other holiday) celebrations. Do not worry about the dairy and eggs going bad over that time period— there is enough alcohol in this concoction to incapacitate the camel George Washington hosted at Mount Vernon for Christmas in 1787.[247] That is to say, the alcohol will act as a preservative and time will not ravage the ingredients, especially when the eggs and dairy are pasteurized and the mixture is kept refrigerated.[248] Just be sure to shake the jar every now and then to ensure the mixture remains homogenous.

---

245. DEGROFF, *supra* note 31, at 220.

246. WONDRICH, *supra* note 4, at 160.

247. GEORGE WASHINGTON, *Cash . . . Contra, 29 December 1787*, LEDGER B #257a ("By the man who brot. [*sic*] A Camel from Alexa[ndria]. For a show . . . . 0.18.0."). Washington paid 18 shillings to secure a visit from the exotic animal to entertain his holiday guests. Mary V. Thompson, *Camel*, MOUNT VERNON, https://lexspirit.link/C6LT.

248. *Rockefeller Microbiologist Tests Safety of Spiked Eggnog*, ROCKEFELLER UNIV. (Dec. 19, 2008), https://lexspirit.link/H8G4. This was only an anecdotal study (not peer reviewed), but the initial findings are fairly compelling. Still, the United States Food and Drug Administration's recommendation is to use *pasteurized* (not raw) dairy and eggs. U.S. Food & Drug Admin., *Alcohol Content Doesn't Matter; Raw Eggs Can Spike Your Nog with Salmonella*, FOOD SAFETY NEWS (Dec. 31, 2018), https://lexspirit.link/30SF.

Skating at Boston (etching) *in* HARPER'S WKLY., Mar. 12, 1859, at 173.

Eggnog[249]

1. Mix the following ingredients together in a large bowl until the contents run evenly off the whisk:[250]
   a. 12 large egg yolks—and *only* the yolks[251]
   b. 1 lb. sugar
   c. 1 tsp. ground nutmeg
2. Combine the following ingredients in a pitcher and gradually incorporate into the mixing bowl:
   a. 1 pint whole milk
   b. 1 pint half-and-half
   c. 1 pint heavy cream
   d. 1 cup spiced rum
   e. 1 cup Cognac[252]
   f. 1 cup Bourbon[253]
   g. 1/4 tsp. salt
3. Pour the contents of the mixing bowl (about 3 quarts) into several large glass jars, seal well, and refrigerate.
4. Letting the mixture sit in the refrigerator for 1–2 months will improve the flavor, but it can also be served after only 24 hours.
5. When serving, pour into a glass and sprinkle freshly ground nutmeg or cinnamon on top.
6. Put the "merry" in "merry Christmas" (it will not take long) by enjoying this remarkably strong beverage with friends and family.

---

249. *My Aged Eggnog Recipe*, ALTON BROWN (Dec. 5, 2014), https://lexspirit.link/ALFN.

250. If you own a stand mixer, this is a perfect time to put it to use.

251. If you are not particularly adept at separating eggs, I suggest purchasing *more* than a dozen eggs so you have some spares on hand.

252. Very Superior Old Pale ("V.S.O.P.") Cognac might seem like overkill here, but I am a fan.

253. I prefer a high-proof Bourbon, such as a Bonded Bourbon (*see* discussion *infra* p. 236).

The Clerk of the
Supreme Court of Texas

Texas history includes a rather infamous batch of Eggnog prepared by none other than the Clerk of the Texas Supreme Court from 1841 to 1861, Thomas J. Green.[254] A native of Tennessee, Green came to Texas in December 1835 as a volunteer in the Texas Revolution. He was assigned to the artillery crew responsible for manning the Twin Sisters[255] and fought at the Battle of San Jacinto.[256]

After the Texas Revolution Green returned to Tennessee and completed his legal studies under the direction of his father, Nathan Green, who was a Tennessee Supreme Court Justice. Green returned to Texas as an attorney in 1837 and served as the Engrossing Clerk of the Texas House of Representatives from 1839 to 1840. In 1841, he became the Clerk of the Supreme Court of the Republic of Texas.[257]

---

254. Tiffany S. Gilman & Blake Hawthorne, *A Brief History of the Texas Supreme Court Clerk's Office*, 5 J. TEX. SUP. CT. HIST. SOC'Y 34, 35–36 (2016). Green's tenure spanned the period Texas was an independent republic, part of the United States, and part of the Confederate States of America.

255. The Texian Army had only two small cannons at San Jacinto (either four- or six-pounders, nobody knows for sure) that were affectionately nicknamed the "Twin Sisters." Those cannons were generously donated to Texas by the people of Cincinnati, Ohio. Interestingly, despite being otherwise well-equipped, the Mexican Army at San Jacinto fielded only one cannon: a comparatively gigantic 12-pounder. HARRIGAN, *supra* note 240, at 178.

256. This was the equivalent of the Siege of Yorktown for the Texas Revolution in that it effectively ended the war. The afternoon attack by the Texians caught the resting Mexican Army off guard, and the battle lasted for only 18 minutes. Mexican forces suffered 858 casualties compared to the Texian Army's 41. *Id.* at 180.

257. L.W. Kemp, San Jacinto Veteran Biographies 82–83 (unpublished manuscript), https://lexspirit.link/PLSG.

In those days, the Supreme Court of the Republic of Texas moved around a lot, and it was not solely because the justices (and clerk) were riding circuit[258] to various venues to hold hearings. The formal or de facto location of the capital of the Republic of Texas (where the court often resided) tended to change frequently.[259] Whenever Green was not coordinating the official business of the court or journeying between cities with the justices, he was permitted to moonlight as a soldier.[260] He saw quite a bit of military action during his tenure as clerk because in the decade Texas was a sovereign nation it was customary for alternating Texian[261] and Mexican raiding parties to cross the border, menace the local citizenry for a few days, and then retreat back to their respective side of the Rio Grande.[262] These incidents were never accompanied by a formal declaration of war, but they may as well have been.

In a September 1842 episode of these skirmishes, the French-born Mexican General Adrián Woll managed to capture and briefly occupy San Antonio. Perhaps nobody in Texas was more surprised by the attack than the judge, clerk, and attorneys in San Antonio's district court because Mexican soldiers suddenly stormed into the courtroom and

---

258. "Riding circuit" refers to the now outdated practice in which judges (especially appellate justices) held court in the various towns of a judicial circuit. This was before the days of permanent, established courthouse complexes, and it was more efficient for the judge to ride his horse to the next venue to hold court. It might surprise you to learn this practice was only discontinued in the United States in 1911. *Circuit Riding*, BLACK'S LAW DICTIONARY 305.

259. Over the course of a decade the government of the Republic of Texas assembled in the following cities: Washington-on-the-Brazos, Columbia, Velasco, Galveston, Harrisburg, Houston, and Austin. "City" is quite a charitable term to use when describing most of those settlements at the time.

260. Gilman & Hawthorne, *supra* note 254, at 35–36.

261. This is not a misspelling of the word "Texan." It refers to someone who was a citizen of the Republic of Texas.

262. HARRIGAN, *supra* note 240, at 226–29.

intervened in an ongoing proceeding![263] Woll withdrew to Mexico a short time later, but his brief presence in the city was enough to cause a panic throughout the region. Determined not to leave such an incursion unanswered, President Sam Houston ordered General Alexander Somervell to lead a retaliatory raid into Mexico. Seeing as the Supreme Court of the Republic of Texas was not presently in session, both Clerk Thomas Green and Chief Justice John Hemphill decided to join Somervell's punitive expedition as officers.[264] Unfortunately, Somervell was an ineffective leader, and his expedition's sole accomplishments were the pillaging of Laredo and the desertion of 200 soldiers.[265] Disgusted, Somervell ordered the remainder of his army to march back to San Antonio, and some of the men—including Chief Justice Hemphill—complied.[266] However, 300 of the 500 remaining soldiers disobeyed the order and chose to raid the Mexican town of Mier instead. Although this venture came to be known as

---

263. FEHRENBACH, *supra* note 240, at 478; GEN. THOMAS J. GREEN, JOURNAL OF THE TEXIAN EXPEDITION AGAINST MIER 30 (New York, Harper & Brothers 1845).

264. *Washington [County] Troops*, TEL. & TEX. REG., Nov. 2, 1842, at p. 2, col. 5, https://lexspirit.link/OHNV; James P. Hart, *John Hemphill—Chief Justice of Texas*, 3 SW. L.J. 395, 400 (1949). Judges in the Republic of Texas were apparently fearsome warriors when the occasion called for it. On March 19, 1840, Hemphill (who at the time was the District Judge of the Fourth Judicial District of the Republic of Texas) was involved in a meeting with 12 Comanche chiefs in the San Antonio Council House. The Texians refused to let the chiefs leave the meeting until certain kidnapped civilians were returned, but there is some doubt today as to whether those chiefs were even responsible for those kidnappings. When the chiefs realized they were not free to leave, they attacked their captors. In the violent and gruesome fracas that followed (remembered by some as a massacre), Hemphill was wounded, but the judge managed to disembowel his assailant with a Bowie knife. *Id.* at 397–98; JOHN HENRY BROWN, INDIAN WARS AND PIONEERS OF TEXAS 78 (Austin, L.E. Daniell 1896).

265. HARRIGAN, *supra* note 240, at 229.

266. Hart, *supra* note 264, at 401.

the "Mier Expedition," it was really a mutiny, and the Clerk of the Supreme Court of the Republic of Texas was their second-in-command.[267]

The Mier Expedition went poorly, to say the least, and the Texians surrendered to a much larger Mexican force at Mier on December 26, 1842. It was not that the Texians were defeated in battle—despite being outnumbered 9:1, they may have killed 430 and wounded 230 Mexican soldiers, while suffering only 10 dead and 23 wounded themselves.[268] The real impetus for surrender appears to have been a combination of the Texian commander being wounded, the supply of rations and gunpowder running low, and the promise of favorable treatment as prisoners of war.[269]

The terms of surrender were either not well defined or were a complete ruse because the Texians were not treated as prisoners of war. In order to discourage any organized escape attempts, Green and the other officers were immediately separated from the other soldiers.[270] Even so, shortly after this precaution was taken 181 of the Texians managed to overpower their captors and escape. However, nearly all of the men who escaped were recaptured after spending a month starving and searching for water in the desert.[271] The dictator of Mexico, Antonio López de Santa Anna, ordered for every recaptured Texian be executed, but diplomats from the United States and Great Britain convinced *el Presidente* to walk that order back to a

---

267. GREEN, *supra* note 263, at 70.
268. *Id.* at 107–08. Contemporary estimates of casualties are often overstated (especially by Texians). But even if you discount Green's figures, the Texians inflicted brutal casualties on the enemy while losing relatively few men.
269. BROWN, *supra* note 264, at 141.
270. GREEN, *supra* note 263, at 129.
271. FEHRENBACH, *supra* note 240, at 479–80.

decimation.[272] Considering Santa Anna's track record with prisoners (e.g., the Alamo and Goliad), this amount of "leniency" was fairly extraordinary. In a now infamous event, 159 white beans and 17 black beans were placed in a pitcher and the recaptured Texian escapees each drew a bean. Those selecting a black bean were shot. Prisoners that drew a white bean were sent to the fortress at Perote, where Green and the other officers (who never managed to escape) were being held.[273]

Evidently, the Texians' imprisonment at Perote was not all doom and gloom: In his 1845 narrative of the entire affair, Green recounted how the captive Texians marked the occasion of the seventh anniversary of their 1836 victory at the Battle of San Jacinto. Somehow, they managed to bribe their captors into smuggling them 7 gallons of Mezcal, 7 gallons of donkey milk, 30 dozen eggs, and a loaf of sugar. With those ingredients in hand, the prisoners gathered every available jar and utensil and proceeded to make an "egg-nog as never before was seen or drank under the nineteenth degree of north latitude."[274] The Eggnog was distributed among the men in abundant quantities, and the soon-drunken Texians proceeded to loudly sing songs and make toasts. All that racket alarmed the guards, who feared the prisoners were attempting to escape. But when the soldiers investigated the commotion, they found their drunken captives were hardly in a condition to stand—let alone stage a prison break—and

---

272. "Decimation" is often used to describe a large amount of destruction, but the term has a much older technical meaning. Originally, decimation was a punishment used in the Roman Legion where every 10th soldier in a unit was executed to punish the entire unit's cowardice or mutiny. *Decimation*, BLACK'S LAW DICTIONARY 511.

273. WONDRICH, *supra* note 4, at 163–64.

274. GREEN, *supra* note 263, at 259.

left them alone to enjoy the rest of their holiday (and subsequent hangover).[275]

Several months later, on July 2, 1843, Green and 15 other prisoners managed to escape by tunneling out of their cell, sneaking out of the fortress, and making their way back to Texas. The remaining prisoners were eventually released in September 1844. The Mier Expedition is remembered as the worst debacle in the fledgling republic's skirmishes with Mexico.[276]

Somehow, despite his role in leading a mutiny, Green was permitted to resume his role as the Clerk of the Supreme Court of the Republic of (and soon-to-be State of) Texas. He held the office until the outbreak of the Civil War, when he resigned to join the 5th Texas Cavalry Regiment. Thomas Green would never return to the judiciary and was killed on the battlefield in 1864.[277]

---

275. *Id.* at 259–60.

276. *Id.* at 305–26.

277. Green was killed in action on April 12, 1864, at the Battle of Blair's Landing in Louisiana. The battle began when several gunboats and transports from a Federal flotilla became stranded on the banks of the Red River, where they were spotted by Confederate forces. Green, who by that time had been promoted to the rank of brigadier general, arrived on the scene of the ongoing battle "well-fortified with Louisiana rum." He personally led a suicidal cavalry charge against the Federal positions and was killed when a cannon shot took the top of his head off. JOHN D. WINTERS, THE CIVIL WAR IN LOUISIANA 359 (La. St. Univ. Press 1991) (1963).

The Archive War[278]

During the period of Green's captivity, a small civil war of sorts occurred in the Republic of Texas. Thankfully, no one was physically harmed in the Archive War, and pride was the only casualty. Despite lasting only two days, the conflict helped to solidify Austin as the permanent capital of Texas.

In 1836, brothers John Kirby Allen and Augustus Chapman Allen purchased a half league of land situated where the White Oak and Buffalo Bayous converged for $5,000 from Elizabeth Parrott.[279] Pandering for investment and hoping to host the capital of the newly minted republic, the Allen brothers named the new settlement "Houston," and "[t]o further push the enterprise they made liberal use of printer's ink."[280] That is, the brothers paid to have weekly advertisements extolling the virtues of the City of Houston run in several newspapers.[281]

Sam Houston thought "Houston" was a great name for a city (of course he did), and during his first term as the President of the Republic of Texas he convinced the Texas

---

278. Anyone who has ever experienced the wrath of an irritated librarian or records professional will identify with this story.

279. BROWN, *supra* note 264, at 358. Elizabeth Parrott is sometimes mistaken for a sister-in-law of Stephen F. Austin because her first husband was named John Austin. John was one of the original settlers in Austin's colony, but he was not related to Stephen F. Austin—or at best he would have been a *very* distant relation.

280. *Id.*

281. A[ugustus] C[hapman] Allen, *The Town of Houston*, TEL. & TEX. REG., Aug. 30, 1836, at p. 3, col. 3, https://lexspirit.link/O1I1; A.C. Allen, *The City of Houston: The Present Seat of Government of the Republic of Texas*, TEL. & TEX. REG., Jan. 3, 1837, at p. 4, col. 3, https://lexspirit.link/B1HC (featuring the updated advertisement after Houston became the capital).

Congress to move the capital there.[282] John Allen also deserves a lot of the credit for Congress's adoption of the City of Houston as the capital because he happened to be serving a term in that very Congress when he invited the legislature to funnel money into his investment.[283] However, like the Congress of the Republic of Texas in 1836, we will choose to look the other way when confronted with this fact.

The City of Houston's location had some real advantages. It was only a stone's throw from the Gulf of Mexico, and the nearby port of Galveston was practically a bustling metropolis in 1837. Unfortunately, Houston was also prone to flooding (it still is) and constituted little more than a shanty town at the time. One visitor, while impressed with the spirit of its inhabitants, called Houston "one of the muddiest and most disagreeable places on earth."[284] Unfortunately, the "disagreeable" conditions of the city he co-founded with his brother contributed to John Allen's untimely demise from "congestive fever" (likely malaria) in 1838.[285]

The Constitution of the Republic of Texas did not permit consecutive-term presidencies, so Sam Houston was forced to step down in 1838.[286] His successor, Mirabeau B. Lamar, hated the primordial conditions of the

---

282. Joe Holley, *Allen Brothers: The Wheeling-Dealing Duo Who Turned Mud into Gold*, HOUS. CHRON. (May 19, 2016), https://lexspirit.link/CMKC.

283. BROWN, *supra* note 264, at 358.

284. *May 10, 1837*, DIARY OF JOHN WINFIELD SCOTT DANCY, VOL. I, at 41 (on file with the University of Texas at Austin Dolph Briscoe Center for American History, Jo[h]n Winfield Scott Dancy Papers, box 4Zc170). Be it ever so humble, there's no place like home.

285. BROWN, *supra* note 264, at 358. John Allen was only 28.

286. REP. OF TEX. CONST. art. I, § 2 (1836) ("The first President elected by the People shall hold his office for the term of two years, and shall be ineligible during the next succeeding term; and all subsequent Presidents shall be elected for three years, and be alike ineligible . . . .").

City of Houston (and Sam Houston), and he wasted little time in urging Congress to form a commission to locate a more suitable location for the capital.[287] Lamar was struck by the natural beauty of a place along the Colorado River while hunting in the Texas Hill Country several years earlier, and he suggested the commissioners consider the area around the town of Waterloo for the capital. The commission was equally impressed by the location, and on December 27, 1838, the Texas Congress incorporated the City of Austin (absorbing the settlement of Waterloo) and declared it the new capital of Texas.[288]

Sam Houston was an outspoken critic of Lamar's decision to move the capital away from his favorite city: "He [Houston] feared that Indians could burn the town, destroy the Archives, and murder the people and that he (using an oath) would not risk his scalp, 'up in that d[amne]d hole, called Austin!'"[289] Houston's bruised ego was probably doing a lot of the talking, but Austin *was* on the bleeding edge of the frontier and made a fair target for raiding Comanches. Austin was also within range of Mexican raiding parties. While it was worrisome that government officials' lives were potentially placed at risk by virtue of Austin's location, the vulnerability of the

---

287. An Act for the Permanent Location of the Seat of Government, 3d Cong., 1st Sess. (Rep. of Tex., Jan. 14, 1839), *reprinted in* LAWS OF TEXAS, 1822–1897, VOL. 2, at 161–65 (Austin, Gammel Book Co. 1898) [hereinafter LAWS OF TEXAS]; Dorman H. Winfrey, *The Texan Archive War of 1842*, 64 SWN. HIST. Q. 171, 172 (1960). Despite this, a prominent street in downtown Houston is named for Lamar.

288. An Act to Incorporate the City of Austin, 4th Cong., 1st Sess. (Rep. of Tex., Dec. 27, 1839), *reprinted in* LAWS OF TEXAS, *supra* note 287, at 386–91. Upon its incorporation as a city, the settlement of Waterloo was renamed Austin in honor of Stephen F. Austin, the "Father of Texas."

289. Winfrey, *supra* note 287, at 173–74 (quoting *The Seat of Government and Gen'l Houston*, TEX. CENTINEL, Aug. 5, 1841, at p. 2, col. 1, https://lexspirit.link/LW5S).

Archives of the Republic of Texas was also of major concern. The Archives held the *only* complete collection of land titles and government records, and losing those documents to a fire set by raiders was a frightening prospect.[290]

Unsurprisingly, when Sam Houston was re-elected President in 1841, he immediately set to work on moving the capital back to . . . well, Houston. Congress was not interested and voted the concept down several times. Out of spite, a frustrated Sam Houston would reside in the City of Houston whenever Congress was not in session.[291]

On March 5, 1842, Mexican General Rafael Vásquez briefly captured San Antonio with a surprise military incursion. Vásquez withdrew from Texas a few days later, but Sam Houston was understandably concerned that the invasion had come within 80 miles of the Republic of Texas's capital. Panic gripped the nation because nobody knew if another invasion would follow (or was already underway). In the face of such uncertainty, Congress moved its sessions to Washington-on-the-Brazos (and later, Houston), and Secretary of War George W. Hockley took the precaution of burying several caches of the Archives' documents to protect them from harm.[292] On March 10, 1842, Sam Houston ordered Hockley to have the entire Archives moved to Houston.[293] That responsibility was delegated to Colonel Henry Jones, the military commander in Austin.

Colonel Jones and the rest of the local populace were not about to let the Archives be moved to Houston.

---

290. *Id.* at 171.

291. *Id.* at 174.

292. Hart, *supra* note 264, at 400; JOURNALS OF THE SIXTH CONGRESS OF THE REPUBLIC OF TEXAS, VOL. 3, at 16–17 (Tex. Libr. & Hist. Comm'n 1945) [hereinafter SPECIAL SESSION JOURNAL].

293. *Id.* at 17.

Austinites were aggravated that Sam Houston had written off the capital, thereby tanking local land values and gutting the residents' business ventures. Houston's order was ignored, and the people of Austin posted armed guards to prevent the movement of the Archives, which were the last vestiges of government remaining in the city.[294]

Sam Houston viewed the actions of the Austinites as tantamount to "treason and insurrection," and he dispatched a strongly worded letter to Colonel Jones ordering him to stand down.[295] Jones refused. At President Houston's request, on June 27, 1842, a special session of Congress was convened in the City of Houston to reconsider moving both the capital and the Archives to Houston.[296] Congress again declined to move either and expressed outrage at Sam Houston's earlier order to Hockley to move the Archives, which was given without obtaining congressional approval beforehand.[297]

Enter the aforementioned Mexican General Adrián Woll, who repeated Vásquez's feat of occupying San Antonio in September 1842, prompting the Somervell and Mier Expeditions.[298] Convinced Austin was still vulnerable to an attack and because Congress would not authorize the removal of the Archives, Sam Houston believed it was his duty to act unilaterally. He secretly ordered the Texas Rangers to move the Archives to Washington-on-the-

---

294. Winfrey, *supra* note 287, at 175–76.
295. DeJean Miller Melton, *Winning the Archive War: Angelina Eberly Takes Her Shot*, 4 J. TEX. SUP. CT. HIST. SOC'Y 35, 43 (2015).
296. SPECIAL SESSION JOURNAL, *supra* note 292, at 99, 106.
297. Winfrey, *supra* note 287, at 178.
298. *See* treachery *supra* p. 80.

Brazos—an action later determined to be unconstitutional.[299]

Texas Rangers Colonel Thomas I. Smith and Captain Eli Chandler arrived outside the records building in Austin before dawn on December 30, 1842, with 20 men and three wagons. The men quietly began loading the contents of the Archives into the wagons. Their clandestine mission benefited from a frigid rainstorm that inspired most of the local populace to remain indoors that morning, blissfully unaware of the treachery afoot.[300]

The men nearly succeeded in loading the entirety of the records without detection when Angelina Eberly, the keeper of a nearby inn, noticed their activities. Eberly quietly alerted her neighbors and soon returned with a small but ferocious mob. For good measure, the rabble brought along the city's six-pound cannon.[301]

I feel safe in speculating Angelina Eberly was a woman of few words because she made no formal demands of the men loading the Archives into the wagons before she fired the cannon at them.[302] Eberly's subtle expression of disapproval put several holes in the Land Office but harmed no one. Completely unscathed (for the moment),

---

299. Winfrey, *supra* note 287, at 183. The Archives were to be housed at the capital unless the Texas Congress determined they should be moved—which they had not. Sam Houston's use of executive fiat did not supersede the enacted law establishing Austin as the capital of Texas. Melton, *supra* note 295, at 44.

300. *Id.* at 45.

301. *Id.* at 46; Winfrey, *supra* note 287, at 179–80.

302. Traditionally, Eberly is said to have fired the cannon, but there are conflicting and vague accounts that cast some doubt on this. Other recollections indicate Eberly merely fired the cannon as a signal to alert the town and was not aiming it at anyone or anything in particular. This might be a case of people not letting history get in the way of a good story. Either way, historians generally agree the cannon was intentionally aimed to the left of the men loading the wagons when it was fired, and it was not the cannoneer's intention to hit anyone. Melton, *supra* note 295, at 46–47.

Colonel Smith's men decided it was an opportune time to leave Austin, so they departed with the records they had already loaded. Unfortunately, their escape was less than rapid because they were using oxen, not draft horses, to pull the wagons.[303] To give you some idea of how slowly oxen travel, the angry mob had no qualms about limbering up the cannon and bringing it with them in their pursuit of the rascals.

Early the next morning and about 20 miles out of town, the armed citizenry caught up with the men who "stole" the Archives. Leaning against the cannon they brought with them, they respectfully "requested" that the Archives be returned to Austin at once. Finding himself in dire straits, Colonel Smith reluctantly complied.[304] With the conflict satisfactorily resolved, the hospitable people of Austin hosted Smith's men to a fine New Year's dinner that evening, and all ill will was soon forgotten.[305]

Since being returned on December 31, 1842, the Archives have remained in Austin, and the city remains the capital of Texas. For her part in preserving Austin's role as the capital of Texas, Eberly was honored with a larger-than-life bronze statue in downtown Austin in 2004. The statue is located at Sixth Street and Congress Avenue near the spot where the incident occurred, and it dramatically depicts a barefoot[306] Eberly in a flowing dress as she lights the fuse of a cannon.[307] She is also the unofficial patron saint of librarians and archivists—at least in the State of Texas.

---

303. Winfrey, *supra* note 287, at 180.

304. *The Archives*, TEL. & TEX. REG., Jan. 11, 1843, at p. 2, col. 3–4, https://lexspirit.link/D0ZE.

305. Winfrey, *supra* note 287, at 181; Melton, *supra* note 295, at 48.

306. I attribute this to artistic license, but it is ridiculous to surmise Eberly was not wearing shoes on that cold and rainy morning.

307. HARRIGAN, *supra* note 240, at 230.

John Karst, *Mrs. Eberly Firing Off Cannon* (etching) *in* D.W.C. Baker, A Texas Scrap-Book: Made Up of the History, Biography, and Miscellany of Texas and Its Peoples pl. 13 (New York, A.S. Barnes & Co. 1875).

§11

The Penicillin and the Decorative Doctor

The Penicillin is another modern invention of Sam Ross, meaning it has a pretty short history.[308] Sometimes this variation on the Whiskey Sour and Gold Rush cocktails gets mistaken for an old classic, but Ross invented the cocktail in 2005 while bartending at Milk & Honey® after emigrating to New York City from Melbourne, Australia.[309] Ross was experimenting with the newly released line of Compass Box® Scotches and wanted to incorporate a particularly smoky variant, The Peat Monster®, into a cocktail.[310] His pairing of ginger's mild spiciness with honey and smoky Scotch was pure genius, and his creation is now known worldwide. It is likely the most famous cocktail of the 21st century (so far).

---

308. Ross, if you remember, also had a hand in creating the Paper Plane. *See* Paper Plane *supra* p. 63.

309. SIMONSON, *supra* note 211, at 170–71; *see* Whiskey Sour recipe *supra* note 31.

Gold Rush: 2 oz. Bourbon, ¾ oz. fresh-squeezed lemon juice, and ¾ oz. honey syrup (*see* recipe *infra* p. 168). Combine those ingredients with ice in a cocktail shaker, shake well, and serve "on the rocks." PETRASKE, *supra* note 212, at 107.

310. SIMONSON, *supra* note 211, at 170–71; PETRASKE, *supra* note 212, at 127.

Ross suggests enjoying this cocktail without a straw so you can experience the full aroma of the Islay Scotch. I fully endorse that idea. The characteristic smoky flavor is derived from peat-burning fires used to imbue the malted barley with a "smoky, iodine-like and medicinal profile" before being fermented and distilled into whiskey.[311] If you do not like peaty Scotch,[312] this may not be the drink for you. Still, the Penicillin is extraordinary enough to try at least once. Doctor's orders!

Hablot K. "Phiz" Browne, *The Woolsack Is to Decide a Suit at Law* (etching) *in* CHARLES J. LEVER, NUTS AND NUTCRACKERS 194 (London, Bradbury & Evans 1845).

---

311. *Our Process*, LAPHROAIG, https://lexspirit.link/80AG.

312. I will be the first to admit peaty Scotch is not my personal favorite. I love the idea of it, but my taste buds are not quite as ambitious as my ideals. Even so, I really enjoy the Penicillin.

Penicillin[313]

1. Combine the following ingredients in a cocktail shaker with ice:
   a. 2 oz. blended Scotch
   b. 3/4 oz. fresh-squeezed lemon juice
   c. 3/4 oz. honey-ginger syrup (recipe follows)
2. Cap the cocktail shaker and shake vigorously for 20–30 seconds.
3. Garnish an old fashioned glass with some candied ginger and add a large piece of ice.
4. Double strain the contents of the shaker into the glass and pour 1/4 oz. of Islay Scotch on top.[314] *Do not* stir this spirit into the mixture.
5. Serve "on the rocks."

Honey-Ginger Syrup

Like agave nectar, honey is too thick to mix directly into a cocktail and needs to be diluted first. This also offers an opportunity to infuse ginger into the syrup for some extra flavor. Combine 1 cup of honey, 1 cup of water, and a 6-inch peeled and sliced piece of ginger in a saucepan. Bring the mixture to a boil and then reduce to a simmer for 5 minutes. Refrigerate overnight and strain into a bottle. If refrigerated, it should keep for several weeks.

---

313. SIMONSON, *supra* note 211, at 170–71; PETRASKE, *supra* note 212, at 127.

314. Ross recommends 10-year-old Laphroaig® Scotch for this libation, but any Islay Scotch (all of which feature a characteristic peat-forward flavor) will do the trick.

The Decorative Doctor

It is a cruel irony that otherwise talented professionals are sometimes terrible at managing their financial affairs. That most likely was the case for one San Antonio doctor who filed for bankruptcy in the late 2000s.[315] As it turned out, he also might have made a decent attorney—but not really.

A brief sidebar on bankruptcy law is warranted here, as it will enhance your appreciation of the physician's cleverness. While bankruptcy is a federal matter, the Bankruptcy Code permits state law to grant debtors property exemptions (e.g., personal property and homestead exemptions) above and beyond those available under federal law.[316] These exemptions allow a debtor to prevent certain property from being seized on account of unpaid debts. There are some special situations that make exemptions unavailable (e.g., a lien or a mortgage encumbering the property),[317] but they are often a powerful tool for debtors both inside and outside of bankruptcy. In the context of a Chapter 7 liquidation, if a particular asset is not exempt, it becomes the property of the bankruptcy estate and may be sold by the trustee.[318] Any sales proceeds are first applied to the costs of sale and then to creditors' claims.[319] Although extremely unlikely to exist, any surplus is payable to the debtor.

Many of the Texas personal property exemptions are fairly intuitive (e.g., professionally prescribed health aids

---

315. *In re* Wilkinson, 402 B.R. 756 (Bankr. W.D. Tex. Apr. 10, 2009).

316. 11 U.S.C. § 522(b)(1), (3)(A) ("[A]n individual debtor may exempt from property of the estate . . . any property that is exempt under . . . State or local law . . . ."). The federal bankruptcy exemptions are found at 11 U.S.C. § 522(d).

317. *See* Tex. Prop. Code § 42.002(b) (2020).

318. *See* 11 U.S.C. §§ 541, 704.

319. *See id.* § 726.

and the family Bible), but several are a nod to the state's heritage (e.g., 2 horses and 12 head of cattle).[320] One such exemption from the latter category is the statutory allowance for a debtor to claim up to two firearms as exempt.[321] The idea behind the firearm exemption is a Texan who hunts needs both a shotgun for hunting birds and a rifle for other game, but that same provision would also permit a cowboy to keep two six-shooters, thereby allowing the pilgrim to show up armed for his date with destiny in front of the local saloon at high noon tomorrow.[322] With that legal framework in mind, we can now return to the story about the cash-poor physician.

The two-firearm limit was a problem for the bankrupt doctor because he collected antique firearms.[323] He owned a veritable arsenal[324] of 23 valuable guns, including several cavalry carbines from the 1860s and a few flintlock rifles from the 18th century (complete with their bayonets). How would he ever decide which two of his beloved guns would remain safe from his creditors?

As it turned out, he did not decide at all. The clever doctor unilaterally determined 17 of his favorite antique firearms were no longer "guns" at all but were—in fact—*home furnishings*. He lovingly affixed each of his new decorations to individualized wooden plaques (complete with brass nameplates) and mounted them on the walls of his home.[325] Because Texas law permits a family to designate up to $100,000 (cumulative total) of

---

320. TEX. PROP. CODE § 42.001–.002.

321. *Id.* § 42.002(a)(7).

322. *In re* Schwarzbach, Bankr. No. 87-30817, 1989 WL 360742 at *4 (Bankr. W.D. Tex. May 22, 1989); *In re Wilkinson*, 402 B.R. at 766.

323. *Id.* at 758–59.

324. Whether or not this qualifies as an arsenal in Texas is debatable.

325. *In re Wilkinson*, 402 B.R. at 759.

unencumbered personal property in a variety of categories (including home furnishings) as exempt, the doctor figured he would be enjoying his new wall ornaments for years to come.[326] He was mistaken.

Upon the bankruptcy trustee's timely objection, the court ordered the doctor's new decorations to be taken down and sold for the benefit of his creditors. While his abuse of the exemptions was evident, the judge still felt the need to issue a written order examining the ordinary usage of the words "firearm" and "home furnishing":

> One visiting the Wilkinsons' home could well comment "that's a very nice firearm you have mounted up there on the wall," and no one would wonder what he or she was talking about. By the same token, one would be surprised if, in response to the query, "what's that firearm," Wilkinson were to reply, "that's not a firearm, that's a home furnishing."[327]

The doctor was neither the first Texan to object to a levy on his firearms, nor will he be the last. But, as the Supreme Court of Texas observed in 1857, "the right to keep and bear arms cannot be infringed by legislation, yet, strange as it may be, it must succumb before the power of a creditor; at least [if] not expressly protected by Statute."[328]

---

326. TEX. PROP. CODE § 42.001(a)(1), .002(a)(1). Both the doctor and his wife filed for bankruptcy, so they received the "family" exemption amount. A single debtor's cumulative personal property exemption under this provision is $50,000.

327. *In re Wilkinson*, 402 B.R. at 764.

328. Choate v. Redding, 18 Tex. 579, 581 (1857). This opinion was authored by Chief Justice Hemphill, who took part in a military expedition while on the bench! *See* discussion *supra* p. 81.

↑ ↑ ↓ ↓ ← → ← → B A

§12

Cuba Libre and the Mauser Model 1893

C uban revolutionaries and American troops once rallied around the battle cry of "free Cuba!" or, in Spanish, "¡Cuba libre!"[329] The cocktail bearing that same name is little more than a combination of rum, Coca-Cola®, and lime juice. That's it. This cocktail is just a "Rum & Coke" with lime juice and a fancy name. It is so easy to make that college students probably still put the rum and lime juice (if any) right into a Coca-Cola bottle as they head off to class. Sometimes there is an elegance to simplicity, but other times it is really just laziness. I will let you decide where this cocktail falls along that spectrum.

This highball cocktail appears to have been invented in Cuba just after the end of the Spanish–American War. With the copious quantities of light rum being produced on the island, the arrival of Coca-Cola in Cuba circa 1900 provided the perfect mixer for the sugar cane-based

---

329. To be fair, Americans were more enthusiastic about the rallying cry, "Remember the Maine! To hell with Spain!" TOM GJELTEN, BACARDI AND THE LONG FIGHT FOR CUBA: THE BIOGRAPHY OF A CAUSE 72 (Penguin Books 2008).

liquor.[330] One can easily imagine United States soldiers and newly liberated Cubans raising a glass of this cocktail and toasting to a free Cuba, saying, *"¡Por Cuba libre!"*

Fausto Rodríguez, who served as a messenger for the United States Army Signal Corps during the Spanish–American War, claimed to have witnessed the creation of the Cuba Libre.[331] In fact, he later signed a not-so-contemporaneous affidavit to that effect:

Fausto Rodriguez, being duly sworn, deposes and says:

. . . .

One afternoon, in August 1900, I went with him to the ███████████ Bar, and he drank Bacardi Rum and Coca-Cola. I just drank Coca-Cola, being only 14 years old.[332] On that occasion, there was a group of soldiers at the bar, and one of them asked Mr. ███████████ what he was drinking. He told them it was a Bacardi and Coca-Cola and suggested they try it, which they did. The soldiers liked it. They ordered another round and toasted Mr. ███████████ as the inventor of a great drink.[333]

---

330. *Id.* at 98.

331. *Id.* at 260.

332. The 14-year-old's abstention from alcohol is commendable, but in 1900 Coca-Cola contained cocaine—a "significant" amount of it. Dan Lewis, *What Happened to the Cocaine in Coca-Cola?*, BUS. INSIDER (Feb. 24, 2012), https://lexspirit.link/Q483. The formula used today is narcotic-free, but it still requires dried coca leaves to manufacture, which happen to be illegal to import into the United States. Fortunately, the Coca-Cola Company has an agreement with the United States Drug Enforcement Administration that allows it to legally import dried coca leaves from Peru and Bolivia for this limited purpose.

333. Bacardi®, *So That's How "Rum & Coke" Was Invented!*, LIFE, May 20, 1966, at 125, https://lexspirit.link/P0UU.

If you think the redactions in the affidavit are suspicious, you are not alone. When Rodríguez swore to that story in October 1965, he was an advertising executive for Bacardí®, and the affidavit appears to have been produced primarily for a joint Coca-Cola–Bacardí advertising campaign. The May 20, 1966 edition of *Life*® magazine contained a photo of the signed affidavit (with the names of Rodríguez's companion and the bar redacted) with the caption, "So that's how "Rum & Coke" was invented!"[334] Even if the affidavit is suspect, the general time and place of the Cuba Libre's creation is supported by it.

Of course, by the time Rodríguez signed his affidavit, the name "Cuba Libre" had been replaced by the moniker "Rum & Coke" (although, some say the cocktail by that name omits the lime juice typically found in a Cuba Libre). By 1965, Americans were no longer in the mood to drink to the longevity of a "free Cuba" after the Cuban Revolution (1953–1959), the failed Bay of Pigs Invasion (1961), the Cuban Missile Crisis (1962), a trade embargo (1962–2017), and the island succumbing to that dirty, dirty word: *communism*.[335]

Politically motivated nomenclature aside, the mixture of Coca-Cola, rum, and lime juice quickly became a permanent part of Cuba's cocktail scene after its invention. Basil Woon's Prohibition-era account of Cuba's bustling cocktail, cigar, and gambling scene, *When It's Cocktail Time in Cuba* (1928), briefly—but prominently—mentions the Cuba Libre.[336] However, Woon was far more impressed

---

334. *Id.*
335. GJELTEN, *supra* note 329, at 260.
336. BASIL WOON, WHEN IT'S COCKTAIL TIME IN CUBA 183 (Horace Liveright 1928).

with the Daiquiri[337] (one of Ernest Hemingway's favorites) and devoted nearly two pages to describing that cocktail.[338] Speaking of Hemingway, the expatriate American novelist lived in Havana for several years and was a discerning cocktail connoisseur.[339] Unfortunately, he does not appear to have thought very highly of the Cuba Libre because he included the following exchange in *To Have and Have Not* (1937):

> "What will you have?" asked Freddy.
> "What's the lady drinking," Harry asked.
> "A Cuba Libre."
> "Then give me a straight whiskey."[340]

Unlike Hemingway, I really enjoy the Cuba Libre. However, I prefer to distance myself from a sophomoric "Rum & Coke" by using Coca-Cola produced with *real* sugar cane (not corn syrup). It comes in glass bottles and is often referred to as "Mexican Coke" because it is produced there. So, the next time you hear someone order a Rum & Coke at a bar you can retort, "You mean a *Cuba Libre*?" I sure wouldn't, but you go right ahead.

---

337. <u>Daiquiri</u>: 1-½ oz. white rum, 1 oz. simple syrup, ¾ oz. fresh-squeezed lime juice. Combine those ingredients with ice in a cocktail shaker, shake well, and serve "up" with a lime wheel for garnish. DeGroff, *supra* note 31, at 124.

338. Woon, *supra* note 336, at 38–39.

339. *See* Philip J. Greene, To Have and Have Another: A Hemingway Cocktail Companion (Revised and Expanded) 74–81 (Perigee Books 2015). If you are a fan of both Hemingway and alcohol, I guarantee you will enjoy this book.

340. Ernest Hemingway, To Have and Have Not 93 (Scribner Classics 2010) (1937). I cannot underscore how significant a disparagement of the Cuba Libre this little bit of dialogue represents. Hemingway's prose was terse. Short sentences. Few words. Sick burn.

Cuba Libre[341]

1. Combine the following ingredients in a highball glass:
    a. Enough ice to fill 3/4 of the glass
    b. 1-1/2 oz. Bacardí® Gold Rum
    c. 1/2 oz. fresh-squeezed lime juice[342]
    d. 4 oz. Coca-Cola® (or enough to fill the glass)
2. Gently stir the contents of the glass with a bar spoon.
3. Garnish the glass with a lime wedge and serve with a straw.
4. Keep the rest of the bottle of Coca-Cola around in case the drinker would like to top off the glass.

---

341. DEGROFF, *supra* note 31, at 152. Unlike many of the other cocktails in this book, the Cuba Libre does not require exact measurements. Feel free to estimate volumes and adjust the proportions to suit your taste.

342. While the presence of citrus juice usually means a cocktail (or components of it) will benefit from being shaken to mix the ingredients, the Cuba Libre has such a small quantity of lime juice that a gentle stirring should suffice. However, especially if producing several batches of the libation, there is no harm in shaking the rum and lime juice ingredients with ice, straining the mixture into the highball glass, and then adding the Coca-Cola. It seems fairly self-evident, but shaking Coca-Cola is not a great idea.

The Mauser Model 1893

When Colonel Theodore Roosevelt led the charge of the (dismounted) 1st United States Volunteer Cavalry (commonly remembered as the "Rough Riders") up Kettle and San Juan Hills in Cuba, his rag-tag regiment of Ivy League socialites, lawmen, cowboys, hunters, and gamblers carried the carbine version of the United States Army's first standard issue smokeless powder rifle: the U.S. Magazine Rifle, Caliber .30, Krag-Jørgensen (the "Krag"), chambered in the round-nosed .30-40 Krag cartridge.[343] What made the volunteer unit's successful charge even more impressive is the fact that the Spaniards had them badly outgunned—literally.

The German-designed Mauser Model 1893 wielded by their Spanish opponents was chambered in the pointed 7x57mm Mauser cartridge, which gave the Spaniards vastly superior range, bullet velocity, and accuracy. Those advantages left the Americans running for cover during much of the Spanish–American War.[344] Making matters worse, Waffenfabrik Mauser, A.G. ("Mauser") had developed an ingenious stripper clip system that allowed for five rounds of ammunition to be rapidly loaded into their rifle.[345] While the Krag also held five rounds, each

---

343. CLAY RISEN, THE CROWDED HOUR: THEODORE ROOSEVELT, THE ROUGH RIDERS, AND THE DAWN OF THE AMERICAN CENTURY 82, 205–11 (Scribner 2019). As its name suggests, the Krag-Jørgensen's design was not domestically developed. Instead, it was licensed from its Norwegian inventors. *New Army Rifle*, N.Y. TIMES, Sept. 4, 1892, at 15, https://lexspirit.link/FPUW.

344. RISEN, *supra* note 343, at 159; *The Krag-Jorgensen Gun: It Is Inferior in Many Respects to the Mauser Used by the Spaniards*, N.Y. TIMES, Aug. 16, 1898, at 4, https://lexspirit.link/RD1D. The Spanish Mauser's 7x57mm cartridge had a muzzle velocity of 2,330 feet per second—300 more than the Krag's .30-40 cartridge!

345. John Sheehan, *Battlefield Tack Driver: The Model 1903 Springfield in WWI*, GUNS MAG., Oct. 2006, at 67–68.

one had to be individually loaded into the rifle by means of a loading gate located on the side of the receiver. In short, the Krag was clumsy and cumbersome to reload— particularly if someone was shooting at you. You can probably still find unfired cartridges in Cuba that were dropped by United States soldiers in 1898 as they frantically tried to reload under fire.

Recalling the inadequacies of the Krag, when Teddy Roosevelt became President in 1901 he ordered the Chief of the United States Army Ordnance Department, Brigadier General William Crozier, to develop a suitable replacement.[346] Ordnance examined some of the captured Mauser rifles, built a replica, changed a few minor features, and christened the "new" rifle the U.S. Rifle, Caliber .30, Model of 1903 (the "M1903 Springfield").[347] It could be loaded with stripper clips and was virtually a clone of Mauser's rifle, but the Springfield Armory manufactured it with a beautiful American walnut stock.

To complement the M1903 Springfield's capabilities, a more powerful cartridge was adopted in 1906: the U.S. Cartridge, Ball, Caliber .30, Model of 1906 (the ".30-'06" [pronounced "thirty-aught-six"]).[348] The bullet's pointed design was a huge improvement over the round-nosed rifle

---

346. It is worth noting that Crozier was promoted directly to Brigadier General from the rank of Captain when he became Chief of Ordnance. That ruffled a lot of feathers.

347. ALEXANDER ROSE, AMERICAN RIFLE: A BIOGRAPHY 264–67 (Random House 2008). Interestingly, some changes from the Mauser 1893's design made the M1903 Springfield slightly worse, such as the two-piece firing pin, which was a holdover from the Krag. These were weak attempts to ward off patent infringement lawsuits. Sheehan, *supra* note 345, at 68; WILLIAM H. HALLAHAN, MISFIRE: THE HISTORY OF HOW AMERICA'S SMALL ARMS HAVE FAILED OUR MILITARY 274 (Charles Scribner's Sons 1994).

348. The .30-'06 was technically preceded by the round-nosed .30-'03, but the .30-'03 was already woefully obsolete at the time of its adoption.

bullets of the past, but it bore a striking resemblance to the *Spitzgeschoß/Spitzgeschoss* (German for "pointed projectile") bullet designed by Arthur Gleinich that had been transferred to Mauser's parent company, Deutsche Waffen-und Munitionsfabriken, A.G. ("DWM"). You do not need to be a gunsmith—or an attorney—to recognize that the United States' new rifle and cartridge practically rolled out the red carpet for the Kaiser's weapon manufacturers to file patent infringement claims. When Crozier recognized this problem, he was determined to save his reputation at all costs.

Rather than wait for Mauser to discover the patent infringement issue on their own, Crozier decided to preemptively seek settlement. On March 15, 1904, he dispatched a letter to Mauser about the potential infringement on their stripper clip system (without even mentioning the similarities in the M1903 Springfield's design to the Mauser rifle). Mauser was invited to have its attorney contact the Ordnance Department to determine "what, if any, of [the] features [were] covered by [their] patents and if so, to arrive at an agreement as to the royalties which should be paid therefore."[349] The invitation was gladly accepted, and Mauser's attorneys ultimately identified two striper clip patents and five rifle patents being infringed upon by the "American" designs.[350] Months

---

349. *Royalties for the Use and Manufacture of Patented Articles*, 11 COMP. DEC. 489, 492–93 (1905).

350. The seven patents being infringed upon were: (i) Small Lock for Breech Bolts of Guns, U.S. Patent No. 590,271 (filed Dec. 2, 1895); (ii) Safety Lock for Breech Bolts of Guns, U.S. Patent No. 547,933 (filed Apr. 26, 1894); (iii) Magazine for Breech Loading Firearms, U.S. Patent No. 527,869 (filed Sept. 15, 1893); (iv) Shell Extractor for Bolt Guns, U.S. Patent No. 477,671 (filed Feb. 29, 1892); (v) Shell Extractor for Bolt Guns, U.S. Patent No. 467,180 (filed May 22, 1891); (vi) Cartridge Pack for Magazine Guns, U.S. Patent No. 547,932 (filed Apr. 26, 1894); and (vii) Cartridge Holder for Magazine Guns, U.S. Patent No. 482,376

of secret negotiations eventually culminated in a settlement agreement on May 5, 1905, which provided for up to $200,000 of royalties to be paid to Mauser over time.[351] It was not a cheap solution, but Crozier managed to avoid public embarrassment—for a while, anyway.

It was not long after the Mauser settlement when a representative from DWM visited Crozier and asserted that the .30-'06 cartridge infringed on their Spitzgeschoss patent.[352] Ordnance's attorneys advised Crozier that DWM had a fairly weak case—apparently the United States had independently researched pointed bullets in the past.[353] Crozier decided to string DWM along to delay the filing of any potential lawsuit. That would keep the patent issues out of the public eye for the time being—even if the United States stood a fair chance at prevailing in court.

The strategy worked for seven years, but eventually DWM filed suit in the United States Court of Claims on July 18, 1914, seeking $250,000 in damages.[354] Fortunately (at least for Crozier), just 10 days later DWM's suit was put on hold because World War One broke out in Europe. The average American could not have cared less

---

(filed June 8, 1892). If you appreciate the minimalistic elegance of technical drawings, you might enjoy looking at these patent records.

351. 11 COMP. DEC. at 490 (discussing the Comptroller's findings in relation to a near-final draft of the settlement agreement, which included the $200,000 cap on royalties); CLARK S. CAMPBELL, THE '03 SPRINGFIELD 51 (Fadco Publ'g 1957).

352. *See* Projectile for Hand Firearms, U.S. Patent No. 841,861 (filed Feb. 20, 1905), *reissued as* U.S. Patent Re. No. 12,927 (filed Jan. 8, 1909); CAMPBELL, *supra* note 351, at 51.

353. *Id.* A March 30, 1894 report by Lt. Col. J.P. Farley mentioned the testing of pointed bullet designs, but the report was never widely circulated and did not provide a clear picture as to their effectiveness. Interestingly, the French also adopted pointed bullets shortly after the Spitzgeschoss was introduced. Pointed bullets were apparently a worldwide phenomenon, whether they represented stolen technology or were independently developed.

354. HALLAHAN, *supra* note 347, at 277.

about a German company's suit against the government for patent infringement while the United States' allies were waging war against the Kaiser.

Crozier's good fortune continued when the United States entered the war in 1917 because Congress passed the Trading with the Enemy Act.[355] The act, once amended in 1918, empowered a newly established department, the Office of the Alien Property Custodian, to seize patents belonging to the United States' enemies and license them for domestic use during the war. The United States was deeply reliant on imported dyes, chemicals, and medicines from Germany, and the statute facilitated the domestic production of those items by breaking the virtual monopoly German firms had over those products through their patents.[356] The legislation was destined to cause an uproar overseas that would outlast the war. Predictably, Congress left the determination of how claims against the United States would be resolved for another day.[357]

DWM's patent was seized on October 16, 1919, and Ordnance—despite previously asserting the .30-'06 did not infringe on the Spitzgeschoss design—boasted the seizure of DWM's patent saved the government an estimated $800,000 in royalty fees![358] On October 24, 1919, the Court

---

355. Trading with the Enemy Act, ch. 106, 40 Stat. 411 (1917), *amended by* Act of Nov. 4, 1918, ch. 201, sec. 7(c), 40 Stat. 1020, 1020–21. Interestingly, the bullet patent was seized *after* the Armistice because the Trading with the Enemy Act was only amended to permit the seizure of enemy patents on November 4, 1918—one week before the fighting ceased. *Id.*

356. *See* United States v. Chem. Found., Inc., 272 U.S. 1, 10 (1926); United States v. Chem. Found., Inc., 294 F. 300, 310–11 (D. Del. 1924).

357. Trading with the Enemy Act § 12, 40 Stat. at 424.

358. 1922 Rep. Alien Prop. Custodian 812, 834; Closing Arguments on Behalf of Defendant at 187, *Chem. Found., Inc.*, 294 F. 300 (D. Del. 1924) (No. 502); Defendant's Motion to Dismiss Petition (Oct. 16, 1919) at 1, 7, Deutsche Waffen-und

of Claims dismissed DWM's pending case against the United States because the bullet patent had been seized by the Alien Property Custodian, meaning DWM no longer had standing to pursue the claim.[359] With that, Ordnance had successfully dodged yet another bullet. Idiomatically, this was a pointed bullet—shaped exactly like the Spitzgeschoss.

Ironically, Crozier's tenure was never marred by patent scandals, but he *was* blamed for wartime munitions shortages.[360] In particular, he was raked over the coals for having refused to adopt the brilliantly engineered Lewis Gun (a light machine gun)—allegedly over some personal vendetta against its inventor, Isaac Newton (not kidding) Lewis.[361] Crozier took no responsibility for his shortcomings, and President Woodrow Wilson relieved him of his Ordnance command and put him out to pasture in December 1917.[362]

When the guns fell silent on November 11, 1918, the United States was faced with the task of sorting out the mess the Great War and the Trading with the Enemy Act left in their wake. To that end, Congress eventually passed

---

Munitionsfabriken, A.G. v. United States, 54 Ct. Cl. 203 (dismissed Oct. 24, 1919) (No. 32,872), https://lexspirit.link/ZNXO.

359. *Id.* The fighting might have ceased in 1918, but the United States was technically at war with the Central Powers until the Knox–Porter Resolution was signed by President Harding on July 2, 1921. The joint resolution also declared the Alien Property Custodian would retain ownership of enemy property until Germany and Austria-Hungary made provisions to compensate Americans for property losses sustained during the war. S.J. Res. 16, 67th Cong. § 5, 42 Stat. 105, 106–07 (1921).

360. *Lack of Ordnance Laid to Congress*, N.Y. TIMES, Dec. 12, 1917, at 1, 3, https://lexspirit.link/OQTM; HALLAHAN, *supra* note 347, at 335–46.

361. *American Gun, Rejected by U.S., Wins for British*, N.Y. TIMES, Sept. 18, 1916, at 1, 4, https://lexspirit.link/EK6U; HALLAHAN, *supra* note 347, at 296–346.

362. *Id.* at 343.

the Settlement of War Claims Act of 1928 (the "Settlement Act of 1928"), which created the Office of the War Claims Arbiter to adjudicate claims of foreign nationals against the United States arising from the Alien Property Custodian's property seizures.[363] Section 3(d)–(f) of the Settlement Act of 1928 capped the aggregate awards to German nationals at $100 million, plus 5% statutory interest to be assessed for the period from July 2, 1921 (the date of the Knox–Porter Resolution and official end of the war from the United States' standpoint), to December 31, 1928.[364] Aggrieved parties' sole remedy for property seizures lay with the War Claims Arbiter, and section 8 of the act specified the Arbiter's decisions would be final and not subject to appeal.[365]

In 1928, DWM's postwar successor entity, Berlin-Karlsruher Industriewerke, A.G. ("BKI"), filed a claim to recover lost royalties resulting from the Alien Property Custodian's seizure of the Spitzgeschoss patent.[366] Much of the literature concerning this case is patently untrue. It is often maintained that BKI was awarded damages on July 2, 1921, the United States appealed the decision, and the parties settled the case on December 31, 1928.[367] The first date corresponds with the Knox–Porter Resolution and predates BKI's (re-)filing the case. Additionally, decisions by the War Claims Arbiter were not appealable. Finally, the so-called "settlement date" matches the end

---

363. Settlement of War Claims Act of 1928, ch. 167, § 4, 45 Stat. 254, 256–57.

364. *Id.* § 3(d)–(f), 45 Stat. at 257–58.

365. *Id.* §§ 4(q), 8(a), 45 Stat. at 260, 267.

366. Berlin-Karlsruher Industriewerke, A.G. (formerly Deutsche Waffen-und Munitionsfabriken, A.G.) v. United States, Docket No. 316 (1928); Gordon Lyle, *Springfield Patent Troubles*, AM. RIFLEMAN, Dec. 1949, at 52, 53, https://lexspirit.link/5NI5.

367. *See* ROSE, *supra* note 347, at 278; HALLAHAN, *supra* note 347, at 277–78; CAMPBELL, *supra* note 351, at 51–52.

point of the statutory interest period under the Settlement
Act of 1928. In fact, records in the National Archives
definitively show the War Claims Arbiter had not
considered the case by either date because the United
States rejected a $250,000 pretrial settlement offer from
BKI on May 16, 1930![368]

Here is what *actually* happened: On December 15,
1931, the War Claims Arbiter completed his arduous
review of claims under the Settlement Act of 1928. Of the
1,069 patent claims filed, the Arbiter awarded 387
claimants compensation for lost royalties.[369] BKI received
$300,000 in damages for the Spitzgeschoss claim, plus
$112,520.55 in statutory interest, for a grand total of
$412,520.55.[370] The Germans may have lost the Great
War, but BKI was effectively compensated for the very
bullets the United States used to turn the tide of the
conflict.[371] The company also managed to extract more

---

368. Off. Alien Prop. Custodian, Memoranda: Negotiations for
Settlement 59, https://lexspirit.link/PKCX (May 16, 1930: "Docket No.
316 (resumed): General discussion. Lillienthal asked for $250,000.").
369. Alexander Holtzoff, *Enemy Patents in the United States*, 26 AM.
J. INT'L L. 272, 279 (1932).
370. Letter from Dr. Johann G. Lohmann, German Prop. Comm'r,
to A.A. Ballantine, Asst. Sec'y Treas. (Jan. 21, 1932),
https://lexspirit.link/ZV9X (confirming one half of the award was
received by BKI); Lyle, *supra* note 366, at 55.
371. While the American Expeditionary Forces exclusively used the
.30-'06 rifle cartridge during the Great War, most soldiers (60–75%)
were issued the U.S. Rifle, Caliber .30, Model of 1917 (the "M1917
Enfield")—and *not* the M1903 Springfield. When the United States
entered the war in 1917, the Springfield Armory was unable to produce
enough M1903 Springfield rifles to equip the military. Fortunately,
Remington®, Eddystone, and Winchester® were producing the Rifle,
.303 Pattern 1914 (the "P14 Enfield") for Great Britain and were able
to quickly retool to produce a .30-'06 version of the P14 Enfield—the
M1917 Enfield. Maj. Richard O. "Dick" Culver, Jr., *The U.S. Rifle,
Caliber .30, M1917*, OFF. DIR. CIVILIAN MARKSMANSHIP PROGRAM (2003),
https://lexspirit.link/BRNO. But isn't copying someone else's rifle
design *exactly* the sort of shenanigans that led to the claims discussed

money from a single (potentially dubious) patent claim than Mauser had for seven clear-cut infringement claims.

Das Model *von* 1903 and the ever-so-pointy .30-'06 cartridge may have been knockoffs of their German counterparts, but at least the United States copied the very best designs in existence at the time. Despite being a legal nightmare, both the rifle and cartridge were unqualified successes and were used in various roles by the military through the 1970s. As for Teddy Roosevelt, he was delighted with the rifle, and in 1903 he requested Crozier have a special one made for him.[372] Roosevelt paid $42.13 for M1903 Springfield #6,000,[373] and it accompanied the outdoorsman on his adventures for the rest of his life.

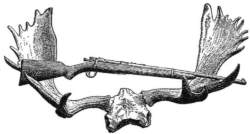

Springfield Rifle No. 6,000, Model 1903 (etching), *in* THEODORE ROOSEVELT, A BOOK-LOVER'S HOLIDAYS IN THE OPEN 356 (Charles Scribner's Sons 1916).

---

in this chapter?! "Borrowing" designs from allied nations proved far less problematic.

372. LT. COL. WILLIAM S. BROPHY, THE SPRINGFIELD 1903 RIFLES 232–37 (Stackpole Books 1985).

373. M1903 SPRINGFIELD #6,000, SAGAMORE HILL NAT'L HISTORIC SITE (NAT'L PARK SERV.), https://lexspirit.link/YDLW; Memorandum from Col. Frank H. Phipps, Ordnance Dept. (Feb. 19, 1904), https://lexspirit.link/7NGX. The serial number of this rifle is often misstated as being #0009, but the Springfield Armory never put leading zeros before a low-digit number. Despite being counterintuitive, the information on the receiver of Roosevelt's rifle is intended to be read from the *left* side of the rifle. Brophy, *supra* note 372, at 233–34. Because the serial number happens to face toward the right side of the rifle, it is often read upside down. Roosevelt also identified the rifle as #6,000 in a 1916 book. THEODORE ROOSEVELT, A BOOK-LOVER'S HOLIDAYS IN THE OPEN 356 (Charles Scribner's Sons 1916).

§ 13

Blood and Sand and Getting Away with Murder

The name "Blood and Sand" conjures up visions of a murder mystery novel set in the Caribbean, or a refreshing rum-based cocktail, doesn't it? Well, neither of those impressions end up being correct. "Blood and Sand" is a reference to bullfighting, and this cocktail has the distinction of being one of the few Scotch Whisky-based cocktails.

Adapted from a 1908 Spanish novel[374] by the same name, *Blood and Sand* (1922) is an American silent film starring the heartthrob Rudolph "The Latin Lover" Valentino as a talented (and married) matador with a penchant for bullfighting and wealthy, seductive widows.[375] To find out whether his wife or a bull kills him first, you can either watch the original black-and-white

---

374. VICENTE BLASCO IBÁÑEZ, SANGRE Y ARENA (Francisco Sempere y Compañía 1908).

375. BLOOD AND SAND (Paramount Pictures 1922).

silent film or one of two subsequent remakes featuring sound.[376]

Not much is known about the precise origin of the Blood and Sand cocktail, but everyone seems to agree it was invented around the time the movie premiered. Even if that basic history is fairly intuitive, why Scotch is an ingredient of a cocktail named for a film about a Spanish bullfighter is something we may never know. The Blood and Sand made its print debut in *The Buckstone Book of Cocktails* (1925), and the following recipe is derived from that book's recipe.[377]

This is a unique cocktail with some unlikely ingredient pairings that work together flawlessly. As a testament to that, I find many people who claim to dislike whiskey seem to enjoy this cocktail quite a lot! I think the cherry liqueur, orange juice, and sweet vermouth join forces to tone down the tenacity of the Scotch.

While the original recipe calls for regular orange juice, I usually opt for blood orange juice because it pairs well with both the cocktail's name and the other ingredients. Plus, it helps distance the Blood and Sand from a Screwdriver (a cocktail consisting of orange juice and vodka). Because of this substitution, I have bumped the volume of juice up to a full ounce. If you are using regular orange juice (and I *definitely* do not mean juice poured from a carton), you should only use 3/4 oz. Importantly, unlike the Penicillin,[378] you should avoid using a peaty/smoky Scotch in this beverage.

---

376. *See* BLOOD AND SAND (20th Century Fox 1941); *see also* BLOOD AND SAND (20th Century Fox 1989). Judging from the frequency of those remakes, I would say we can expect another one fairly soon.

377. "ROBERT" BUCKBY & GEORGE STONE, THE BUCKSTONE BOOK OF COCKTAILS 14 (Union Press 1925).

378. *See* Penicillin recipe *supra* p. 95.

Blood and Sand[379]

1. Combine the following ingredients in a cocktail shaker with ice:
    a. 1 oz. fresh-squeezed blood orange juice[380]
    b. 3/4 oz. blended Scotch
    c. 3/4 oz. Heering® Cherry Liqueur
    d. 3/4 oz. sweet vermouth
2. Cap the cocktail shaker and shake vigorously for 20–30 seconds.
3. Garnish a coupe glass with a blood orange wedge.
4. Double strain the contents of the shaker into the coupe glass and serve "up."

---

379. BUCKBY & STONE, *supra* note 377, at 14.; CRADDOCK, *supra* note 7, at 30.

380. Blood oranges are only seasonally available, but you can reliably find them from December through April.

Getting Away with Murder

For better or worse, the 19th century had no shortage of larger-than-life personalities. Perhaps no person embodied the negative side of this phenomenon better than Major General and Congressman Daniel E. Sickles, the O.J. Simpson of the 19th century. He assembled a "dream team" of attorneys—including Edwin Stanton, who later became Abraham Lincoln's Secretary of War—and was the subject of the "trial of the century." However, unlike O.J., Sickles readily admitted to having committed the murder he was prosecuted for.

On February 27, 1859, Congressman Sickles (D-NY) looked out the window of his home and spotted the District Attorney for the District of Columbia, Philip Barton Key II.[381] This was an unwelcome sighting because two days earlier Sickles received an anonymous letter informing him that Mrs. Sickles was having an affair with Key. When he confronted his wife with this allegation, she confessed her infidelity and divulged that Key's method of initiating one of their "outings" together involved waving a white handkerchief outside a window of the Sickles' home.[382] Needless to say, as Sickles watched Key retrieve a white handkerchief from his pocket, it was as if a matador was waving a red cape to taunt a bull.

After arming himself with an array of pistols, the Congressman stormed outside and screamed, "You have dishonored my bed and family, you scoundrel—prepare to die!" As soon as Key spotted Sickles advancing toward him,

---

381. *O say can you see* who Key's father was? None other than the famed attorney-laureate, Francis Scott Key. *See* discussion *infra* p. 148.

382. In addition to being a murderer, Sickles was also an attorney, which explains why he forced his wife to write out a confession of her transgressions in torrid detail. It was a double standard because Sickles himself was a notorious philanderer.

he frantically thrust his hand into his pocket, and it may have appeared as if he was retrieving a weapon. Sickles drew a derringer and shot at Key, but the shot merely grazed the District Attorney, who then threw the object he had retrieved from his pocket at his assailant—a pair of opera glasses.[383] Undeterred, Sickles drew another derringer and hit Key in the upper-right thigh with his second shot.

The wounded District Attorney fell to the ground at Sickles's feet—clearly unarmed and unable to fight—and began pleading for his life. Ignoring Key's appeals for mercy, Sickles shot him in the chest at point-blank range with a revolver and walked away.[384] Key was carried into a nearby house and died shortly thereafter.

The murder took place right by the White House and was witnessed by everyone in Lafayette Square on that Sunday afternoon. Incredulous bystanders watched as Sickles calmly hired a carriage and departed. He headed to the home of the current Attorney General of the United States, Jeremiah S. Black, where he surrendered without further incident. As soon as a Deputy District Attorney was appointed to replace the one Sickles killed, the congressman was charged with murder.[385]

---

383. JAMES A. HESSLER, SICKLES AT GETTYSBURG: THE CONTROVERSIAL CIVIL WAR GENERAL WHO COMMITTED MURDER, ABANDONED LITTLE ROUND TOP, AND DECLARED HIMSELF THE HERO OF GETTYSBURG 11 (Savas Beatie 2009).
384. *Philip Barton Key Shot Dead in the Street by Daniel E. Sickles*, N.Y. TIMES, Feb. 28, 1859, at 1, https://lexspirit.link/8Y5S.
385. United States v. Sickles, 27 F. Cas. 1074, 1076–77 (D.C. Crim. Ct. 1859).

Homicide of P. Barton Key by Hon. Daniel E. Sickles at Washington on Sunday, February 27, 1859 (etching) in HARPER'S WKLY., *Mar. 12, 1859, at 169.*

Sickles readily confessed to the *actus reus*[386] of the charge, but insisted he lacked the *mens rea*[387] to support a murder conviction. Having recently learned about Key's affair with his wife, Sickles maintained he was temporarily driven insane when he saw Key waving the white handkerchief and had no control over his actions. As such, Sickles entered a plea of not guilty by reason of *temporary insanity* (an affirmative defense that had yet to be successfully employed in court).[388]

When the trial began, Sickles's attorneys artfully sidestepped the testimony of several witnesses who described Sickles as collected and thoughtful when he shot Key. Surprisingly, the defense never put a physician on the stand to testify as to Sickles's mental health.[389] Instead, Sickles's attorneys proclaimed that mental illness, like certain physical maladies, could strike without warning and then completely resolve a short time later.[390] In this case, "a short time later" was synonymous with the word "instantly," but it was (apparently) a compelling argument. So much so that the judge permitted the jury charge to include the following instruction: "The law does not require that the insanity . . . exist for any definite period, but only that it exists at the moment when the act occurred with which the accused stands charged."[391]

---

386. The wrongful act constituting a crime. *Actus Reus*, BLACK'S LAW DICTIONARY 45.

387. "The state of mind that the prosecution, to secure a conviction, must prove that a defendant had when committing a crime." *Mens Rea*, BLACK'S LAW DICTIONARY 1181.

388. Other viable strategies might have included using a "heat of passion" argument to reduce a murder charge to manslaughter or— better still—learning to solve disputes in a civilized manner.

389. Robert M. Ireland, *Insanity and the Unwritten Law*, 32 AM. J. LEGAL HIST. 157, 159–60 (1988).

390. *Id.* at 162.

391. *Sickles*, 27 F. Cas. at 1075.

While Sickles *did* have a fantastic team of attorneys, "temporary insanity" was code for a then-prevailing unwritten—but widely accepted—rule that an outraged husband could justifiably kill the rascal responsible for seducing his wife.[392] This line of thinking certainly explains the contents of the defense attorneys' dramatic opening statements, which lasted two days and, among other things, quoted *Othello*, the *Bible*, and Roman law. "You are here to fix the price of the marriage bed," John Graham declared to the jury at one point.[393] "There are certain wrongs which are not protected against at all by human laws, and therefore the only law which protects us against them is that which is traced in the human bosom by the finger of God—the law of human nature; the law of human instinct."[394] The inexperienced Deputy District Attorney never stood a chance.

On the 20th day of trial, the jury deliberated for just over an hour and returned a verdict of "not guilty."[395] Sickles was practically carried out of the courtroom on the shoulders of jubilant spectators. In the end, his wife's infidelity—and not his mental state when he committed the murder—was responsible for his freedom.[396] It was the first time the affirmative defense of temporary insanity was successfully used in the United States.[397]

---

392. Ireland, *supra* note 389, at 157.

393. JOSEPH W. DONOVAN, MODERN JURY TRIALS AND ADVOCATES: CONTAINING CONDENSED CASES, WITH SKETCHES AND SPEECHES OF AMERICAN ADVOCATES 135 (G.A. Jennings Co., Inc., 5th ed. 1924).

394. *Id.* at 142.

395. *Twentieth and Last Day's Proceedings; Verdict of Not Guilty*, N.Y. TIMES, Apr. 27, 1859, at 1, 8, https://lexspirit.link/JS25. This article took up the *entire* front page of *The New York Times* (and then some). Daily accounts of the trial were published under the sympathetic heading, "The Sickles Tragedy."

396. HESSLER, *supra* note 383, at 17.

397. Ireland, *supra* note 389, at 162 n.11.

Sickles's insanity may have been temporary, but his vanity and incompetence proved to be permanent. When the Civil War broke out, Sickles was instrumental in recruiting four regiments of New York volunteers for the Excelsior Brigade. Despite having zero military experience, he decided he should be their Brigadier General. Unfortunately, on March 17, 1862, the Senate refused to confirm Sickles's commission, which severely bruised his ego.[398] He appealed to President Abraham Lincoln (a Republican) for help, and Lincoln (the kind soul) sent a letter to the Senate urging them to reconsider. The second time the matter was put to a vote Sickles was narrowly confirmed with a 19–18 vote.[399] Thanks in no small part to a gratuitous amount of saber rattling,[400] the amateur soldier was eventually promoted to the rank of Major General[401] and given command of the entire Federal III Corps—consisting of about 10,600 men.

---

398. 12 S.J. EXEC. PROC., 37th Cong., 2d Sess. 166 (1862).

399. *Id.* at 257, 285.

400. "An ostentatious display of military power." *Saber Rattling*, MERRIAM-WEBSTER'S COLLEGIATE DICTIONARY 1093. Cavalry sabers, unlike most other swords, have a curved blade because they are designed for slashing—as opposed to chopping or running someone through. A leather sheath is suitable for a straight-bladed sword but is not very durable when used for a curved blade. This is why sheaths for sabers were usually made from metal. A sword in a leather sheath will not rattle, but a saber in a metal sheath makes quite a lot of noise! Hence, why the phrase is "saber rattling" and not "sword rattling." *Compare* U.S. Model 1840 Cavalry Saber (supplied with an iron scabbard), *with* U.S. Model 1840 Non-Commissioned Officer's Sword (supplied with a leather scabbard).

401. Recite the following "patter song" aloud as quickly as possible:
For my military knowledge, though I'm plucky and adventury,
has only been brought down to the beginning of the century;
but still in matters vegetable, animal, and mineral,
I am the very model of a modern Major-General.
I Am the Very Model of a Modern Major-General, from THE PIRATES OF PENZANCE; OR, THE SLAVE OF DUTY (Arthur Sullivan & W.S. Gilbert 1879).

Some months later on July 1, 1863, Sickles's III Corps arrived in Gettysburg, Pennsylvania, on the evening of the first day of the Battle of Gettysburg.[402] Major General George Meade, who had only assumed command of the Army of the Potomac three days earlier, also arrived that evening, and he positioned the Federal army in a strong defensive position along Cemetery Ridge. By dawn, the ends of the Federal position were anchored on geographic features that served as natural barriers to an assault. Meade's extreme right flank (to the north) ended on Culp's Hill, and his left flank (to the south) was bordered by Little Round Top.[403] As long as his flanks were secure, Meade could reliably run communications and reinforcements quickly from one end of the battlefield to the other. It was tactically brilliant.

On the morning of the second day, Sickles sat astride his favorite horse, Tammany,[404] gazing at the landscape that lay before him. Meade had entrusted Sickles with holding the extreme left flank of the entire Federal Army, and III Corps's assigned position extended from where II Corps's lines ended along Cemetery Ridge to just shy of Little Round Top (*see* map *infra* p. 124).[405]

Unfortunately for Meade, Sickles spied some elevated ground with a peach orchard three-quarters of a mile ahead of his assigned position. At the Battle of Chancellorsville two months before, Sickles sought to occupy a patch of elevated ground called Hazel Grove, but he was ordered to pull back. The Confederates subsequently occupied Hazel Grove and dominated

---

402. HESSLER, *supra* note 383, at 94–95.

403. *Id.* at 106.

404. Sickles was associated with the Tammany Hall political machine. *Id.* at 14.

405. *Id.* at 114.

Sickles's position with artillery.[406] Sickles resolved to hold the high ground this time, and the peach orchard would become known as *the* Peach Orchard as a result.[407]

The Chief of Artillery, Brigadier General Henry Hunt, surveyed the elevated ground with Sickles and admitted the Peach Orchard was—in some ways—a superior place to position III Corps's cannons and men because of its higher elevation. This was especially true considering Sickles's assigned position placed a portion of III Corps in low, marshy ground.[408] However, Hunt also told Sickles *not* to occupy the Peach Orchard without Meade's permission and apprised him of several reasons why advancing to the Peach Orchard was a bad idea: (i) III Corps would be entirely unsupported if they were three-quarters of a mile ahead of the entire Federal Army; (ii) if Sickles disobeyed Meade's order to extend the defensive line, he would abandon Little Round Top and leave the left flank of the entire Federal Army vulnerable to attack; (iii) Sickles's lines would be spread dangerously thin because he lacked the manpower to hold the advanced position; (iv) the defense of the Peach Orchard would create a salient that would allow the Confederates to simultaneously fire at Sickles's men from *both* a northwestern and southwestern direction; and (v) the ground was within range of Confederate artillery.[409] Sickles ignored Hunt (a West Point graduate) and at 2:00 p.m. ordered III Corps to advance.[410] Meade was not informed.

---

406. STEPHEN W. SEARS, CHANCELLORSVILLE 312–13 (Mariner Books 1996).

407. STEPHEN W. SEARS, GETTYSBURG 250–52 (Houghton Mifflin 2003) [hereinafter GETTYSBURG].

408. HESSLER, *supra* note 383, at 116.

409. *Id.* at 114–18.

410. *Id.* at 131.

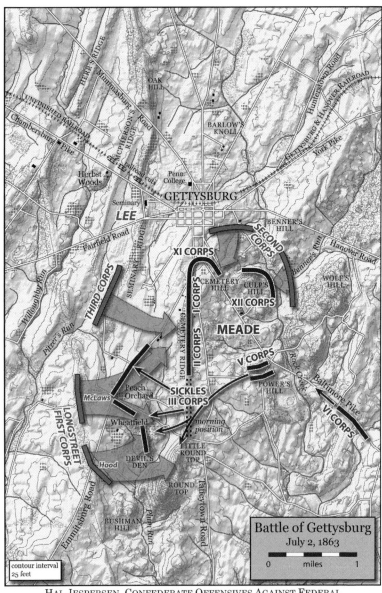

HAL JESPERSEN, CONFEDERATE OFFENSIVES AGAINST FEDERAL
POSITIONS AT THE BATTLE OF GETTYSBURG, JULY 2, 1863 (2021).

Earlier that same day, Confederate General Robert E. Lee tasked Lieutenant General James Longstreet with finding and attacking the Federal Army's left flank.[411] Longstreet's scouts reported the Peach Orchard in front of the southernmost Federal position was unoccupied (at least when they surveyed it), and Longstreet intended to use the area to launch an offensive on the left flank of the Federal Army. By sheer dumb luck, Sickles managed to completely surprise Generals Lee and Longstreet by depriving them of the Peach Orchard.[412] Unfortunately for Sickles, his luck had run out because III Corps was in a terrible position to defend against the onslaught headed their way.

Around the time Longstreet's men spied Sickles's new position, Meade was inspecting the defensive line along Cemetery Ridge and found empty fields where III Corps was supposed to be.[413] A livid Meade, upon locating Sickles, is said to have exclaimed, "General Sickles, this is neutral ground, our guns command it, as well as the enemy's. The very reason you cannot hold it applies to them!"[414] But it was too late: Longstreet's attack on Sickles's untenable position began in earnest, and a furious barrage of artillery rained down on the Peach Orchard. The bombardment was followed by an unrelenting assault by Longstreet's First Corps.[415] The isolated Federal defenders fought bravely but were soon overwhelmed and withdrew to the east in disorder—

---

411. *Id.* at 122.
412. *Id.* at 140.
413. JOHN GRAY & JOHN ROPES, WAR LETTERS OF JOHN CHIPMAN GRAY AND JOHN CODMAN ROPES, 1862–1865, at 256, 318 (Houghton Mifflin 1927).
414. GETTYSBURG, *supra* note 407, at 263.
415. *Id.* at 265–300.

leaving a giant hole in the Federal lines. By the end of the day 40% of III Corps was killed, wounded, or missing.[416]

As he supervised III Corps's withdrawal from atop his horse, Sickles's lower right leg was all but severed from his body by a 12-pound cannonball.[417] To his credit, the gravely wounded Sickles put on a brave face, encouraged his demoralized troops, and even puffed on a cigar as he was carried away on a stretcher.[418] He would lose his leg.

Meanwhile, an incensed Meade was forced to throw V Corps into his left flank to prevent the entire Federal Army from collapsing in the face of the Confederate offensive.[419] The heroic defense of Little Round Top by Colonel Joshua Chamberlain and the 20th Maine (along with other elements of V Corps) ultimately secured the left flank of the Federal Army—and saved the day.[420]

After seeing Sickles carried off the field on a stretcher, an onlooking officer from II Corps is said to have remarked, "The loss of his leg is a great gain to us, whatever it may be to him."[421] Another general would later posit that, had Sickles not lost his leg, he would have been court-martialed for his actions.[422] Sickles came very close to single-handedly losing the Battle of Gettysburg—and possibly the entire war—for the Union. But time apparently heals all wounds because in 1897 he received the Medal of Honor for his "gallantry" at Gettysburg![423]

---

416. HESSLER, *supra* note 383, at 228.

417. *Id.* at 204. Miraculously, his horse was unharmed.

418. GETTYSBURG, *supra* note 407, at 301; HESSLER, *supra* note 383, at 206–12 (demonstrating Sickles's cigar smoking antics are plausible).

419. *Id.* at 151.

420. GETTYSBURG, *supra* note 407, 292–97.

421. *Id.* at 301.

422. GRAY & ROPES, *supra* note 413, at 256.

423. S. COMM. VETERANS' AFFS., 96TH CONG., MEDAL OF HONOR RECIPIENTS, 1863–1978, at 218 (Comm. Print 1979) ("[Sickles] displayed most conspicuous gallantry on the field vigorously contesting the

The Civil War changed many men, but Sickles's swagger was not tempered by the loss of his leg. The surgeon that amputated Sickles's leg knew the newly established Army Medical Museum was looking for "specimens of morbid anatomy" and asked for permission to send Sickles's leg to the museum.[424] "Whose leg deserves to be exhibited, if not mine?" was probably the response he received from his patient. The remains of Sickles's leg were sent to the museum in a small, coffin-shaped box accompanied by a greeting card that read, "With the compliments of Major General D.E.S."[425] At least Sickles had a sense of humor.

Upon seeing his leg in the museum for the first time, Sickles is said to have angrily exclaimed, "What have you done with my foot?! That should have been shown too!"[426] Only the bones of his shattered tibia and fibula were preserved by the museum, and they were displayed next to a 12-pound cannonball similar to the one that caused the wound. The detached (but otherwise uninjured) foot was not deemed to be medically interesting.

Sickles lived to the ripe old age of 94 and, despite his disappointment with certain aspects of its display, is reported to have visited his leg at the museum on the yearly anniversary of its amputation. Today, the shattered bones of Sickles's leg remain on display to the public in the National Museum of Health and Medicine in Silver Spring, Maryland (the successor to the Army Medical Museum).[427] He would be absolutely delighted to know that.

---

advance of the enemy and continuing to encourage his troops after being himself severely wounded.").

424. Tim Clarke, Jr., *Sickles' Leg and the Army Medical Museum*, 179 MIL. MED. 1051, 1051 (2014).

425. HESSLER, *supra* note 383, at 224.

426. *Id.* at 315.

427. Clarke, *supra* note 424, at 1051.

Hablot K. "Phiz" Browne, *O'Connell Taking the Oaths*
(etching) *in* JAMES GRANT, SKETCHES IN LONDON pl. 9
(London, Wm. Tegg 1838).

§14

The Aviation and
Jump Jets

German immigrant Hugo Ensslin, a bartender at the Hotel Wallick (once located on Times Square), probably invented the Aviation cocktail, as his book, *Recipes for Mixed Drinks* (1916), contains the first published reference to the tipple.[428] Unfortunately for Ensslin, his book did not receive much attention at the time. It had a bland, brown cover and was not flashy or entertaining.[429] Making matters worse, the Eighteenth Amendment (Prohibition) went into effect only a few years after its publication.[430] Still, Ensslin's book is invaluable today because it is a time capsule of what Americans were drinking before Prohibition took the cocktail scene underground and overseas for over a decade.

By the time Prohibition was repealed in 1933, Ensslin's dated publication was eclipsed by Harry Craddock's masterpiece, *The Savoy Cocktail Book* (1930). While

---

428. HUGO ENSSLIN, RECIPES FOR MIXED DRINKS 7 (Fox Printing House 1916).

429. James Wilson, *The Most Influential Cocktail Book To Date*, WASH. POST (Oct. 11, 2011), https://lexspirit.link/FIPT.

430. *See* U.S. CONST. amend. XVIII, *repealed by* U.S. CONST. amend. XXI.

Craddock's book also included the Aviation, it inexplicably omitted the cocktail's signature ingredient: crème de violette.[431] As its name suggests, crème de violette is a hue of purple. When the liqueur is combined with lemon juice, the resulting mixture is a sky-blue color—from which this cocktail derives its name. During the decades Craddock's (incorrect) recipe was dominant, people must have been pretty confused as to why a pale, yellow-colored cocktail was called the "Aviation!" We know Craddock was familiar with crème de violette because it is an ingredient of the Atty Cocktail, which appears directly above the Aviation on the same page. As a result, it is likely the omission of crème de violette in his recipe for the Aviation was entirely accidental.

The "incorrect" recipe being disseminated, combined with the fact that crème de violette (never very common to begin with) virtually disappeared from the face of the earth for several decades, meant the original formulation for the Aviation was effectively lost for many decades.[432] Luckily, in the 1990s an archaeological bartender named Paul Harrington was digging through old cocktail books in the library and discovered the long-lost "correct" recipe in Ensslin's book. It is doubtful it will ever be forgotten again.

The Aviation has a certain level of obscurity to it such that you can order one to show you are a member of the elite, learned fraternité of mixologists—an act called a "Bartender's Handshake." Not every bartender will have heard of the Aviation or will have a bottle of crème de violette, but ordering this cocktail can make a real impression.

---

431. CRADDOCK, *supra* note 7, at 25.
432. Robert Simonson, *The Rise and Fall of the Aviation Cocktail*, PUNCH (Dec. 5, 2017), https://lexspirit.link/GSOW.

Aviation[433]

1. Combine the following ingredients in a cocktail shaker with ice:
   a. 1-1/2 oz. floral-focused gin (not dry)
   b. 3/4 oz. Luxardo® Maraschino Liqueur
   c. 1/2 oz. fresh-squeezed lemon juice
   d. 1/4 oz. crème de violette[434]
2. Cap the cocktail shaker and shake vigorously for 20–30 seconds.
3. Garnish a coupe glass with a Luxardo® Cocktail Cherry.
4. Ensure your seat back and tray table are returned to their full, upright positions.
5. Double strain the contents of the shaker into the coupe glass and serve "up."

---

433. ENSSLIN, *supra* note 428, at 7.

434. Lee Spirits® and The Bitter Truth® each make a crème de violette that will produce a sky-blue color when mixed with lemon juice. The Rothman & Winter® variant of the spirit is also excellent but gives the resulting beverage a purplish hue.

Jump Jets

At 7:58 a.m. on a Monday morning, the paper boy throws the newspaper over a white picket fence, where it lands on the perfectly manicured lawn of a suburban home. Meanwhile, on the second story of the home, Jimmy[435] slicks back his hair after putting on his new Pepsi® t-shirt (75 Pepsi Points®). Satisfied with his hair, he struts out of his bedroom wearing his new black leather jacket (1,450 Pepsi Points). Jimmy knows he will soon become dehydrated in the August heat wearing that jacket, but he walks right out the front door anyway and puts on his shades (175 Pepsi Points) to complete the ensemble. Jimmy *does not* drink Coca-Cola®, and he wants the world to know it.

"Introducing the new Pepsi Stuff® catalog," an unseen narrator boldly proclaims as a group of children, standing in front of their school, flip through a conspicuously branded brochure. In the next shot, a hurricane force wind blows open the windows of a classroom, scattering papers everywhere. The astonished students turn toward the open windows to see what interrupted their studies. "Now the more Pepsi you drink, the more great stuff you're going to get," the narrator aggressively expounds as Jimmy skillfully performs a vertical landing and parks his Pepsi logo-emblazoned McDonnell Douglas® AV-8B Harrier II "Jump Jet" (7,000,000 Pepsi Points) on the school's lawn.[436]

---

435. The protagonist of this commercial is not actually named.

436. Jimmy managed to land a fighter jet on the school's lawn thanks to the Harrier's most salient feature: vertical/short take-off and landing ("V/STOL"). The Harrier's ability to take off and land like a helicopter earned it the nickname "Jump Jet" because it seemed to jump straight up into the sky. Unfortunately, that capability also made the Harrier notoriously difficult to fly. *See* Alex Davies, *The Exhilarating, Exasperating Life of the Harrier Jump Jet*, WIRED (June 6, 2014, 6:03 PM), https://lexspirit.link/OVAI.

"Sure beats taking the bus," remarks the young aviator as he exits the cockpit and goes to class.

Jimmy violated a whole host of airspace regulations (and may have come close to committing an act of war) during that 30-second commercial for the Pepsi Stuff promotional campaign, but he sure looked great doing it.[437] Care to guess which of the featured prizes from the commercial would later form the basis of a lawsuit? I will give you a hint: It was not the black leather jacket.

John Leonard of Seattle, Washington, saw the Pepsi Stuff commercial and decided a Harrier Jump Jet was something he needed in his life.[438] He read the rules of the promotional campaign and learned that, rather than having to purchase a lifetime supply of Pepsi to accumulate 7,000,000 points, he could simply buy supplemental Pepsi Points for 10 cents apiece when ordering a prize from the catalog, provided he redeemed at least 15 "real" Pepsi Points. He secured funding, and in March 1996 Leonard instructed his attorney to send the beverage maker 15 Pepsi Points, a check for $700,008.50, and his completed Pepsi Stuff order form requesting a Harrier.[439]

Pepsi's fulfillment agent responded with a letter explaining, "The Harrier jet in the Pepsi commercial is fanciful and is simply included to create a humorous and

---

437. PEPSI-COLA COMPANY, *Brand Pepsi "Harrier" Rev. PEPX-1514* (BBDO Adver. 1995), https://lexspirit.link/7PDH.

438. Lindsay E. Cohen, *The Choice of a New Generation: Can an Advertisement Create a Binding Contract?*, 65 MO. L. REV. 553, 554–55 (2000). The Author needs a Lockheed® SR-71 "Blackbird" in *his* life. Send money.

439. Conspicuously absent from the catalog and order form was the Harrier featured in the commercial. Undeterred, Leonard wrote "1 Harrier Jet" on the form and submitted it. Leonard v. PepsiCo, Inc., 88 F. Supp. 116, 119 (S.D.N.Y. 1999).

entertaining ad."[440] But Leonard was not laughing, and his attorney followed up with a demand letter. Executives did not initially believe Leonard was serious about ordering a Harrier, but—seeing as he had written a check for over $700,000 and retained an attorney—Pepsi filed an action for declaratory judgment in the Southern District of New York. They sought a judicial determination that Pepsi had no obligation to furnish Leonard with a Harrier.[441] Leonard also filed suit, but he inexplicably filed it in a Florida state court—a venue neither party had a connection to. For this reason, the cases were later consolidated in the Southern District of New York.[442]

Judge Kimba M. Wood was likely amused when she read Pepsi's motion for summary judgment, but she nevertheless thoughtfully analyzed the relevant principles of contract law implicated by the pleadings. As a refresher, "[s]ummary judgment is proper when the 'words and actions that allegedly formed a contract [are] so clear themselves that reasonable people could not differ over their meaning.'"[443] In other words, a case need not go to trial if there is no dispute over the material facts and the law precludes one of the parties from prevailing.[444]

Under common law, the formation of a contract requires (i) an offer, (ii) an acceptance of that offer, and (iii) consideration.[445] In those terms, Leonard was arguing

---

440. *Id.* at 120.

441. *Id.* at 119–20.

442. *Id.* at 120–21.

443. *Id.* at 122.

444. FED. R. CIV. P. 56(a).

445. "Consideration" is something (e.g., an act, a forbearance, or a return promise) bargained for and received by a promisor from a promisee. This serves to motivate (and bind) the promisor to do something, and it does not need to be particularly valuable. In fact, the exchange of a single peppercorn (an archetypal example of nominal consideration) will suffice. *Consideration*, BLACK'S LAW DICTIONARY 382.

(i) the commercial constituted Pepsi's offer to sell him a Harrier for 7,000,000 Pepsi Points, and (ii) he accepted that offer by tendering his completed order form and (iii) Pepsi Points/payment. Therefore, according to him, a binding contract existed, and Pepsi owed him a Harrier. Summary judgment would be granted to Pepsi only if Leonard could not possibly show that Pepsi made an offer to sell him a Harrier.

As an initial matter, the *Restatement (Second) of Contracts* makes it clear that advertisements generally do not constitute offers. Rather, they serve as invitations for someone to *make* an offer. That is, unless the advertisement contains language that is "clear, definite, and explicit and leaves nothing open for negotiation"— such that if somebody says, "I accept," a third party would understand *exactly* what the contract is for.[446] But the Pepsi commercial was not definite enough to give anyone the power of acceptance because it directed viewers to reference the catalog for further details about the promotion. Even if it had not done that, the commercial's lack of limiting language, such as "first-come, first-served," meant it was too indefinite to constitute an offer.[447]

On the other hand, while the publication of the *catalog* represented an offer to provide the promotional prizes, the Harrier was conspicuously absent from the list of available

---

Article 2 of the Uniform Commercial Code (the "U.C.C."), which governs the formation of a contract for the sale of goods, does not explicitly require consideration to create a binding agreement. Even so, the concept is often the deciding factor between an enforceable contract and a gratuitous promise. RESTATEMENT (SECOND) OF CONTS. §§ 71, 79 (Am. L. Inst. 1981).

446. *Leonard*, 88 F. Supp. at 122–24 (citing RESTATEMENT (SECOND) OF CONTS. § 26 cmt. b); Lefkowitz v. Great Minneapolis Surplus Store, 86 N.W.2d 689, 691 (Minn. 1957).

447. *Leonard*, 88 F. Supp. at 124 (citing Mesaros v. United States, 845 F.2d 1576, 1581 (Fed. Cir. 1988)).

rewards. The Judge also briefly considered whether the commercial was offering a reward for performance (e.g., offering a reward for the return of a lost dog).[448] That clearly was not applicable either. This meant the only "offer" for a Harrier was Leonard's purported *acceptance* (i.e., his tender of payment with a completed order form for a Harrier). Pepsi had not accepted that offer, and a contract never came into being as a result.

Even if that analysis was incorrect (spoiler: it wasn't), courts never consider the subjective viewpoint of a party when determining whether an offer has been made.[449] Leonard's ludicrous perspective was irrelevant, and the court only needed to consider whether a *reasonable* person would have believed the commercial was offering a Harrier as a promotional prize. The court determined the commercial's inclusion of the Harrier was done in jest,

---

448. One of my law school professors *loved* to use the reward-for-lost-dog scenario as a contracts hypothetical. As the story went, the dog was particularly adept at escaping from the professor's office (where it was confined during the day). True to his nature, the hypothetical dog staged a series of prison breaks that semester. Each time this occurred, the frantic professor would beseech various law students to find his beloved dog, often promising a reward.

Some students would hear about the reward the professor was offering, search for the dog, find him, return him, and then ask for the reward. Others—blissfully unaware of the reward—would simply return the dog, learn of the reward after doing so, and then demand to be paid the reward. One unscrupulous fellow even (hypothetically) stole the dog, waited until the professor offered the reward, and then attempted to collect the reward by returning the dog.

Was anyone entitled to the reward? Was prior knowledge of the reward before returning the dog legally significant? In classic Socratic fashion, these issues were never definitively resolved in class. We later learned the professor's dog had died a few years earlier. He featured the dog in his favorite hypothetical so his companion would never really be gone. What a seamless web; if that doesn't melt your heart, I don't know what will!

449. 1 SAMUEL WILLISTON & RICHARD A. LORD, A TREATISE ON THE LAW OF CONTRACTS § 4:7 (4th ed. 1990).

remarking that, "Explaining why a joke is funny is a daunting task; as the essayist E.B. White has remarked, 'Humor can be dissected, as a frog can, but the thing dies in the process . . . .'"[450] However, Judge Wood still endeavored to beat a dead horse (or frog) as she attempted to explain why the commercial was funny. Perhaps the *real* punchline was Pepsi would never seriously offer a $23,000,000 fighter jet for the equivalent of $700,000 in Pepsi Points![451]

Pepsi was clearly going to prevail, but Judge Wood knew Leonard was not one for picking up on subtleties (e.g., humor). That is why she threw the kitchen sink into her dispositive order: the Statute of Frauds. Because the Statute of Frauds states a signed, written agreement must exist to permit judicial enforcement of a contract for the sale of goods valued at $500 or more (e.g., a Harrier), Leonard's claim failed as a matter of law.[452] While a completed order form can serve as a written record for a contract, Leonard's order form was the *only* offer made for a Harrier—an offer Pepsi rejected. Summary judgment was entered for Pepsi, and the case was closed.

Perhaps to spite Leonard, Pepsi continued running the commercial, but they increased the value of the Harrier to *700,000,000* Pepsi Points. They also added a "just kidding" disclaimer in case anyone was dense enough to purchase $70,000,000 worth of Pepsi Points.[453] Leonard unsuccessfully appealed the case, and much of the funding earmarked for his fighter jet was absorbed by his sizeable legal bills.[454]

---

450. *Leonard*, 88 F. Supp. at 128.
451. *Id.* at 129.
452. *Id.* at 131; N.Y. U.C.C. § 2-201(1) (2020).
453. *Leonard*, 88 F. Supp. at 130.
454. *See* Leonard v. PepsiCo, Inc., 210 F.3d 88 (2d Cir. 2000).

Hablot K. "Phiz" Browne, *Inside* (etching)
in JAMES GRANT, SKETCHES IN LONDON pl. 20
(London, Wm. Tegg 1838).

§ 15

The Sazerac® and *The Star-Spangled Banner*

Y ou may not think of a cocktail as having a patriotic bent, but I would submit to you that the Sazerac® is the All-American cocktail.[455] The Sazerac® is one of the country's earliest cocktails, and it may have even been the first branded cocktail in the world.[456] Branding and capitalism are as American as baseball, raising hell over taxes, and refusing to use the metric system, but the fact that an immigrant created the signature ingredient for this cocktail really seals the deal—for me, anyway.

Antoine Amédée Peychaud was born in 1803 in Saint-Domingue (which was about to become the Republic of Haiti). The child of wealthy French colonists, his family

---

455. Sazerac Company, Inc. has trademarked the phrases "America's First Cocktail®" and "America's Original Cocktail®," which it uses to describe the Sazerac®. AMERICA'S FIRST COCKTAIL, Registration No. 2,962,684 (registered June 14, 2005); AMERICA'S ORIGINAL COCKTAIL, Registration No. 2,955,839 (registered May 24, 2005). The case could be made that the Mint Julep is a better candidate for both of those titles. *See* history of the Mint Julep *infra* p. 231.

456. "Branded," meaning the cocktail calls for ingredients produced by a specific manufacturer.

fled the country in the wake of the Haitian Revolution (1791–1804), and Peychaud ended up in New Orleans.[457] He became a pharmacist and, of greater consequence, brewed his own restorative tonic in the 1830s.[458] Although the concoction was allegedly developed for "medicinal" purposes, it was soon discovered that Peychaud's bitters paired especially well with brandy. Thanks to that secondary application, the pharmacist was soon selling his bitters by the bottle.

By the 1850s, Peychaud's product had become a local staple and was used extensively at the Sazerac Coffee House (more like a bar than a Starbucks®). The use of the word "Sazerac" in the establishment's name was a nod to a popular brand of Cognac, Sazerac de Forge et Fils. The Sazerac Coffee House served brandy and whiskey cocktails made with Peychaud's® Bitters, but it does not appear to have served a Sazerac® cocktail—at least not by that name.

The modern formulation of the Sazerac® (made with rye whiskey) probably came about during the 1870s when Cognac consumption in New Orleans sharply declined.[459] Some of that may have been the "Americanization" of the city, but an even greater influence was Cognac becoming virtually unavailable for several decades after the Civil War. An invasive North American aphid, phylloxera, was unwittingly introduced to France in the course of trade. Soon after its arrival, the bug began devastating the roots

---

457. Philip Greene, *Who Is the Real Father of the Cocktail?*, DAILY BEAST (Apr. 5, 2017, 1:00 AM), https://lexspirit.link/JALN.

458. Wayne Curtis, *History Lesson: The Sazerac*, IMBIBE (July 16, 2019), https://lexspirit.link/YASS. For further material relating to Haitian potions, see *supra* note 22 and accompanying text.

459. Amy Zavatto, *The History and Secrets of the Sazerac*, LIQUOR.COM (Mar. 5, 2019), https://lexspirit.link/RLRG. The Union Blockade made Cognac scarce during the Civil War, but not completely unavailable.

of French grapevines.[460] Suffice it to say, this was a national tragedy for France because the shortage of grapes meant wine and brandy production fell by the wayside. Sazerac de Forge et Fils and many other reputable Cognac producers folded by the mid-1880s. A solution to the problem was eventually found,[461] but New Orleans's pairing of Peychaud's Bitters with rye whiskey would never be undone.

Of course, cocktail history is never quite that simple, and it remains a mystery as to when exactly a *specific* cocktail called the "Sazerac®" came about. People had been mixing Peychaud's Bitters with sugar and liquor for decades, but did they call the concoction a "Sazerac®"? In the 1890s, the current owner of the Sazerac Coffee House and Peychaud's Bitters, Thomas H. Handy & Co., began selling "Sazerac®" brand bottled cocktails. Oddly enough, those premixed cocktails did not come in a Sazerac® flavor, but there were whiskey, brandy, Manhattan, Martini, gin, and vermouth varieties.[462] Confusingly, any of those products could have fairly been called a "Sazerac®" cocktail! In the spirit of eschewing further nuance on the point, I will simply note that cocktail historian David Wondrich believes the first distinct mention of *the* Sazerac® cocktail occurred in March 1899,[463] and I am more than happy to take his word for it.

---

460. Laura Clark, *American Bugs Almost Wiped Out France's Wine Industry*, SMITHSONIAN MAG. (Mar. 9, 2015), https://lexspirit.link/SC1G.

461. Phylloxera attacked the leaves of American grapevines but preferred to devour the roots of French grapevines—killing the plant altogether. The solution was to graft French vines onto American rootstocks, and now most French wine has American roots! *Id.*

462. David Wondrich, *Is the Sazerac a New Orleans Cocktail?*, DAILY BEAST (Apr. 24, 2017, 1:00 AM), https://lexspirit.link/TWTF.

463. *Miscellaneous Notes on Congress*, 19 ALPHA TAU OMEGA PALM 157, 158 (March 1899), https://lexspirit.link/G44K.

Intellectual Property Rights in Cocktails[464]

In case you have not noticed the unrelenting use of the "®" symbol throughout this book, a brief note on intellectual property might be prudent, especially when discussing the Sazerac®.[465] The Founding Fathers considered intellectual property rights to be so fundamental that the Constitution specifically granted Congress the power to create a system to regulate those ownership rights.[466] Some of those rights are applicable to cocktails, and others are not.

To begin with, if you are truly interested in preventing anyone from copying your cocktail recipe, do not *ever* tell anyone how to make it in the first place. Keeping recipes a trade secret[467] is a very effective way to safeguard unique formulas, and the strategy has famously been employed to keep the recipes for Coca-Cola® and Chartreuse® a complete mystery to outsiders. Competitors cannot steal your recipe if they cannot figure out what that recipe is.

---

464. Special thanks go to Michael A. Masse, Ph.D., for his assistance with this material. Much of his career was devoted to the administration of intellectual property rights in polymers. He also happens to be a fantastic human being—and my stepfather. *See generally* Michael A. Masse, Structure and Morphology of Electrically Conducting Poly(*p*-Phenylene Vinylene) (September 1989) (Ph.D. dissertation, U. Mass.), https://lexspirit.link/9YOQ.

465. While standard conventions permit a writer to dispense with the "®" symbol after the first mention of a mark, I have chosen to include the symbol the first time a mark appears in each chapter and on recipe pages. That is, except where the Sazerac® is concerned.

466. U.S. CONST. art. I, § 9, cl. 8 ("The Congress shall have power to . . . promote the progress of science and useful arts, by securing for limited times to authors and inventors the exclusive right to their respective writings and discoveries.").

467. "A formula, process, device, or other business information that is kept confidential to maintain an advantage over competitors." *Trade Secret*, BLACK'S LAW DICTIONARY 1800.

However, in the case of a recipe that is too easily guessed or replicated to be safeguarded, a mixologist must explore other avenues for protection. An original work embodying a sufficient amount of creativity is often eligible for copyright protection under United States law.[468] However, "a mere listing of ingredients or contents, or a simple set of directions [e.g., a cocktail recipe] is uncopyrightable" because it is a mere listing of facts.[469] For the same reason, the name of a cocktail is uncopyrightable because it contains "an insufficient amount of authorship."[470] But if you convey a listing of facts in a unique, literary manner, the novel presentation of that factual material *can* receive copyright protection.[471] The exhibition of information in this book (for better or worse) is an example of that.

On the other hand, while cocktail recipes and names are not eligible for copyright protection, a cocktail *can* receive protection under trademark law if it is "distinctive of the applicant's goods in commerce."[472] A trademark is "any word, symbol, or device, or any combination thereof adopted and used by a manufacturer or merchant to identify his goods and distinguish them from those manufactured or sold by others."[473] A registered trademark reserves the rights in the mark to the owner, and the owner can exert control over others' use of the mark to ensure it meets their standards for quality, among other things. Although not especially common, several cocktails

---

468. *See generally* Copyright Act of 1976, Pub. L. No. 94-553, 90 Stat. 2541 (codified as amended at 17 U.S.C. § 101 *et seq.*).

469. U.S. COPYRIGHT OFF., CIRCULAR NO. 33, at 2 (2021).

470. *Id.*

471. *Id.*

472. *See generally* Lanham Act § 2(f), 60 Stat. at 429 (codified as amended at 15 U.S.C. § 1052(f)).

473. *Id.* § 45, 60 Stat. at 443 (codified as amended at 15 U.S.C. § 1127).

are trademarked.[474] For instance, Tropical Isle, Inc., which owns a chain of bars in New Orleans, trademarked the Hand Grenade® cocktail, which means no other bar can sell a cocktail by that name without their permission.[475] This is considered a venue-based trademark: *That* cocktail can only be purchased at *that* establishment.

But what happens if a distiller—who does not actually sell cocktails to the general public—wants to trademark a cocktail? As it just so happens, Sazerac Company, Inc. (through its subsidiary, Sazerac Brands, LLC) appears to hold a registered trademark for the Sazerac® *cocktail*—or at least they certainly have acted like they do (more on that in a moment). Unfortunately, Sazerac Company, Inc. declined to respond to a letter and several e-mails requesting clarification on this point. In 1955, the company registered a Sazerac® trademark for "alcoholic cocktails" and listed the first commercial use of the mark as occurring in 1895 (probably in reference to the pre-bottled Sazerac® cocktails mentioned *supra* p. 141).[476]

Complaints have been made that the term "Sazerac" when used in relation to an "'alcoholic cocktail' does not function as a trademark" because it is a common term for a cocktail that can be ordered at any bar. Thus, the trademark should be cancelled because it is generic.[477] But

---

474. Philip J. Greene, *Can You Trademark a Cocktail Recipe?*, DAILY BEAST (Sept. 27, 2016, 1:00 AM), https://lexspirit.link/WPKZ.
475. HAND GRENADE, Registration No. 1,806,334 (registered Nov. 23, 1993).
476. SAZERAC, Registration No. 602,218 (registered Feb. 15, 1955); Kate Dingwall, *Inside the World of Trademarked Cocktails*, FORBES (June 23, 2020, 4:50 PM), https://lexspirit.link/5MHM.
477. Answer and Counterclaim at 4–6, *In re* U.S. Trademark Application Serial No. 87/069842 (filed June 13, 2016), Sazerac Brands, LLC v. Carr Spirits, Ltd. (T.T.A.B. Opposition No. 91233152), https://lexspirit.link/7WZM; Lanham Act § 14(c), 60 Stat. at 433 (codified as amended at 15 U.S.C. § 1064(3)).

for argument's sake (and to allow the Author to dispense with noncommittal, hypothetical language), let us be generous (cautious) and assume they *do* hold a valid trademark for this cocktail.[478] Either way, much of the following discussion is also applicable to other distiller-trademarked cocktails, such as the Dark 'n Stormy® (mark held by Gosling Brothers Limited, the producer of Goslings® Black Seal Rum).[479]

Holding a trademark for the Sazerac® cocktail allows Sazerac Company, Inc. to ensure whoever calls a cocktail a "Sazerac®" has used their approved recipe, thereby ensuring the cocktail meets minimum standards of quality. In practice, this means you *must* use specific brands of ingredients to make a Sazerac®—all of which just so happen to be produced by subsidiaries of Sazerac Company, Inc.[480] If your "Sazerac®" deviates from their official recipe, it represents an unauthorized use of their mark. This clever strategy allows them to indirectly use trademark law to control the contents of a cocktail. Recipes

---

478. It is a bit ironic that Sazerac Company, Inc. holds the trademark rights to a word "borrowed" from a popular brand of Cognac in the mid-19th century. I do not mean to imply it does not hold a valid trademark, but it is an interesting foundation on which to build a brand.

479. DARK 'N STORMY, Registration No. 1,657,574 (registered Sept. 17, 1991). When this cocktail is made with a dark rum other than Goslings Black Seal Rum, many bars call the resulting cocktail a "Safe Harbor." Now *that* is a double entendre!

Dark 'n Stormy: Combine 4 oz. of ginger beer and 1-½ oz. of Goslings Black Seal Rum in a highball glass filled with ice. Stir gently and garnish with a lime wedge. DEGROFF, *supra* note 31, at 157. This cocktail is a play on the Moscow Mule (replacing the vodka with rum), and many people add some lime juice and a dash of bitters to it.

480. Herbsaint® Liqueur, Peychaud's® Bitters, and Sazerac® Rye Whiskey are the mandatory ingredients to manufacture a Sazerac® cocktail. In fact, the only ingredients Sazerac Company, Inc. does not produce are the requisite lemon peel and sugar cube! Curiously, Sazerac® Rye Whiskey is a fairly recent modification to the recipe because it was only released in the early 2000s.

themselves are too factual to be copywritten, but trademark law can serve as the proverbial back door into those intellectual property rights.

For a registered holder to maintain their rights in a trademark, they must vigorously defend their rights, lest their mark become abandoned or genericized (e.g., all tissues are commonly referred to as a Kleenex despite that being a specific brand of facial tissue).[481] Sazerac Company, Inc. has really taken this to heart, and their attorneys once sent a demand letter to a small blogger (receiving about 200 hits per day) when she provided an incorrect recipe for the Sazerac®.[482] The courteous—but firm—letter provided the blogger with the *correct* recipe for a Sazerac® and requested she publish a correction to her original blog post.[483] The blogger acquiesced.

The following recipe for the Sazerac® comes straight from Sazerac Company, Inc.'s website.[484] Interestingly, the official directions do not explicitly instruct you to stir the ingredients with ice. If you are so inclined (I am), I suggest doing that on the tail end of step three and then straining out the ice. More importantly, no decent bar on Bourbon Street would shake this cocktail—and neither should you.

---

481. *See* Lanham Act § 14(c), 60 Stat. at 433 (codified as amended at 15 U.S.C. § 1064); *see also* Whitson Gordon, *How a Brand Name Becomes Generic: Pass the Kleenex, Please*, N.Y. TIMES (June 24, 2019), https://lexspirit.link/TLUN.

482. Dr. Becca, *A Sazerac for You*, FUMBLING TOWARDS TENURE (Feb. 22, 2012), https://lexspirit.link/T1XE, *subsequently corrected by* Dr. Becca, *Adventures in Trademark Law: The Sazerac Saga*, FUMBLING TOWARDS TENURE (Mar. 6, 2012), https://lexspirit.link/94VY.

483. Letter from Cooley LLP, on behalf of Sazerac Co., Inc., to "Dr. Becca" (Feb. 29, 2012), https://lexspirit.link/SQFY.

484. This was a voluntary decision. While a trademark can effectively mandate the *ingredients* of a cocktail, a patent would be required to cover the directions/process for making the cocktail.

Sazerac®[485]

1. Pack an old fashioned glass with ice.[486]
2. In a second old fashioned glass, saturate a sugar cube with 3 dashes of Peychaud's® Bitters, then crush the sugar cube with a muddler.
3. Add 1-1/2 oz. of Sazerac® Rye Whiskey (apparently Buffalo Trace® Bourbon is also acceptable, as stated in the demand letter *supra* note 483) to the glass containing the Peychaud's Bitters and sugar.[487]
4. Empty the ice from the first glass and coat the glass with 1/4 oz. of Herbsaint® Liqueur, then discard any excess.[488]
5. Empty the whiskey/bitters/sugar mixture from the second glass into the first glass and garnish with a lemon peel. Serve without any ice in the glass.

---

485. *Sazerac Rye—The Character of New Orleans*, SAZERAC CO., INC., https://lexspirit.link/YJYJ.

486. This technique is called *frappé*, and it chills the serving glass.

487. While Buffalo Trace Bourbon is included in the demand letter as an acceptable alternative because the brand is under common ownership, it would be an interesting (dare I say inappropriate?) choice to use Bourbon in a Sazerac®.

488. Herbsaint Liqueur is an anise-flavored liqueur created in 1934 as an absinthe substitute. Absinthe was banned for nearly a century in the United States, but that is an interesting story for another time.

The Star-Spangled Banner

Speaking of the Sazerac®, another iconic American composition was created with the assistance of serendipity and alcohol. I am, of course, referring to *The Star-Spangled Banner*. Pour yourself a double and enjoy the following double feature concerning our national anthem.

The Poetic Attorney[489]

On September 7, 1814, two attorneys named John Stuart Skinner and Francis Scott Key disembarked from a 60-foot sloop and climbed into a small rowboat.[490] As the pair began rowing toward the place where the British fleet was anchored in Chesapeake Bay, it is not known whether either of the men harbored any apprehension about the

---

489. Aside from a certain poem, Francis Scott Key never wrote a detailed account of these events, but he *did* give an extended oral account to Chief Justice Roger B. Taney. Irritatingly, Taney did not record what Key told him until he wrote a letter to Charles Howard in 1856 (*infra* note 497). Hearsay, anyone? By that time, Taney was 79 years old and almost 42 years had elapsed since the events he was recounting.

John S. Skinner, who had firsthand knowledge of the events, did not feel rushed to memorialize his version of the story either. His account— taking the form of an 1849 letter to the editor of the *Baltimore Patriot and Commercial Gazette* (*infra* note 498)—was written to correct certain inaccuracies he perceived in a May 23, 1849 article. Skinner was 61 years old when he wrote that letter, and 35 years had elapsed since the Battle of Baltimore. GEORGE J. SVEJDA, HISTORY OF THE STAR SPANGLED BANNER FROM 1814 TO THE PRESENT 69–70, 72–73 (Nat'l Park Serv. 1969).

Much of what we know about the events leading up to Key writing the lyrics to *The Star-Spangled Banner* is gleaned from Taney and Skinner's letters. Unfortunately, whether as a result of old age, the passage of time, hearsay, or a combination of those factors, the letters contradict one another in several key respects. Historians have been tasked with reconciling those details, and I can only hope this retelling does not muddy the waters any further!

490. MARC LEEPSON, WHAT SO PROUDLY WE HAILED: FRANCIS SCOTT KEY, A LIFE 56 (Palgrave Macmillan 2014).

task at hand.[491] The War of 1812 was raging in the United States, and while advancing toward enemy vessels in a rowboat was normally a foolhardy errand, the men approached under a flag of truce.

Two weeks earlier, on August 24, 1814, around 4,500 British troops under the command of Major General Robert Ross routed a numerically superior—but poorly trained—American army about nine miles outside of Washington, D.C.[492] With the now-undefended capital left vulnerable to attack, President James Madison, his Cabinet, Congress, and most of the local residents fled the city. By midafternoon Ross had marched his army into the capital, and British troops spent the next 26 hours looting, plundering, and setting fire to federal buildings— including the Presidential Mansion (not yet called the White House) and the Capitol.[493]

By providence, a freak storm with gale force winds materialized just as the invaders began to withdraw from the devastated city.[494] The storm was so fierce it extinguished many of the remaining structure fires, injured and killed several Redcoats, and spawned several tornados—one of which threw a pair of British cannons across the road.[495] Washington, D.C., may have constituted little more than a heap of storm-damaged, smoldering ruins, but we can take some satisfaction in knowing that Mother Nature is an American.

---

491. ALLEN D. SPIEGEL, MURDER AND MADNESS, MILITARY MATTERS, AND MANAGED MEDICINE: MEMORABLE MILESTONES AND MOMENTS 138–42 (Heritage Books 2007).

492. LEEPSON, *supra* note 490, at 47.

493. MARC FERRIS, STAR-SPANGLED BANNER: THE UNLIKELY STORY OF AMERICA'S NATIONAL ANTHEM 15 (MJF Books 2014); LEEPSON, *supra* note 490, at 50–51.

494. *Id.* at 51.

495. *The Tornado That Stopped the Burning of Washington*, NAT'L CONST. CTR. (Aug. 25, 2015), https://lexspirit.link/IGDW.

After the storm abated, Ross ordered his troops to make their way back to the British fleet. During this mobilization a series of incidents occurred that culminated in the arrest of an elderly Maryland physician named Dr. William Beanes.[496] Fortunately for Dr. Beanes, he was well liked and had friends in high places. He counted Francis Scott Key among those friends, and the esteemed attorney appealed to government officials for assistance.

Following some initial diplomatic posturing that proved ineffective, President Madison dispatched John S. Skinner, the United States Agent for Prisoner Exchange, to accompany Key on his quest to secure the noncombatant's release. Key's brother-in-law, Roger B. Taney (who later became the fifth Chief Justice of the Supreme Court of the United States) remarked that the elderly doctor "was treated as a culprit, and not as a prisoner of war."[497] It was a good thing Key and Skinner showed up when they did—otherwise the poor doctor might have died in custody.

---

496. FERRIS, *supra* note 493, at 16. Dr. Beanes was the leader of a posse that arrested several British soldiers who were caught looting farms in the area. One of those prisoners escaped, and a retaliatory raiding party was dispatched by Major General Ross and Rear Admiral George Cockburn to arrest Dr. Beanes. LEEPSON, *supra* note 490, at 52–53.

497. Letter from Roger B. Taney, Chief Justice of the Supreme Court of the United States, to Charles Howard, Esq. 9 (Mar. 17, 1856), https://lexspirit.link/6S9A [hereinafter Taney Letter]. After obtaining the existing microfilm of this letter, I discovered whoever was responsible for scanning it many decades ago neglected to scan the back of the first page. While the letter had been transcribed in several books over the course of the last century and a half, upon deciphering Justice Taney's heavily slanted cursive I discovered several words were either omitted or changed in those publications. That rendered me curious enough to request a scan of the missing page. Once apprised of the situation, the archivists at the Library of Congress were kind enough to carefully scan the *entire* letter for me (in color, no less).

Now, let us return to the all-attorney regatta taking place in Chesapeake Bay: A short time after Key and Skinner rowed alongside the H.M.S. *Tonnant*, they were greeted by British Major General Ross and the Commander-in-Chief of the North American Station, Vice Admiral Sir Alexander Inglis Cochrane. Seeing as the Americans arrived just in time for dinner, the gentlemanly Vice Admiral invited the guests to dine with him and the other British officers aboard his flagship. Cochrane may have detested Americans, but he had impeccable manners.

What transpired next is disputed. Skinner claimed he had a private conversation with Major General Ross in the Vice Admiral's cabin while Key remained at the dinner table that evening.[498] Reportedly, it was at this private meeting with Skinner that Ross agreed to release Dr. Beanes.[499] If Skinner's version of events is correct, then Key's intercession on the doctor's behalf—the only reason for him being there—was unnecessary. Taney's recollection of what Key told him is that Key was actively involved in the negotiations for Dr. Beanes's release.[500]

---

498. John S. Skinner, *Attack of the British on Baltimore—Mr. Ingersoll's History*, BALT. PATRIOT & COM. GAZETTE, May 29, 1849, at p. 2, col. 2 [¶ 7], https://lexspirit.link/PXIZ [hereinafter Skinner Letter].

499. SVEJDA, *supra* note 489, at 63, 72. Ross was persuaded to release the doctor after he was presented with several letters from captured British officers attesting to how diligently Dr. Beanes had tended to their wounds after the Battle of Bladensburg. SPIEGEL, *supra* note 491, at 139.

500. "And after a good deal of conversation and strong representations from Mr. Key as to the character and standing of Doctor Bean[e]s, and of the deep interest which the community in which he lived took in his fate, Genl. Ross said that Doctor Bean[e]s deserved much more punishment than he had received, but that he felt himself bound to make a return for the kindness which had been shown to his wounded officers, whom he had been compelled to leave at Bladensburg—and upon that ground and that only he would release him." Taney Letter, *supra* note 497, at 7–8.

While Taney's account lacks a definitive timeline, it gives the impression it may have taken several days to secure the doctor's freedom. Wherever the truth may lie, Ross *did* agree to free Dr. Beanes, and the Americans remained with the British fleet for several days while Skinner discussed other business with the enemy.[501]

Arguably, a more historically consequential (and undisputed) fact is British officers drank plenty of wine with dinner, and a significant amount of it cleared the Vice Admiral's table during the tenure of the Americans' visit.[502] So much so that it appears to have been responsible for Key and Skinner being privy to several detailed conversations concerning the planned invasion of Baltimore, which would kick off with an overland assault on September 12, 1814. The Americans politely held their tongues but listened intently. After all, you should never interrupt your enemy while they are making a mistake!

Once Skinner's other business with the British was concluded, the Americans prepared to depart on their merry way—but they were stopped by the Vice Admiral. "Ah, Mr. S[kinner] after discussing so freely as we have done in your presence, our purposes and plans, you could hardly expect us to let you go on shore now in advance of us," Cochrane remarked.[503] The British prudently recognized they probably should not allow their guests to inform their friends of the details of the impending attack on Baltimore. Several Royal Marines were tasked with guarding the "honored guests" until after the offensive. Key and Skinner continued to be treated well, but

---

501. Skinner Letter, *supra* note 498, at p. 2, col. 3 [¶ 18].

502. Skinner later recounted one mealtime incident by leading with the following: "[Admiral Codrington], after the wine had been in free circulation, allowed himself to remark, with somewhat unbecoming freedom . . . ." *Id.* at p. 2, col. 2 [¶ 5].

503. *Id.* at p. 2, col. 3 [¶ 18].

Dr. Beanes was kept in his present, deplorable accommodations for the time being.

The two American agents were initially detained aboard the frigate H.M.S. *Surprise*, but just before the attack on Baltimore began, all three Americans (including Dr. Beanes) were transferred back to the sloop Key and Skinner arrived in.[504] That is, once the sloop was relieved of its sails and tethered to a British vessel.[505] It was from the deck of that vessel the men witnessed the naval bombardment of Fort McHenry, which began on the morning of September 13, 1814, and continued until just before dawn the next day.[506]

When the Congreve "rockets' red glare" and "bombs bursting in air" abruptly ceased lighting up the sky before sunrise on the 14th, Key and Skinner feared the Fort had surrendered.[507] Much to their elation, this was not the case: The British stopped firing because they were abandoning the assault. When he beheld the stars and stripes waving above Fort McHenry at dawn, Key—who was a talented amateur poet—was inspired to compose a

---

504. Taney Letter, *supra* note 497, at 10.

505. The ship from which Key witnessed the bombardment of Fort McHenry is often incorrectly cited as being the H.M.S. *Minden. See, e.g.,* Colleen Walsh, *Star-Spangled Beauty,* HARV. GAZETTE (Sept. 11, 2014), https://lexspirit.link/VZGK. This is impossible because the *Minden* was stationed in India in 1814. *[News from] Madras,* BOMBAY GAZETTE, Oct. 19, 1814, at 2 ("Salutes from the Fort, from Chepauk Palace, H.M. Ship *Minden,* and from the *Asia,* announced the embarkation of the General . . . ."). Unfortunately, the identity of the cartel ship from which Key watched the bombardment from may never be known for certain. The most plausible theory is that it was a 60-foot sloop operated by John Ferguson called the *President.* SVEJDA, *supra* note 489, at 61, 64; LEEPSON, *supra* note 490, at 56; Skinner Letter, *supra* note 498, at p. 2, col. 3 [¶ 18] ("Seeing no help for it, I demanded that we should then be returned to our own vessel—one of Ferguson's Norfolk Packets, under our own 'Star Spangled Banner,' during the attack.").

506. LEEPSON, *supra* note 490, at 61–63.

507. Taney Letter, *supra* note 497, at 11.

poem. He titled it *The Defence of Fort M'Henry*, but it soon became known as *The Star-Spangled Banner*.[508]

Key composed the words of his poem to be sung to the tune of a "bawdy, boozy ballad," *To Anacreon in Heaven*, which was the club song of the Anacreontic Society of London, a convivial gentlemen's organization in England that gathered to partake in music, food, and drink.[509] It was a popular tune in the United States at the time, with an everyday familiarity comparable to that of *Yankee Doodle*. The tune we sing today differs slightly from the original, but Key's lyrics persist. Oddly enough, in spite of its instant popularity, *The Star-Spangled Banner* would not officially be adopted as the United States' national anthem until 1931—nearly 117 years after it was written![510]

---

508. Taney states Key jotted down some notes on the back of a letter during the bombardment, wrote a draft on the way to shore, and transcribed a final draft of the poem at a Baltimore hotel (probably the Indian Queen Tavern). *Id.* at 12–13. Skinner's account, on the other hand, gives the impression Key did not begin writing the poem until after he arrived at the hotel in Baltimore. Skinner Letter, *supra* note 498, at p. 2, col. 3 [¶ 19].

509. FERRIS, *supra* note 493, at 21; LEEPSON, *supra* note 490, at 66. There has been some debate as to whether Key wrote a poem (that just so happened to fit with a song) or if he was deliberately composing lyrics to be sung to the tune of *To Anacreon in Heaven*. His poem matches the meter of the tune so well the general consensus is Key deliberately wrote a *song*—and not merely a poem. *Id.* at 67–69.

510. An Act to Make *The Star-Spangled Banner* the National Anthem of the United States of America, ch. 436, 46 Stat. 1508 (1931) (codified as amended at 36 U.S.C. § 301(a)).

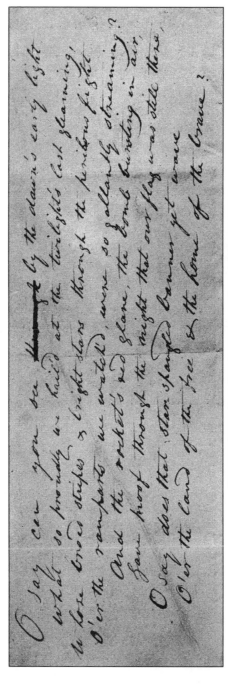

FRANCIS SCOTT KEY, THE DEFENCE OF FORT MCHENRY (1814),
Object No. 54,315, H. FURLONG BALDWIN LIBR., MD. CTR. HIST. & CULTURE
(detail of the first verse from Key's handwritten manuscript).

Stravinsky's National Anthem[511]

When considering the more recent history of Key's composition, Igor Fyodorovich Stravinsky may not initially come to mind, but perhaps he should. Stravinsky was one of the most notable composers of the 20th century and led an interesting life. He is best remembered for a trio of Russian ballets—*The Firebird, Petrushka,* and *The Rite of Spring*—that each feature extensive use of his signature elements: dissonant chords and unusual rhythmic patterns. Buckle up because this warrants a slight detour into music theory for a moment.

Traditional classical music uses certain chord structures which are perceived as sounding "pleasant" to the listener. These are called consonant chords, and they form the harmonic foundation of Western music. Dissonant chords, on the other hand, are often experienced by the listener as being harsh or edgy, and they foster an uncomfortable need for resolution. Stravinsky never viewed this dissonance as "wrong" or unpleasant. He saw dissonant chords as an underutilized color of the musical palate and employed them to enhance the storytelling aspect of his music.

Likewise, Stravinsky's rhythmic motifs were distinctive, to say the least. His music often featured highly irregular rhythms with ever-changing time signatures and repeated patterns of rhythms (individually referred to as an ostinato, or ostinati in the plural). Despite not necessarily being complementary to one another,

---

511. Special thanks to Dr. James Worman, Professor of Music Education at Trinity University, who introduced me to Stravinsky's music, provided some helpful context on dissonant chords for this chapter, and put up with my "spirited" trombone playing for a total of five years (not a victory lap—that includes my graduate studies). Christina Beeler also provided helpful legal insights for this section.

Stravinsky occasionally superimposed these ostinati over each other in a chaotic manner. What initially struck the listener as a series of nonsensical moving parts was eventually developed into a sense of motion, progression, and resolution.[512] The combination of Stravinsky's vibrant rhythms and dissonant harmonies created an avant-garde musical collage for audiences. While his pieces were initially perceived as chaotic and aggressive, over time listeners learned to appreciate Stravinsky's vision and embraced his works as valid musical expression. He is revered as a composer that both rocked the foundations of Western music and broadened the horizons of that same order.

Given his unique approach to music, it is not terribly surprising that Stravinsky enjoyed amusing himself by rewriting various countries' national anthems into decidedly less-than-traditional arrangements.[513] He composed four separate versions of *The Star-Spangled Banner* alone, and one of those was premiered by the Boston Symphony Orchestra on January 14, 1944. Ahead of the concert Stravinsky was asked how he had modified the national anthem. His response was intriguing: "I gave it the character of a real church hymn . . . not that of a soldier's marching song or a club song, as it was originally. I tried to express the religious feelings of the people of America."[514] The public's interest was piqued.

On the night of the premiere, Stravinsky turned around to conduct the audience in singing *The Star-*

---

512. *See* Gretchen Horlacher, *The Rhythms of Reiteration: Formal Development in Stravinsky's Ostinati*, 14 MUSIC THEORY SPECTRUM 171 (1992).

513. H. Colin Slim, *Stravinsky's Four Star-Spangled Banners and His 1941 Christmas Card*, 89 MUSICAL Q. 321, 321–22 (2006).

514. *Revises Nation's Anthem*, N.Y. TIMES, Jan. 13, 1944, at 16, https://lexspirit.link/30X3.

Spangled Banner to his modified setting. It was an unmitigated disaster.[515] Even though the piece contained only a few "mildly dissonant" chords and was largely unaltered from a rhythmic standpoint, the audience was completely flummoxed by the unfamiliar supporting harmonies and contrapuntal lines.[516] The confounded audience stopped singing midway through the performance, and one review of the concert described the spectacle as "a performance of the customary version [of the national anthem] by an orchestra which either cannot read or cannot play music." Some of the negative reception may have been amplified by the public's patriotic fervor during World War Two. Still, Stravinsky was up front about the spirit of his modifications to the tune, and the audience cannot have fairly expected a "vanilla" version of the song. But the controversy was only just beginning.

On Saturday, January 15, 1944, the Boston Police Commissioner appeared in Stravinsky's dressing room and informed him that performing a modified version of *The Star-Spangled Banner* was a crime punishable by a $100 fine in Massachusetts. That night's performance was to be broadcast live on the radio, and the police had already taken the liberty of removing Stravinsky's offensive arrangement from the music stands. Stravinsky voluntarily agreed to perform a traditional version of the national anthem for the broadcast, and that was the official end to the matter.[517] Even so, a rumor circulated that Stravinsky was arrested for breaking the law. It was patently untrue. He was not even fined.

---

515. *Revised Anthem Played*, N.Y. TIMES, Jan. 15, 1944, at 11, https://lexspirit.link/ML76.

516. FERRIS, *supra* note 493, at 178; Slim, *supra* note 513, at 367.

517. *Stravinsky Liable to Fine*, N.Y. TIMES, Jan. 16, 1944, at 41, https://lexspirit.link/VJKE.

The 1917 Massachusetts law Stravinsky violated predates the United States' adoption of *The Star-Spangled Banner* as the national anthem, and it remains on the books today! The statute provides, in relevant part, that a public performance of *The Star-Spangled Banner* with "embellishment" is punishable by a "fine of not more than one hundred dollars."[518] That was serious money in 1917! More importantly, the law appears to be facially unconstitutional—especially when reviewed in light of today's jurisprudence.

The First Amendment to the Constitution provides that "Congress shall make no law . . . abridging the freedom of speech . . . ."[519] Notice that Congress is not allowed to pass such a law, but the First Amendment is silent on a *state* government's ability to curtail free expression. This was intentional. James Madison's proposal for a separate amendment prohibiting *states* from violating "the rights of conscience, or the freedom of the press, or the trial by jury in criminal cases" was rejected by Congress.[520] The Fourteenth Amendment (which specifically curtails state action) eventually changed that dynamic, and the Supreme Court has since interpreted the Due Process Clause of the Fourteenth Amendment to

---

518. Relative to the Manner of Rendering *The Star-Spangled Banner*, 1917 Mass. Acts 318 (codified as amended at MASS. GEN. LAWS ch. 264, § 9 (2020)). Truthfully, the language of the statute leaves some doubt as to whether Stravinsky's modifications to, and performance of, the national anthem violated the law, but the legislative intent was clearly to discourage modifications to *The Star-Spangled Banner*.

519. U.S. CONST. amend. I.

520. LINDA R. MONK, THE BILL OF RIGHTS: A USER'S GUIDE 225 (Hachette Books, 5th ed. 2018) (quoting 1 ANNALS OF CONG. 783–84 (1789) (Joseph Gales ed., 1834)).

apply most of the Bill of Rights (including the First Amendment) to the states.[521]

The First Amendment protects a plethora of speech, including viewpoints and commentaries on political, social, economic, educational, religious, and cultural issues.[522] The Supreme Court has routinely held that "speech" encompasses much more than mere words[523] and have recognized that "[m]usic is one of the oldest forms of human expression."[524] Accordingly, Stravinsky's performance of his arrangement of *The Star-Spangled Banner* implicated his right to free expression under the First and Fourteenth Amendments.

But not all speech is entitled to the same level of protection, and lesser degrees of judicial scrutiny apply to government restrictions on speech that is commercial in nature or considered to be low value because it could not possibly be involved in the exposition of ideas.[525] Generally speaking, however, the regulation of speech that is *content based*—meaning the topic, idea, or message being

---

521. Gitlow v. New York, 268 U.S. 652, 666 (1925) ("[W]e may and do assume that freedom of speech and of the press—which are protected by the First Amendment from abridgement by Congress—are among the fundamental personal rights and 'liberties' protected by the due process clause of the Fourteenth Amendment from impairment by the States."); U.S. CONST. amend. XIV. Rights have been selectively (gradually) applied to the states in piecemeal fashion over time—a process called selective incorporation.

522. Roberts v. U.S. Jaycees, 468 U.S. 609, 622 (1984).

523. Stromberg v. California, 283 U.S. 359, 369 (1931).

524. Ward v. Rock Against Racism, 491 U.S. 781, 790 (1989).

525. *See, e.g.*, Cent. Hudson Gas & Elec. Corp. v. Pub. Serv. Comm'n, 447 U.S. 557 (1980) (commercial speech); Miller v. California, 413 U.S. 15 (1974) (obscenity); Gertz v. Robert Welch, Inc., 418 U.S. 323 (1974) (defamation); Riley v. Nat'l Fed'n of the Blind, 487 U.S. 781 (1988) (fraud); Brandenburg v. Ohio, 395 U.S. 444 (1969) (incitement of imminent lawless action); Chaplinsky v. New Hampshire, 315 U.S. 568 (1942) (fighting words); Watts v. United States, 394 U.S. 705 (1969) (true threats); Giboney v. Empire Storage & Ice Co., 336 U.S. 490 (1949) (speech integral to criminal conduct).

expressed itself is regulated—is "presumptively unconstitutional."[526] Indeed, "the government's benign motive, content-neutral justification, or lack of 'animus toward the ideas contained' in the regulated speech" is wholly irrelevant when a restriction is based on content because the "marketplace of ideas" is being suppressed.[527]

If a content based restriction on speech is imposed by the government, it will only be upheld as constitutional if "the restriction furthers a compelling interest and is narrowly tailored to achieve that interest."[528] This is commonly referred to as the "Strict Scrutiny Test" because few government interests and restrictions will pass muster. Massachusetts's justifications for the law—both then and now—are not likely to be compelling, and in all probability the broad restriction was (and is) unconstitutional.

This is not to say that a *private* entity cannot restrict free speech (they often can), but in Stravinsky's case the Boston Police Commissioner was enforcing a state law that effectively removed the public's ability to parody, fugue, modulate, syncopate, or purposefully butcher *The Star-Spangled Banner*. As such, Stravinsky should have been free to perform his rendition of the national anthem over the airwaves that evening—provided he still wanted to.[529]

---

526. Reed v. Town of Gilbert, 576 U.S. 155, 163 (2015).

527. *Id.* at 165 (quoting Cincinnati v. Discovery Network, Inc., 507 U.S. 410, 429 (1993)).

528. *Id.* at 171.

529. "[Free speech] may indeed best serve its high purpose when it induces a condition of unrest, creates dissatisfaction with conditions as they are, or even stirs people to anger." Terminiello v. Chicago, 337 U.S. 1, 4 (1949).

Hablot K. "Phiz" Browne, *A Scene in the House* (etching)
in JAMES GRANT, SKETCHES IN LONDON pl. 10
(London, Wm. Tegg 1838).

§ 16

The Bee's Knees and Brown M&M's®

In 1904, a cocktail called "Gin and Honey" appeared in a French book of English and American cocktail recipes.[530] While it merely consisted of equal parts gin and honey stirred together (potentially at room temperature), it was likely a crude precursor to this chapter's namesake cocktail.[531] What we now call the Bee's Knees may have been invented by a bartender at The Ritz® Paris named Frank Meier, but the first publication to include the cocktail (by that name) was William T. Boothby's *World Drinks and How to Prepare Them* (1930).[532] While being the first to publish a cocktail recipe often indicates the author invented the cocktail, the

---

530. FRANK P. NEWMAN, AMERICAN-BAR: BOISSONS ANGLAISES & AMÉRICAINES TELLES QU'ON LES PRÉPARE 43 (2d ed. 1904).

531. Armin Zimmerman, *Bee's Knees*, BAR-VADEMECUM (Feb. 28, 2021), https://lexspirit.link/I0G8.

532. WILLIAM T. BOOTHBY, "COCKTAIL BILL" BOOTHBY'S WORLD DRINKS AND HOW TO PREPARE THEM 17 (Recorder Printing & Publ'g Co. 1930). Interestingly, Boothby's recipe employs both lemon and orange juice.

general consensus is Boothby simply beat Meier to the printing press.[533] These things happen.

But there was another interloper vying to be known as the creator of the Bee's Knees. An April 22, 1929 article in *The Standard Union* attributed the cocktail to an American socialite residing in Paris at the time, Margaret Brown (remembered as the "The Unsinkable Molly Brown").[534] Brown was a positively fascinating woman who, among other things, survived the sinking of the R.M.S. *Titanic* and ran for a seat in the United States Senate in 1914—which was before women even held the right to vote in an election.[535] However, as extraordinary as she was, I doubt Brown invented this cocktail. Even so, the 1929 article *does* provide further evidence the Bee's Knees originated in Paris.

Legend has it the reason this cocktail became a Prohibition classic is because the sweetness of the honey helped to mask the harshness of the garbage "bathtub gin" people were making at home.[536] That theory is intuitive, but I also think the beverage is delicious in its own right. Gin is a bitter spirit, so combining it with lemon juice and honey makes for a well-balanced cocktail.

---

533. Jim Sabataso, *Happy Hour History: The Bee's Knees*, PASTE MAG. (Dec. 29, 2014, 12:02 PM), https://lexspirit.link/IHDX.

534. *Bars in Paris for 'Madame' Close Doors to Mere Male*, STANDARD UNION, Apr. 22, 1929, at 3, https://lexspirit.link/9D4A ("The 'Bee's Knees' is an invention of Mrs. J.J. Brown of Denver and Paris, widow of the famous miner, and is a rather sweet combination including honey and lemon."). I do not believe the writer of this column ever tried a Bee's Knees because I would not describe it as being overwhelmingly sweet. The honey ingredient's flavor is fairly nuanced.

535. Andrea Malcomb, *'No Pink Tea': Mrs. Brown for Senate*, MOLLY BROWN HOUSE MUSEUM, https://lexspirit.link/9MPR.

536. OXFORD COMPANION, *supra* note 6, at 76.

A Word About Gin

You might be surprised to learn juniper berry derived liquor has not always been quite so bitter and in want of sweetness. Gin has a surprisingly complex history and is the product of governmental regulation. Genever, the precursor to modern dry gin, was invented in the Kingdom of the Netherlands sometime during the late 1500s.[537] It is a distilled malt wine made from a grain (rye, corn, or wheat), juniper berries, and other assorted botanicals and more closely resembles a juniper-flavored whiskey than dry gin.[538] In some ways, it is both less understated and sweeter in flavor than its progeny—but exceptions will always abound.

The British obsession with genever (and eventually, gin) began in the late 1600s when the spirit made its way across the North Sea. Part of the spirit's migration to England is attributed to King William III (William of Orange), who was actually Dutch. While importing a monarch might seem to be an uncommon occurrence, surprise opportunities for promotion did occur—though it was usually as a result of someone's head being separated from their body. William's predecessor, James II (his wife's father), was forced to abdicate in 1688 in what became known as the "Glorious Revolution." (By the way, James managed to retain his head.) With the throne vacant, Parliament offered William of Orange and his wife, Mary II of England, a joint monarchy if they agreed to embrace the 1689 English Bill of Rights.[539] They accepted the

---

537. Stephanie Moreno, *Gin & Genever: A Gin-troduction*, DISTILLER BLOG (Jan. 20, 2018), https://lexspirit.link/0PB0.

538. Most modern gin is manufactured by infusing a neutral spirit (essentially vodka) with botanicals.

539. An Act Declaring the Rights and Liberties of the Subject and Setleing the Succession of the Crowne 1689, 1 W. & M., 2d sess., c. 2 (Eng.); MONK, *supra* note 520, at 14.

invitation and formally adopted what would become a precedent for the United States' Bill of Rights.

The new King and Queen of England were understandably concerned about having ascended to the throne of an empire with a large trade deficit, particularly when it came to France and the Kingdom of the Netherlands. To solve that malady, the pair enacted protectionist tariffs on a variety of imported goods, including wine, beer, brandy (specifically targeting French Cognac), genever, and other spiritous drams.[540] Domestic distilling was also subsidized.[541] Because genever had become popular but was expensive to import from the Netherlands, the English began producing (imitating) it domestically. They soon modified the recipe to suit their tastes and domestically available ingredients. An unfortunate byproduct of the expansion in British distilling was the societal catastrophe known as the Gin Craze (1700–1750), but I will not even attempt to delve into that subject here. In any case, the English transformed genever into the ubiquitous dry gin encountered everywhere today thanks to protectionist tariffs and subsidized domestic distilling.[542]

---

540. *See* Ralph Davis, *The Rise of Protection in England 1689–1786*, 19 ECON. HIST. REV. 306 (1966); *see also* Excise Act 1688, 1 W. & M. c. 24, § 1 (Eng.) (doubling tariffs on beer, wine, and liquors for one year); Taxation Act 1690, 2 W. & M., 2d sess., c. 10, § 1 (Eng.) (extending heightened tariffs for four more years); House of Commons (Disqualification) Act 1693, 5 W. & M. c. 7, § 26 (Eng.) (extending tariffs for a further 16 years). The outbreak of the Nine Years' War with France in 1688 brought a prohibition on all trade with France, meaning no amount of money could be paid to legally import products from France. An Act for Prohibiting All Trade and Commerce with France 1688, 1 W. & M. c. 34, § 1 (Eng.).

541. An Act for the Encourageing the Distilling of Brandy and Spirits from Corne and for Laying Severall Dutyes on Low Wines or Spirits of the First Extraction 1690, 2 W. & M., 2d sess., c. 9 (Eng.). "Corne" referred to gains *generally*—not just the yellow stuff on the cob.

542. OXFORD COMPANION, *supra* note 6, at 315–16.

Gin's ascendancy did not happen overnight in the United States. In 1850, 2,400 gallons of English dry gin cleared the port of New York—a figure dwarfed by the 720,000 gallons of Holland genever unloaded that same year.[543] American imports of gin would not surpass genever until the 1890s. This timing corresponds with the rising popularity of the Martini[544] in the United States, which is fitting because dry gin pairs much better with vermouth than genever does.[545]

You could try making a Bee's Knees with genever as a throwback to the base spirit's heritage, but a floral-focused gin will better complement the honey and citrus notes of the cocktail. Even so, whatever spirit you choose, I am certain it will be the Bee's Knees. *Proost!*

Hablot K. "Phiz" Browne, *Lawyer with Punch* (etching)
in CHARLES J. LEVER, NUTS AND NUTCRACKERS 94
(London, Bradbury & Evans 1845).

---

543. WONDRICH, *supra* note 4, at 71–72.
544. *See* Martini recipe *supra* note 71.
545. WONDRICH, *supra* note 4, at 72.

Bee's Knees[546]

1. Combine the following ingredients in a cocktail shaker with ice:
   a. 2 oz. floral-focused gin
   b. 3/4 oz. honey syrup (recipe follows)
   c. 1/2 oz. fresh-squeezed lemon juice
2. Cap the cocktail shaker and shake vigorously for 20–30 seconds.
3. Garnish a coupe glass with a lemon peel twist.
4. Double strain the contents of the shaker into the coupe glass and serve "up."

Honey Syrup

If you put raw honey into a cocktail shaker with ice, you are in for a *very* bitter cocktail. The chilled honey will congeal and stick to the walls of the cocktail shaker—and will not go into your drink.[547] Fortunately, diluting the honey into a syrup avoids this sticky situation. To make a simple syrup out of honey, combine it with water in a saucepan at a 1:1 ratio over low heat. Stir until combined and then bottle the mixture. If refrigerated, it should keep for several weeks.

---

546. DEGROFF, *supra* note 31, at 63.
547. I learned this lesson the hard way. If you have managed to successfully mix honey directly into a cocktail without diluting it beforehand, you may have been using "fake" honey. Believe it or not, honey is the world's third most faked food! *See* Larry Olmstead, *Exclusive Book Excerpt: Honey Is World's Third Most Faked Food*, FORBES (July 15, 2016, 4:00 AM), https://lexspirit.link/QSDD.

Brown M&M's®

Speaking of gin, do you know what else was not associated with sobriety and came from the Netherlands? Legendary guitarist Eddie Van Halen![548] Van Halen® was an American hard rock band formed in the 1970s, and it made Eddie a household name. The Dutch guitarist did not invent "whammy bar" vibrato, string bending, or fret tapping, but he perfected the combination of those techniques (and more) to become a rock-and-roll virtuoso.

Eddie was notorious for modifying his guitars with parts from other models, and one of his most iconic guitars (aside from the original "Frankenstrat") was affectionately nicknamed "Bumblebee." The Bumblebee was a chaotically striped yellow and black guitar made for Eddie by Wayne Charvel, and it debuted on the back of the *Van Halen II* (1979) record sleeve.[549] The guitar saw extensive use on Van Halen's 1979 *World Vacation Tour* and quickly became a fan favorite because of its outlandish paint job.[550] The appearance of Bumblebee also coincided with the first sighting of a curious contract provision that is the subject of the remainder of this chapter.

---

548. Eddie Van Halen got sober for good in 2008. Sadly, he died of cancer in 2020 while I was writing this chapter. He was a remarkable person—specifically because he had the fortitude to overcome his addictions. *See* Chuck Klosterman, *Billboard Cover: Eddie Van Halen on Surviving Addiction, Why He's Still Making Music and What He Really Thinks of David Lee Roth (and Other Past Van Halen Bandmates)*, BILLBOARD (June 19, 2015), https://lexspirit.link/WNM6.

549. VAN HALEN, VAN HALEN II (Warner Bros. 1979). Bumblebee is also a "Frankenstrat" because it is a Fender Stratocaster®-style guitar cobbled together from an array of other guitars. *'79 Bumblebee*, EVH GEAR, https://lexspirit.link/HKT2.

550. The original Bumblebee was retired when Eddie switched back to using his original Frankenstrat. The guitar was eventually buried with Pantera's guitarist, "Dimebag" Darrell Abbot, in 2004. Abbot credited Eddie as being a significant influence for him, and the permanent parting gift was a sign of friendship from Eddie. *Id.*

Whenever Van Halen arrived at a venue before a concert, one of the first things lead singer David Lee Roth did was look for a bowl of M&M's® chocolate candies backstage.[551] If the bowl of M&M's included the brown-colored variant of the candy, the dressing room would get trashed by the band. While it is not uncommon for famous musicians to harbor eccentric superstitions or make oddly specific requests for their dressing rooms, that was not (entirely) the reason for Roth's displeasure—it was contractual.

When musicians execute a contract to perform at a venue, they customarily attach their rider[552] as an appendix to the agreement. The main body of the agreement typically includes the terms of compensation and the performance dates for the band, and the rider often specifies the band's technical requirements and any special (but mandatory) requests. Van Halen's rider famously included a provision specifying that, while M&M's *must* be available backstage, no brown-colored M&M's were allowed.[553]

Yes, you read that correctly.

No.

Brown.

M&M's.

---

551. Julie Zeveloff, *There's a Brilliant Reason Why Van Halen Asked for a Bowl of M&M's with All the Brown Candies Removed Before Every Show*, Bus. Insider (Sept. 7, 2016, 8:04 AM), https://lexspirit.link/OBQA.

552. "An attachment to some document, such as a legislative bill or an insurance policy, that amends or supplements the document." *Rider*, Black's Law Dictionary 1581.

553. Van Halen, Contract Rider 40 [Food Requirements (Band)] (1982).

```
Munchies

    Potato chips with assorted dips
    Nuts
    M & M's (WARNING: ABSOLUTELY NO BROWN ONES)
    Twelve (12) Reese's peanut butter cups
    Twelve (12) assorted Dannon yogurt (on ice)
```

VAN HALEN, CONTRACT RIDER 40 [Food Requirements (Band)] (1982)
(contract provision reproduced on the Author's 1955 Olympia SM 3).

Van Halen included this unusual requirement in their rider because they wanted to know whether a venue had actually read the document. The band was fed-up with arriving at venues with nine eighteen-wheelers of equipment (most bands had three or fewer) only to discover the building's girders could not support the 850 PAR lamps (gigantic, heavy stadium lights), the floor could not support the weight of the stage, or the doors were too small to accommodate the gear which needed to be brought in.[554] So, if Roth spotted brown M&M's backstage, the crew knew they needed to check the stage setup because there might be a technical error or a major safety hazard.

While a deviation from an agreement's terms constitutes a breach of contract, a *material* breach of contract occurs when a party fails to comply with a provision so integral to the parties' agreement the nonbreaching party is *entirely* excused from performing their end of the bargain—at least until the breach is cured (if curable).[555] Considered in isolation, putting brown M&M's in Van Halen's dressing room probably did not constitute a material breach of contract. But, on the other hand, a venue's dangerous stage setup would be serious enough to permit Van Halen to cancel or delay a concert without being penalized.

---

554. DAVID LEE ROTH, CRAZY FROM THE HEAT 97–98 (Ebury Press 2000).
555. *See* RESTATEMENT (SECOND) OF CONTS. § 237.

But determining whether a deviation from the terms of a contract constitutes a material breach is often a fact-intensive inquiry, and it can be very expensive to litigate such issues.[556] To avoid that headache, the parties to an agreement will often specify what breaches are to be considered material enough to permit the other party to suspend their performance without facing repercussions. This is why—according to David Lee Roth—article 126 of the band's rider contained an acknowledgment that "There will be no brown M&M's in the backstage area, upon pain of forfeiture of the show, with full compensation."[557] Curiously, no copies of a Van Halen rider containing this exact provision have surfaced publicly—not yet anyway. The 1982 rider contains the only verifiable reference to brown M&M's. Still, Roth *would* be in a position to know what the band's rider said. Who am I to second guess him?

While a ban on brown M&M's initially sounds as mad as a March hare, Van Halen took safety seriously and creatively deployed contract law to reveal potential hazards. So, the next time you enjoy one of those round chocolate candies, remember that brown M&M's once functioned as the rock-and-roll equivalent of a canary in a coal mine.

---

556. *See id.* § 241.
557. ROTH, *supra* note 554, at 98.

§ 17

South Pacific Punch and Rumrunner High Jinks

outh Pacific Punch will be this book's only foray into the rum-soaked, cocktail umbrella-adorned, and tropical world of Tiki. Tiki is a mythical creation because it mixes Caribbean rum with Polynesian aesthetics (two cultures that never interacted historically)—but that might be a slight oversimplification of the genre. Even so, the theme was something of a self-fulfilling prophecy because today you find Tiki cocktails on any island paradise your travels take you. The trailblazer of Tiki was Donn Beach (born Ernest Raymond Beaumont Gantt), who opened his Hollywood restaurant, Don the Beachcomber®, right after Prohibition was repealed.[558] The concept was a hit, and the next 40 years became known as the "Era of Tiki."

Beach's successful concept was emulated by many establishments, but one restaurant imitated Don the Beachcomber a little too closely. In 1958, Harry J. Batt, Sr.

---

558. Ian McNulty, *Revisiting Polynesian Restaurant Bali Ha'i at Pontchartrain Beach*, BESTOFNEWORLEANS.COM: GAMBIT (May 16, 2010, 11:00 PM), https://lexspirit.link/C8CV.

opened the Pontchartrain Beach Comber in New Orleans.[559] Even if "[i]mitation is the sincerest [form] of flattery,"[560] Donn Beach was not amused by the restaurant parroting his own establishment's name and promptly sued Batt for trademark infringement. Batt wisely backed down and then not-so-wisely risked yet another lawsuit by changing his restaurant's name to Bali Ha'i at the Beach, which was a reference to a song from Rodgers and Hammerstein's *South Pacific* (1949).[561]

Miraculously, the pair of musical magnates never sued Batt, but perhaps he had a hunch they would not: In 1954, a Tiki restaurant named Bali Hai (note the absence of the apostrophe) opened in San Diego and had been operating unmolested for several years—and still is today.[562] Seeing as both restaurants were "borrowing" intellectual property from *South Pacific*, Batt probably figured the San Diego establishment's owners would not quibble with him over the name either. He appears to have been correct, and Bali

---

559. Seale Paterson, *Nostalgia: Bali Ha'i*, MYNEWORLEANS.COM (Nov. 1, 2018), https://lexspirit.link/USF7.

560. REV. CHARLES CALEB COLTON, LACON; OR MANY THINGS IN FEW WORDS: ADDRESSED TO THOSE WHO THINK 113 (London, Longman, Hurst, Rees, Orme & Brown, 4th ed. 1820).

561. *South Pacific*'s island matriarch, Bloody Mary (also of cocktail fame *supra* p. 33), sings *Bali Ha'i*:

> *Most people live on a lonely island,*
> *lost in the middle of a foggy sea.*
> *Most people long for another island,*
> *one where they know they will like to be.*

> *Bali Ha'i may call you,*
> *any night, any day.*
> *In your heart you'll hear it call you,*
> *come away, come away.*

Bali Ha'i, from SOUTH PACIFIC (Richard Rodgers & Oscar Hammerstein II 1949).

562. *History*, BALI HAI REST., https://lexspirit.link/ERMO.

Ha'i at the Beach went on to become a New Orleans staple until it closed in 1983. It outlasted both the golden age of Tiki and the Pontchartrain Beach theme park located next door.

South Pacific Punch was on Bali Ha'i at the Beach's menu and would have been served in a mug featuring the molded face of a Polynesian deity.[563] The drinkware was grandiose, but it fit right in because the restaurant had a thatched roof and was decorated with bamboo paneling, seafaring artifacts, and murals depicting picturesque scenes from Polynesia. The décor might sound tacky by today's standards, but the tropical fantasy it brought to life is fondly remembered by those who had the pleasure of visiting the establishment. But how essential was the scenery? Let me put it this way: If you enjoy a South Pacific Punch from a regular glass on the couch in your living room, it will still be a delicious cocktail. Maybe not *as* delicious as it would be if served in a Tiki mug with an excessively elaborate garnish illuminated by the flickering flames of a tiki torch—but a worthy endeavor nonetheless.

---

563. JEFF BERRY, BEACH BUM BERRY'S REMIXED: A GALLERY OF TIKI DRINKS 111 (Club Tiki Press 2014).

South Pacific Punch[564]

1. Combine the following ingredients in a cocktail shaker with ice:
    a. 2 oz. Puerto Rican gold rum
    b. 1 oz. Jamaican dark rum
    c. 1 oz. fresh-squeezed lime juice
    d. 1 oz. fresh-squeezed orange juice
    e. 1/2 oz. passion fruit syrup[565]
    f. 1/2 oz. falernum[566] (a recipe follows)
2. Cap the cocktail shaker and shake vigorously for 20–30 seconds.
3. Fill a highball glass or Tiki mug with plenty of crushed ice, insert a straw, and garnish with a sprig of spearmint, pineapple leaves, and a cocktail umbrella.
4. Double strain the contents of the shaker into the vessel, don a Hawaiian shirt, and enjoy.

Falernum #9[567]

Combine 6 oz. Wray & Nephew® Overproof White Rum, the zest of 9 limes, 2 tbsp. slivered almonds, 40 whole cloves, and (by weight) 1-1/2 oz. of peeled, sliced ginger in a jar. Seal the jar and let the mixture soak. After 24 hours, strain the contents through a cheesecloth and add 14 oz. of 2:1 ratio simple syrup, 4-1/2 oz. of fresh-squeezed lime juice, and 1/4 tsp. of almond extract. Shake well and bottle. If refrigerated, it should keep for several weeks.

---

564. This recipe was introduced to me by Ray Jones, a talented band director, tuba virtuoso, and Tiki enthusiast. BERRY, *supra* note 563, at 111.

565. Liber & Co.® makes excellent cocktail syrups, and their passion fruit syrup is no exception.

566. John D. Taylor® Velvet Falernum is also perfectly acceptable.

567. BERRY, *supra* note 563, at 197. This recipe represents the culmination of mixologist Paul Clarke's eight prior falernum experiments.

Rumrunner High Jinks

The term "rumrunning" describes the activities of certain enterprising outlaws who made a lucrative living smuggling alcohol into the United States throughout the "noble experiment" known as Prohibition.[568] Although, if you want to get technical about it, "rumrunning" refers to maritime alcohol smuggling and "bootlegging" is its landlubbing relative. Some of those smugglers—and their attorneys—were downright clever and showed an aptitude for circumnavigating federal laws passed to enforce Prohibition. What follows are a few vignettes of challenges encountered by law enforcement during this period and one extended account of a maritime debacle.

Loopholes in the Volstead Act

The Eighteenth Amendment to the Constitution went into effect on January 17, 1920, and banned the manufacture, sale, and transportation of intoxicating liquor.[569] Although *consuming* alcohol was still technically legal, the Feds figured any existing stockpiles of alcohol would dry up soon after Prohibition went into effect. When Americans managed to keep their buzz going—meaning they were being resupplied—the government turned to Prohibition's enforcement arm: the Volstead Act.[570]

Among other things, the Volstead Act provided that whenever law enforcement discovered someone "in the act of transporting" alcohol, the vehicle, liquor, and driver were subject to seizure.[571] But clever defense attorneys

---

568. Andrew Norris, *Rum Row: The Sinking of the Rum Runner I'M ALONE*, 24 TUL. J. INT'L & COMP. L. 1, 3 (2015). "Noble experiment" was President Herbert Hoover's pet name for Prohibition.

569. *See* U.S. CONST. amend. XVIII.

570. *See* Volstead Act, ch. 85, § 26, 41 Stat. 305, 315–16 (1919).

571. *Id.* § 26, 41 Stat. at 315.

were quick to point out the statute's use of the phrase "act of transporting" made prosecution under the statute dubious if a vehicle was stationary when the liquor was discovered.[572] This was not a very persuasive argument, but it did garner a few laughs from the legal community.

The Volstead Act also provided that once a vehicle was impounded, "unless good cause to the contrary [was] shown by the owner, [a court was to] order a sale by public auction of the property seized."[573] This provision spawned an interesting method of installment sale. A bootlegger would purchase a vehicle on credit and make the required down payment—only a fraction of the vehicle's total cost— and the car dealer would retain title to the vehicle until it was fully paid off. If the bootlegger was caught smuggling liquor with the vehicle (meaning the vehicle was seized), the dealer would show the judge the vehicle's title and swear they were ignorant of the bootlegger's nefarious purpose for obtaining the vehicle.[574] This, they argued, was "good cause to the contrary" under the Volstead Act, and the vehicle should be spared from the auction block and returned to them. It was not uncommon for car dealers to collect the keys right after the hearing. The dealer was happy because they could resell the vehicle and keep the bootlegger's payments. The bootlegger would spend some time in prison, but at least they did not have much invested in the vehicle they lost. It was an amicable, if collusive, relationship.

---

572. Frank Buckley, *Forfeiture of Vehicles for Unlawful Movement of Liquor Under the National Prohibition Act Under the Revised Statutes*, 4 B.U. L. REV. 183, 184–85 (1924).

573. Volstead Act § 26, 41 Stat. at 315–16. The vehicle was sold— not the alcohol.

574. Buckley, *supra* note 572, at 187–88.

America's Northern Neighbor[575]

A Canadian barrister once remarked, "It is maintained by officials of the United States that their efforts to suppress smuggling from the sea have been generally successful; if this is a fair statement of the case, the liquor still plentifully available must be either of the fruit of home enterprise, or have been imported from across the Canadian border."[576] The learned counselor was merely pointing out what was already common knowledge: Prohibition transformed the Canada–United States border into the most well-stocked bar in the hemisphere.

Canada did not exactly encourage this behavior, but it did not discourage it either—at least not at first.[577] In fact, Canadians were entering into contracts to supply smugglers with product, and the parties expected Canadian courts to enforce those agreements—even if the alcohol was clearly destined for the United States. One such contract enforcement action was *Walkerville Brewing Co. v. Mayrand*.[578] Mayrand owned a dock on the Detroit River (constituting the border with the United States) and signed an exclusivity agreement with Walkerville Brewing in which he promised to exclusively export Walkerville's beer. But Mayrand evidently had excess capacity in his warehouse because he began exporting other brewers' beer too. Walkerville sought to enjoin that behavior.[579]

---

575. Fun fact: The Canadian Supreme Court Justice's ceremonial robes are red with white fur trim. The justices would look right at home at the North Pole! *See Judges of the Court*, SUP. CT. CAN., https://lexspirit.link/P1R0; *see also* Charles M. Yablon, *Judicial Drag: An Essay on Wigs, Robes and Judicial Change*, 1995 WIS. L. REV. 1129.

576. Marjorie Owen, *The Courts and the Rum-Running Business*, 8 CAN. BAR REV. 413, 413–15 (1930).

577. Norris, *supra* note 568, at 9–10.

578. *See* Walkerville Brewing Co. v. Mayrand (1929), 63 O.L.R. 573 (Can. Ont. C.A.).

579. *Id.* at 574–75, 577.

The equities of the case favored the brewer, and the court awarded Walkerville a preliminary injunction lasting until the day the trial was scheduled to begin.[580] The trial was postponed, but when Walkerville filed a routine motion to extend the preliminary injunction, a different judge denied the motion. The judge explained that his denial was premised on public policy grounds because the underlying contract was to supply alcohol to be smuggled into the United States—which was illegal under the laws of the United States.[581] The brewery appealed the ruling.

The appellate court did not find the lower court's rationale for denying the extension to be entirely problematic. (Although, one concurring justice *did* devote several paragraphs to lambasting the lower court for judicial activism.[582]) Their concern revolved around how a Canadian judge had taken judicial notice of the illegality of importing alcohol into a foreign country. The judge had not cited any United States statutes or heard any evidence as to whether—under United States law—it was illegal to import alcohol.[583] For that reason, the preliminary injunction was reinstated. While the appellate court's professionalism and adherence to civil procedure is admirable, I am not entirely certain it was inappropriate or unreasonable for the judge to take judicial notice of the fact that the end goal of Canada's burgeoning export industry was illegal in the United States.

---

580. Owen, *supra* note 576, at 415.
581. *Walkerville Brewing*, 63 O.L.R. at 577–79.
582. *Id.* at 580–81.
583. *Id.* at 575–76, 579–80. *See supra* note 84 and accompanying discussion related to the concept of judicial notice.

Seafaring Shenanigans

While enforcing Prohibition on land was difficult, maritime enforcement proved nearly impossible. The United States Coast Guard had neither the vessels nor the personnel to blockade the flow of liquor into the country. Compounding this problem, rumrunners had a habit of sending fake distress signals at coordinates that ensured any well positioned Coast Guard vessel was drawn far away from their smuggling operations. After the authorities wised up to this trick, the rumrunners began deploying small, agile decoy vessels called Mosquito Boats. These boats would conspicuously speed away from the rumrunning vessel and make a beeline for shore, and the commotion drew the attention of the Coast Guard away from the rumrunner and their customers. If the Coast Guard was able to intercept one of the Mosquito Boats, they were disappointed to find a sober crew operating a dry vessel.[584]

While the Coast Guard could board a United States vessel just about anywhere they found one, they could only board foreign-flagged vessels within the United States' own territorial waters. The conventional wisdom at the time was a nation's territorial waters extended three nautical miles from shore (the "Three-Mile Limit").[585]

---

584. Norris, *supra* note 568, at 4.

585. From the late-17th century to the mid-20th century, the dominant (albeit informal) international policy was that a nation's territorial waters extended to a point one marine league (three nautical miles) from shore. Despite the effective range varying from being woefully shorter to significantly further during those centuries, the "utmost range of a cannon ball" (a proxy for control) was thought to comport with this distance, and Secretary of State Thomas Jefferson cited that convention when he announced the United States' adoption of the Three-Mile Limit in 1793. Letter from Thomas Jefferson, Secretary of State of the United States, to Certain Foreign Ministers in the United States (Nov. 8, 1793), *reprinted in* THE PAPERS OF THOMAS

Recognizing this jurisdictional issue, rumrunning vessels were typically Canadian- or British-flagged vessels, and they were never to be found within three nautical miles of the United States. Instead, their cargo was sold at sea "over the railing" to small, local boats on a first-come, first-served basis.[586] Almost any class of vessel could venture just beyond the Three-Mile Limit in fair weather, so something needed to change to stem the inflow of liquor from the high seas.

To their credit, Congress quickly responded to this challenge by passing the Tariff Act of 1922, which purported to extend the Coast Guard's authority to "hail and stop"[587] vessels to a distance of four leagues (12 nautical miles) from shore.[588] Only seaworthy vessels were likely to venture that far out, and customers needed more than a mere rowboat to pick up their cargo. Ironically, this expanded jurisdiction had the effect of encouraging a single buyer with a large vessel to purchase the entire shipment of alcohol, which was more efficient— if somewhat less lucrative for the rumrunners—than the prior ad hoc sales.

Great Britain and its dominion, Canada, were not amused by the United States' unilateral expansion of its territorial waters, and the government was informed that "any attempt on the part of the [Coast Guard] to seize a British [or Canadian] ship outside the three-mile limit would be regarded by His Majesty's Government as

---

JEFFERSON, VOL. 27, at 328–30 (John Catanzariti ed., 1997); CHARLES CHENEY HYDE, INTERNATIONAL LAW, CHIEFLY AS INTERPRETED AND APPLIED BY THE UNITED STATES, VOL. 1, at 251–55 (Little, Brown, & Co. 1922).

586. Norris, *supra* note 568, at 7–8.

587. This is the maritime equivalent of "stop and frisk." *See* Terry v. Ohio, 392 U.S. 1 (1968).

588. Tariff Act of 1922, ch. 356, § 518, 42 Stat. 858, 979.

creating a very serious situation."[589] To avoid an awkward situation, the United States needed to find a diplomatic solution to permit enforcement of Prohibition beyond the Three-Mile Limit. Fortunately, the British were in a mood to negotiate because they had grown weary of crossing the Atlantic in dry vessels. Whether intentionally omitted or not, enforcement mechanisms for the Eighteenth Amendment lacked a carve-out permitting internationally voyaging vessels to have alcohol on board when they docked in the United States. Captains either had to risk prosecution by hiding the alcohol or throw it all overboard before approaching within three nautical miles of shore. Understandably, that second option was completely unpalatable.[590]

The United States was willing to make an exception for internationally voyaging vessels so long as any alcohol on board was placed under seal within its territorial waters. In return, it wanted the ability to police foreign vessels further from shore. Those terms were deemed acceptable, and the United States and Great Britain formalized their bargain by signing the Convention for the Prevention of Smuggling of Intoxicating Liquors (the "1924 Treaty").[591]

The 1924 Treaty permitted the Coast Guard to board Canadian- and British-flagged vessels at no greater distance from shore "than can be traversed in one hour by the vessel suspected of endeavoring to [smuggle liquor into

---

589. Letter from H.G. Chilton, British Chargé d'Affaires, to Charles E. Hughes, U.S. Secretary of State (July 10, 1923), *reprinted in* PAPERS RELATING TO THE FOREIGN RELATIONS OF THE UNITED STATES 1923, VOL. 1, at 163, 164 (1938).

590. Norris, *supra* note 568, at 11. A sensible impression, indeed— only tea should be thrown overboard.

591. *See* Convention for the Prevention of Smuggling of Intoxicating Liquors, arts. II, III, U.S.-Gr. Brit., Jan. 23, 1924, T.S. No. 685 [hereinafter 1924 Treaty].

the United States]."[592] This was a vessel-specific distance, but any area within 12 nautical miles of shore was generally considered fair game. Rumrunners adjusted their rendezvous points accordingly, and business largely continued as usual. But the shortcomings of the 1924 Treaty would be exposed five years later in a dramatic incident that strained diplomatic relations.

The Vessel Arctic (etching)
in HARPER'S WKLY., Mar. 12, 1859, at 164.

---

592. *Id.* art. II(3).

The Final Voyage of the S.S. *I'm Alone*[593]

In March 1929, a notorious rumrunning vessel named the S.S. *I'm Alone* was operating in the Gulf of Mexico. A 125-foot wooden hulled British schooner registered in Canada, it was built for the express purpose of smuggling liquor.[594] Its captain, Jack Randell, was something of a daredevil and was known for taunting the Coast Guard whenever he was pursued.[595] Over the previous year, the crew of the *I'm Alone* amassed a small fortune running liquor into New Orleans. In fact, thanks in part to the crew's efforts, the Big Easy was aptly known as the "wettest city in America" at the time (*of course* it was), but the Coast Guard was working hard to rid the city of the moniker.[596]

The *I'm Alone* left Belize on March 12, 1929, laden with 500 cases of rye whiskey, 300 cases of Johnny Walker® Scotch, 110 demijohns of Bacardí® Rum, and 200 cases of other assorted liquor.[597] The customs papers carried on board stated the cargo was destined for Bermuda (like hell it was). Favorable conditions saw the *I'm Alone* arrive at the specified rendezvous point near New Orleans on March 20, 1929—nearly two full days ahead of schedule. To kill time, Captain Randell decided it would be prudent to perform some routine maintenance on the engines. But

---

593. Professor Andrew Norris, a former United States Coast Guard Judge Advocate, does a masterful job of telling the tale of the *I'm Alone* and the legal issues surrounding those events. *See generally* Norris, *supra* note 568.

594. *Id.* at 17–18.

595. *Id.* at 20.

596. *Id.* at 23.

597. *See generally* Jack Randell, I'm Alone (Garden City Press 1930). The author of this book is none other than the *I'm Alone*'s captain.

shortly after dropping anchor the captain noticed the *I'm Alone* was not actually alone at all.[598]

Like the *I'm Alone*, the U.S.C.G.C *Wolcott* was also purpose-built, but its purpose was to enable the Coast Guard to catch rumrunners. The *Wolcott* was a 100-foot cutter capable of sustaining 12 knots for long distances. It was outfitted with a three-inch deck gun and carried an arsenal of assorted small arms. In 1929, the *Wolcott* was under the command of Boatswain Frank Paul, and his crew spotted the *I'm Alone* while patrolling an area frequented by rumrunners. The Coast Guard approached to investigate the suspicious vessel, which they suspected to be the *I'm Alone*. The crew of the *Wolcott* was familiar with the *I'm Alone* because they recently pursued the vessel, but Captain Randell and his crew managed to give them the slip on that occasion. The Coast Guard resented that humiliating episode and was determined to not let the vessel escape if they ever found it again.[599] Even better, the *Wolcott*'s navigator estimated the foreign-flagged vessel was anchored just shy of 11 nautical miles from shore, meaning it was subject to hail and stop under the 1924 Treaty.

After spotting the Coast Guard, Captain Randell ordered the anchor hauled in, started the engines, and prepared to flee to the south. He hoped by heading in that direction he would discourage the Coast Guard from pursuing because the *I'm Alone* would soon leave their jurisdiction—if it was ever within it at all. But Randell had no such luck. Once the crew of the *Wolcott* positively identified the vessel, they were not inclined to let the *I'm Alone* escape again.

---

598. Norris, *supra* note 568, at 24.
599. *Id.* at 23.

The crew of the *I'm Alone* rebuffed an initial boarding attempt as they got underway and ignored the Coast Guard's orders to "heave to." After that, warning shots (blanks) were fired from the *Wolcott's* three-inch deck gun, but this proved wholly ineffective in convincing the crew of the *I'm Alone* to cease their flight. Captain Randell, in true swashbuckling fashion, could be heard yelling to his pursuers, "You can shoot and sink [me] but [I'll] be damned if you will board me!"[600]

The chase had been underway for several hours when, inexplicably, Captain Randell slowed his vessel and motioned for his pursuers to approach. He invited Boatswain Paul to come aboard (alone and unarmed) to have a chat—a *parley*, if you will. The Boatswain accepted the invitation, and the two gentlemen spoke in the cabin of the *I'm Alone* for about an hour and a half. During this interlude Randell told Paul he would rather have his vessel sunk than be captured, and he readily confessed to having a cargo hold full of liquor destined for New Orleans. The two men disagreed as to how far from shore the *I'm Alone* was when the chase began, with Captain Randell vehemently insisting the vessel was over an hour away from shore. Even with this disagreement, the meeting was described by both men as "cordial."[601] Evidently, the bond shared by all seafarers could not be eclipsed by the petty trifles of Prohibition. One might even wonder whether they shared a cocktail!

Socializing concluded, the Boatswain returned to the *Wolcott*, and the chase recommenced in earnest. To ratchet

---

600. Affidavit of Frank Paul, Boatswain of the *Wolcott*, *enclosed in* Letter from A.L. Gamble, Captain, to F.C. Billard, Commandant (Mar. 28, 1929) (on file with the University of Rochester Rare Books Special Collections and Preservation Department, William Roy Valiance Papers 1908–1967, box 120, folder 4).

601. Norris, *supra* note 568, at 27.

up the pressure, live ammunition was fired from the deck gun of the *Wolcott*—although the gun crew intentionally aimed too high. When the three-inch gun jammed, the Coast Guard opened fire with M1903 Springfield[602] rifles and Thompson submachine guns. Randell was hit in the leg, but upon inspecting the wound he discovered the Coast Guard was firing nonlethal bullets made of wax. Undeterred, Randell continued speeding southward as the sun set, and the Coast Guard pursued the *I'm Alone* through the night.[603]

On the morning of the second day of the chase, Randell spied an unwelcome development: The *Wolcott* had been joined by another cutter, the U.S.C.G.C. *Dexter*. The Coast Guard had finally accepted the crew of the rumrunner would not surrender, and the *Dexter*'s crew began putting large holes into the *I'm Alone*'s hull with their deck gun. Grievously damaged, the rumrunning vessel took on water and was soon consigned to Davy Jones. One of the *I'm Alone*'s crew drowned in the rough seas, but the rest of Randell's men were rescued from the Gulf waters.[604]

With that, the chase was concluded, but the conflict was far from resolved: The Coast Guard had sunk a foreign civilian vessel in international waters. While it was true the crew of the *I'm Alone* was armed and smuggling contraband into the United States, Great Britain and Canada were outraged by the Coast Guard's conduct toward a vessel flying the flag of the Commonwealth. The public, on the other hand, was enthralled by the dramatic tale of the pursuit. Less than 24 hours after the sinking, a

---

602. For an extended account of the legal controversy surrounding this weapon, see *supra* p. 104.

603. Norris, *supra* note 568, at 28–30.

604. For their part, the Coast Guard staged a valiant rescue attempt to save the sailor who ultimately drowned. *Id.* at 31–32.

bar in Paris even commemorated the event by creating the *I'm Alone* cocktail.[605]

In accordance with the 1924 Treaty, a tribunal was formed to adjudicate claims against the United States arising out of the incident. The commissioners were tasked with resolving a whole host of factual disputes surrounding the incident.[606] To begin with, was the *I'm Alone* ever subject to the Coast Guard's jurisdiction? Even if the vessel had been anchored more than 12 nautical miles from shore, the *I'm Alone* would have been subject to the United States' jurisdiction if it could have covered the distance to shore in under an hour. Then, there was the issue of the vessel's flight. The 1924 Treaty did not explicitly authorize the Coast Guard to engage in hot pursuit[607] beyond the hail and stop distance. That meant it was unclear whether the Coast Guard could chase—let alone sink—the *I'm Alone* in international waters.[608]

The case languished for several years, and Prohibition was repealed before the tribunal finally issued its decision on January 5, 1935. The commissioners found that the *I'm Alone* was beneficially owned and operated by citizens of the United States and was registered in Canada for the sole purpose of restricting the Coast Guard's jurisdiction over her.[609] While no damages were assessed for the loss of

---

605. STANDARD UNION, *supra* note 534, at 3 ("The Canadian rum schooner had been sunk off the New Orleans coast less than a day before the 'I'm Alone' cocktail appeared."). I wish I knew what was in that cocktail. Equal parts seawater and rum, perhaps?

606. 1924 Treaty, *supra* note 591, art. IV.

607. "The legitimate chase of a foreign vessel on the high seas just after that vessel has violated the law of the pursuing country while within that country's jurisdiction." *Hot Pursuit*, BLACK'S LAW DICTIONARY 887.

608. Norris, *supra* note 568, at 41–43.

609. S.S. "I'm Alone" (Can. v. U.S.), Joint Final Report of the Commissioners, 3 R.I.A.A. 1609, 1617–18 (1935).

the vessel or the cargo, the tribunal awarded the crew of the *I'm Alone* the sum of $25,000 based on its finding that the degree of force employed by the Coast Guard was wholly unjustified.[610] Probably because Repeal effectively extinguished the purpose of the 1924 Treaty, the tribunal's final report omitted findings on the legal issues surrounding hot pursuit under the 1924 Treaty, the *I'm Alone*'s closest approach to shore, and the vessel's top speed. Adding further insult to injury, the tribunal strongly suggested "the United States . . . formally acknowledge [the sinking's] illegality, and . . . apologize to His Majesty's Canadian Government therefor . . . ."[611] To summarize, the United States had to compensate the crew of a rumrunner for the privilege of sinking their vessel and was told to publicly apologize for the actions of their overzealous Coast Guard.

The wreck of the *I'm Alone* lies somewhere at the bottom of the Gulf of Mexico surrounded by broken liquor bottles. It is a fitting monument to the tenacity of Prohibition's rumrunners.

---

610. *Id.* at 1618. The tribunal also found that "none of [the crew] was a party to the illegal conspiracy to smuggle liquor into the United States and sell the same there." This is a surprising conclusion because Captain Randell was pretty cavalier about his illicit intentions. Perhaps this finding is justified by the conclusion that only the crew of the vessel transporting the liquor *into* the United States was committing a crime.

611. *Id.*

§ 18

The Southside(s) and Organized Crime

The Southside's name is either a reference to the south side of Manhattan, the Southside Sportsmen's Club on Long Island, or the South Side of Chicago. Two of those origin stories are more credible than the third, but the third one is somewhat entertaining. I will briefly examine all three.

Many people claim the Southside was invented in New York City's 21 Club®, which was opened in 1922 by Austrian immigrants Jack Kriendler and Charles E. Berns.[612] During Prohibition, locals referred to the 21 Club as "Jack and Charlie's" because both the speakeasy's name and location changed frequently. By all accounts, it was a colorful place incorporating many of the classic elements of a stereotypical speakeasy. The peephole was manned by "Jimmy at the front door" and a series of electric and mechanical devices operated secret doors to hide the liquor in case the police paid a visit.[613] Nobody disputes the Southside was the house drink at the 21 Club, but the

---

612. DEGROFF, *supra* note 31, at 140. Sadly, the 21 Club was yet another restaurant casualty of the COVID-19 pandemic.
613. *Id.*

speakeasy probably did not invent the cocktail.[614] A 1916 book by Hugo Ensslin, *Recipes for Mixed Drinks*, contained a recipe for the Southside and predated the bar's existence by six years.[615] Even so, the recipe in Ensslin's book is for a "Southside Fizz," and the 21 Club may have originally served the cocktail without club soda.

A more likely scenario is the Southside came from the Southside Sportsmen's Club of Long Island.[616] In the early 19th century, Long Island was not the bustling metropolis it is today. Largely uninhabited, it was a popular area for hunting and fishing.[617] To that end, Snedecor's Tavern, which was located on the island and renowned for its Mint Juleps,[618] was converted into a clubhouse for the Southside Sportsmen's Club in 1866.[619] As legend has it, the club concocted a gin variant of a Mint Julep, which eventually evolved into the Southside cocktail. This story seems plausible, and the timeline fits better with Ensslin's 1916 book including a recipe for the Southside.

---

614. OXFORD COMPANION, *supra* note 6, at 662–63.

615. *See* ENSSLIN, *supra* note 428, at 42.

616. Eric Felten, *A Privilege of the Privileged*, WALL ST. J. (Aug. 18, 2007, 12:01 AM), https://lexspirit.link/VX8C.

617. *See* Pierson v. Post, 3 Cai. 175 (N.Y. Sup. Ct. 1805) (recognizing a fox is *feræ naturæ* and property interests in such animals are only acquired through corporal possession). *Pierson v. Post* was the first case in the United States to deal with a situation analogous to someone bid sniping an eBay auction. It involved a contested fox hunt on present-day Long Island, and the case established the "Rule of Capture" that continues to govern ownership of natural resources throughout much of the United States today. Further reading on this important case can be found in the following journal article: Ridgely Schlockverse III, *Mad Dogs and Englishmen: Pierson v. Post [A Ditty Dedicated to Freshman Law Students, Confused on the Merits]*, 17 NOVA L. REV. 857 (1993). By the way, that author's name is a pseudonym.

618. *See* Mint Julep *infra* p. 231.

619. OXFORD COMPANION, *supra* note 6, at 662–63.

The final story for this cocktail credits its name (but not necessarily its origin) to the South Side of Chicago.[620] Prohibition-era Chicago was carved up by organized crime syndicates for the purpose of peddling illegal beer and liquor at fantastic profits. The violence perpetrated by those gangs became the stuff of legend, and one of the gangs from the South Side eventually gained control of the entire city. The Chicago Outfit, as it became known, was led by none other than Alphonse Gabriel Capone.[621] The story goes that the gin served in Chicago's South Side was terrible, and bartenders used the Southside cocktail's citrus and mint elements to mask its shortcomings. Some authorities also insist Capone's favorite cocktail was the Southside, which seems pretty fanciful to me—but it does make for an interesting story.

Similar to the Aviation,[622] the Southside faded into relative obscurity after Prohibition's repeal. Fortunately, the ingredients are not difficult to obtain, and this cocktail is a "Bartender's Handshake" you can comfortably order at most gin joints today. A word of warning though: You most likely will get a slightly different variant of this cocktail every time you order one because nobody can seem to agree on the "correct" formula. There are more variations of the Southside in existence than there are origin stories for the tipple—which is really saying something.

---

620. Felten, *supra* note 616.
621. By the way, it is appropriate to call Al Capone an "O.G." because he *was* an original gangster!
622. *See* Aviation *supra* p. 129.

Southside[623]

1. Combine the following ingredients in a cocktail shaker with ice:
   a. 2 oz. gin
   b. 3/4 oz. fresh-squeezed lime juice (or maybe it should be lemon juice—who knows)
   c. 3/4 oz. simple syrup
2. Cap the cocktail shaker and shake vigorously for 20–30 seconds.
3. Add 5–8 large mint leaves and gently roll[624] the mixture between the lid and base of the shaker.
4. Put a single mint leaf or a lime peel spiral into a coupe glass for garnish.
5. Double strain the contents of the shaker into the coupe glass and serve "up."
6. Prepare to be told, "That's not how you make a Southside!"[625]

---

623. DEGROFF, *supra* note 31, at 140.
624. This gently infuses some of the flavor from the mint leaves into the mixture without overdoing it.
625. This is not something to bring up at the dinner table. Nobody can agree whether this cocktail is served "up," "on the rocks," or as a "fizz." The use of lemon juice versus lime juice is also disputed. Mint, gin, and simple syrup are the only uncontested matters in this case. Debating the other details can quickly lead to fisticuffs.

Several Other Causes of Action

1. For a Gimlet, follow the directions on the prior page but omit the mint.

2. If you follow the recipe on the prior page but swap out the gin for white rum, you will have concocted another classic: a Daiquiri (with mint).

3. Some people also turn the recipe on the prior page into a "Southside Fizz" by serving it in a highball glass with ice and adding 1-1/2 oz. of club soda.[626]

4. Make a Southside Fizz but omit the mint and use lemon juice (instead of lime), and you have a Tom Collins.

5. If you make a Southside Fizz but use white rum in place of gin, that's a Mojito.

6. For a Southside Royale, make a Southside Fizz using Champagne in place of club soda.

---

626. *See* ENSSLIN, *supra* note 428, at 42. Ensslin's recipe uses *both* lemon and lime juice.

Organized Crime[627]

Prohibition was enacted to address the perceived societal evils associated with the consumption of alcohol, but its practical effect was to lay the foundation for a much greater problem: the golden age of organized crime.[628] Organized crime took hold in most major cities during Prohibition, but no city experienced more gang violence than Chicago. As soon as the Eighteenth Amendment went into effect, gangs swiftly carved up the Windy City and an uneasy cartel was formed to corner the market for illegal liquor.[629] With rogue gangs operating outside of the cartel and so much money up for grabs, this status quo did not last very long and the city was soon engulfed in gang wars. The victorious faction in the contest was the aforementioned Chicago Outfit.

A 1931 report written by a Bureau of Internal Revenue[630] agent provides a colorful (but accurate) summary of Capone's ascendancy to the throne of the Chicago Outfit:

---

627. Special thanks to Leo Unzeitig for his assistance with this material.

628. *See* U.S. CONST. amend. XVIII; *see also* JOHN J. BINDER, AL CAPONE'S BEER WARS: A COMPLETE HISTORY OF ORGANIZED CRIME IN CHICAGO DURING PROHIBITION (Prometheus 2017).

629. Cartel-like activities are illegal per se under the Sherman Antitrust Act. But, seeing as bootlegging was also illegal, it is unlikely a bootlegging cartel was concerned their trade practices were considered anticompetitive. *See generally* An Act to Protect Trade and Commerce Against Unlawful Restraints and Monopolies (Sherman Antitrust Act), ch. 647, 26 Stat. 209 (1890).

630. The Bureau of Internal Revenue was the original name of the Internal Revenue Service. The agency was renamed in 1953 after being reorganized. DEPT. TREAS., IRS HISTORICAL FACT BOOK: A CHRONOLOGY, 1646–1992, at 9 (1992).

> Al Capone, a punk hoodlum, came to
> Chicago from New York about 1920, as a
> protégé of John Torrio, who, at the time was
> a lieutenant of Jim Colisimo. The first heard
> [*sic*] of Capone was as a bouncer in a
> notoriously tough joint called the "Four
> Deuces." In the course of time, Colisimo,
> following the path of all good gangsters, was
> "bumped off," and Torrio took control. True
> to tradition, the guns again began to blaze,
> but this time the person behind the gun
> evidently had poor eyesight and Torrio,
> instead of going to the cemetery, took a
> vacation in the hospital. On getting out
> Torrio evidently thought discretion the
> better part of valor, and migrated to New
> York. This left the field clear for Al Capone,
> who promptly muscled in, and due to free
> advertising in the newspapers became the
> "Big Shot" . . . .[631]

Capone was in the business of gambling, operating houses of ill repute, and manufacturing and selling alcohol, and—to put it lightly—business was booming. Bribes flowed freely from his wallet, and whatever money could not buy, his reputation for violence usually could. For example, Capone was once arrested on a vagrancy charge, but the charge was dismissed for a lack of evidence because "no policeman could be found in Chicago who knew of

---

631. Letter from Internal Revenue Agents W.C. Hodgins, Jacque L. Westrich, and H.N. Clagett to the Internal Revenue Agent in Charge 1–2 (July 8, 1931), https://lexspirit.link/VPPU [hereinafter Letter of July 8, 1931]; BINDER, *supra* note 628, at 152.

Al Capone!"[632] To say that people were afraid of him is an understatement.

His reputation was well deserved, and it was further enhanced on February 14, 1929, when a group of five men (two of whom were dressed as police officers) appeared outside the SMC Cartage Company on North Clark Street.[633] The building served as the headquarters for Capone's last major competitor, the North Side Gang, led by George "Bugs" Moran. What transpired next could euphemistically be termed an "anticompetitive business practice." In what became known as the Saint Valentine's Day Massacre, seven people (including some of the North Side Gang's senior leadership) were brutally executed in front of a brick wall with Thompson submachine guns[634] and shotguns.[635] Nobody has ever definitively proven who was responsible for the hit, but Capone certainly benefited the most from the North Side Gang being neutralized.

The federal government had seen enough. Although they were already unsuccessfully trying to enforce Prohibition in Chicago, President Hoover made it clear he wanted Capone's operation shut down. Thanks in part to a blockbuster movie starring Kevin Costner and Sean Connery, Bureau of Prohibition Special Agent Eliot Ness and his team of "Untouchables" receive a lot the credit for

---

632. Letter of July 8, 1931, *supra* note 631, at 2; DENNIS E. HOFFMAN, SCARFACE AL AND THE CRIME CRUSADERS: CHICAGO'S PRIVATE WAR AGAINST CAPONE 135–36 (S. Ill. Univ. Press 1993).

633. *Id.* at 71–72.

634. Aside from "Tommy Gun," another nickname for this firearm is "Chicago Typewriter."

635. BINDER, *supra* note 628, at 186–87. A lookout erroneously reported Moran was inside the garage, which prompted the raid to kick off a bit early. Fortunately for him, Moran was walking toward the garage when he saw his would-be assassins' cars pull up. He wisely decided to turn around and walk in the other direction. It saved his life.

taking down Al Capone.[636] In reality, it was the work of Bureau of Internal Revenue Special Agent Frank J. Wilson that ultimately put Al Capone behind bars, and that is the story I will relate here.

When the Sixteenth Amendment to the Constitution was ratified by the states in 1913, it laid the foundation for Congress to levy a direct income tax not apportioned between the states, and the current system of federal income taxation developed soon thereafter.[637] The next major development in the field of taxation came in 1927, when the Supreme Court held that *all* income—whether derived legally or illegally—was subject to taxation. The opinion also dispelled the myth that the Fifth Amendment's guarantee against self-incrimination meant taxpayers could refrain from reporting illegal income.[638] Following that landmark ruling, the Bureau of Internal Revenue promptly opened investigations into the leaders of the Chicago Outfit. While the government was certainly amenable to collecting revenue from Al Capone's operations, the real objective of the investigation was to

---

636. THE UNTOUCHABLES (Paramount Pictures 1987). That is not to say Ness's efforts should be overlooked because his raids cost Capone a significant amount of money and were very disruptive. *Raids Cost Capone $500,000 in Six Months*, N.Y. TIMES, Sept. 28, 1931, at 40, https://lexspirit.link/EJO2.

637. U.S. CONST. amend. XVI ("The Congress shall have the power to lay and collect taxes on incomes, from whatever source derived, without apportionment among the several states, and without regard to any census or enumeration."). Congress had always possessed the power to collect taxes under the Taxing Clause of the Constitution, with the caveat that it needed to be a direct tax apportioned among the *states* (by population). U.S. CONST. art. I, § 8, cl. 1; § 9, cl. 4. After an 1895 Supreme Court decision held that a tax on the income of an individual represented an unconstitutional unapportioned direct tax, the Sixteenth Amendment was the method by which Congress's taxing power was expanded to encompass a direct tax on an individual's income. *See* Pollock v. Farmers' Loan & Tr. Co., 157 U.S. 429 (1895).

638. United States v. Sullivan, 274 U.S. 259, 262–64 (1927).

shut down the Chicago Outfit's activities. The Feds were frustrated connecting murder and bootlegging directly to Capone had not yet borne any fruit, and they hoped a tax investigation would yield better results.

Special Agent Wilson was probably the best forensic accountant and investigator the government had at its disposal, and all accounts indicate he was both dedicated and brilliant. Even so, when Wilson took over the tax investigation in May 1930, he found himself at an impasse. Capone's spending habits were decidedly lavish, meaning he probably had extensive income.[639] And yet, on paper, the gangster owned very little property, maintained no bank accounts, was not employed, and (except by reputation) did not appear to run any of the Chicago Outfit's businesses.[640] He exclusively used currency (i.e., dollar bills and coins) for his financial affairs, which was more difficult to establish as coming from taxable income—as opposed to already-taxed savings. To prosecute Capone for failing to pay income taxes, Wilson needed to establish a direct link between Capone and the unreported income derived from his bootlegging, gambling, and prostitution[641] activities.[642]

Late one evening, Wilson was scouring records to see if he might have overlooked a clue in the course of his

---

639. Memorandum from Special Agent Frank J. Wilson to Chief of Intelligence Unit, Bureau of Internal Revenue 35–48 (Dec. 21, 1933), https://lexspirit.link/MIFO [hereinafter Wilson Memo].

640. *Id.* at 4.

641. I want to ensure one point is unambiguously clear: Al Capone was not *personally* soliciting clients in this line of trade. He merely received cash derived from the efforts of others.

642. *See* Commissioner v. Glenshaw Glass Co., 348 U.S. 426, 431 (1955) (holding that taxable income is recognized when a taxpayer has "undeniable accessions to wealth, clearly realized, and over which the taxpayer [has] complete dominion."). While this case was decided years after Capone's death, it provides a succinct taxonomy for understanding when a taxpayer must recognize taxable income.

investigation to that point. He was just about to head home when he stumbled upon a brown package tied with string in the back of an old filing cabinet. Inside were three ledgers, one of which contained the accounting records of the Hawthorne Smoke Shop.[643] The business was a known front for a gambling parlor operated by the Chicago Outfit in Cicero. Often at the urging of the West Suburban Citizen's Association of Cook County, a civic group hell-bent on driving Capone out of the area, the police found one reason or another to raid the Hawthorne Smoke Shop every few months. But for all intents and purposes the place remained in continuous operation. The accounting records Wilson was examining were seized from the gambling parlor's safe in an April 26, 1926 raid, but they were apparently never scrutinized in any depth.[644] Wilson changed that.

The ledger pertained to the period from May 1, 1924, to April 26, 1926, and indicated the Hawthorne Smoke Shop generated a net profit of $587,721.95 during that time.[645] It also revealed Capone owned a 41% interest in the gambling parlor in 1924 and a 52% interest in 1925 and 1926.[646] The individual entries were no less significant: A December 2, 1924 entry read, "Frank paid $17,500.00 for Al."[647] "Al" almost certainly was a reference to Capone, but Wilson needed the bookkeeper to testify to that fact and authenticate the records in court. Handwriting analysis indicated the accountant Wilson needed to track

---

643. FRANK J. WILSON & BETH DAY, SPECIAL AGENT: TWENTY-FIVE YEARS WITH THE U.S. TREASURY DEPARTMENT AND SECRET SERVICE 36–37 (Frederick Muller, Ltd. 1966).

644. Wilson Memo, *supra* note 639, at 5.

645. *Id.* at 5.

646. *Id.* at 30, 33.

647. HOFFMAN, *supra* note 632, at 158–59.

down was Louis Shumway.[648] Once agents located Shumway, he reluctantly agreed to testify against Capone and was promptly whisked away into protective custody.[649]

Conveniently for Wilson, Capone himself provided additional evidence of his ownership of the same gambling establishment during a separate raid on May 16, 1925. Within minutes of the raid occurring, an agitated Capone dressed in pajamas and a coat appeared and demanded entry into the building because he was the owner. Once admitted, he walked over to the cash register, opened it, pocketed the contents, and instructed the staff to secure the remaining cash.[650] Evidence of Capone's ownership of the gambling parlor, along with the captured ledger and cooperative bookkeeper, provided Wilson with the foothold he needed to start building a case against Capone.

Even with the captured ledger, the government had few concrete financial records with which to prosecute Capone. To supplement their direct proof of Capone's unreported taxable income, federal prosecutors turned to an untested theory of tax prosecution they would first use to bring down Al's brother, Ralph, in early 1931: the cash expenditure theory.[651] The expenditure theory was an outgrowth of the net worth theory of prosecution, and both theories utilize circumstantial (indirect) evidence to corroborate—or overcome a complete lack of—direct proof of unreported income.[652] Unlike the net worth theory (which is useful when taxpayers convert unreported income into durable assets titled in their name, such as real estate), the expenditure method aims to establish the amount of income earned in a particular year by totaling

---

648. *Id.* at 159.
649. WILSON & DAY, *supra* note 643, at 37–39.
650. Wilson Memo, *supra* note 639, at 7, 10, 13.
651. Holland v. United States, 348 U.S. 121, 126 (1954).
652. Taglianetti v. United States, 398 F.2d 558, 562 (1st Cir. 1968).

the amount of nondeductible goods and services a taxpayer purchases during the year "which are not attributable to the resources at hand at the beginning of the year or to nontaxable receipts during the year."[653] Capone had few assets titled in his name and reported no taxable income during the tax years 1924–1929, but he was estimated to have spent—and therefore made—$1,055,375.07 during that period based on lavish outlays on furniture, clothing, dining, hotels, and money orders.[654]

Even so, this was a difficult theory under which to prosecute Capone, in part because it *assumes* cash expenditures are generally derived from taxable sources.[655] As a result, the expenditure method of prosecution has been criticized as coming dangerously close to putting the onus *on the taxpayer* to show their cash expenditures were derived from nontaxable sources, which toes or crosses the line marking the domain of the Sixth Amendment's guarantee of being "presumed innocent until proven guilty."[656] Not that the government had the benefit of knowing this in 1931, but the Supreme Court has since commented that federal prosecutors may utilize this theory of prosecution in extreme cases of tax evasion, provided the trial court exercises "great care and restraint" in safeguarding the defendant's Due Process rights.[657]

Armed with several avenues upon which to build a case against Capone, Wilson's investigation eventually culminated in two federal grand jury indictments delivered on March 13, 1931, and June 5, 1931, respectively. Those indictments related to Capone's failure to file tax returns and pay income taxes for the years 1924

---

653. *Id.*
654. Wilson Memo, *supra* note 639, at 2.
655. *Holland*, 348 U.S. at 126.
656. *Id.* at 127–29; U.S. CONST. amend. VI.
657. *Holland*, 348 U.S. at 129.

through 1929, inclusive.[658] Facing up to 32 years in prison if convicted, Capone agreed to plead guilty to the tax charges and 5,000 violations of Prohibition in exchange for a two and a half year prison sentence.[659] Prosecutors were happy to negotiate a plea deal because they had serious concerns as to whether their witnesses would show up to testify at trial—if they even lived that long. Assuming they ever took the stand, the prosecutors also were not certain witnesses would testify truthfully for fear of retribution at the hands of the Chicago Outfit.

Federal Judge James H. Wilkerson was unhappy with the (nonbinding[660]) plea deal recommended by the prosecution—and he was particularly annoyed when the newspapers printed stories implying the court would be bound by the plea deal. Hinting he would sentence Capone for a longer prison term than the plea agreement provided for, he remarked, "It is time for somebody to impress upon this defendant that it is utterly impossible to bargain with a federal court."[661] Needless to say, Capone's attorneys immediately moved to withdraw their client's guilty pleas and proceed to trial instead. The motion was granted by the court on July 31, 1931, and prosecutors decided they would only proceed to trial on the tax charges for the time being. Incidentally, Capone would never be tried on Prohibition-related offenses or for any of the other crimes he was alleged to have committed.

---

658. Wilson Memo, *supra* note 639, at 2. There was also a third indictment resulting from Ness's investigation of potential violations of Prohibition laws, but Capone was never tried on those charges.

659. *'Al' Capone Pleads Guilty to Charges; May Get Three Years*, N.Y. TIMES, June 17, 1931, at 1, 18, https://lexspirit.link/M1KL; HOFFMAN, *supra* note 632, at 160.

660. FED. R. CRIM. P. 11(c).

661. *Capone Begs a Trial as Court Bars Deal*, N.Y. TIMES, July 31, 1931, at 12, https://lexspirit.link/FQ2J.

Seeing as bribery had worked so well for Capone in the past, it was not terribly surprising he somehow obtained a listing of the jury pool before *voir dire*[662] began. When Judge Wilkerson was informed that Capone was engaging in jury tampering, he cleverly did absolutely nothing about it so the Chicago Outfit would believe their efforts had gone unnoticed. Wilkerson then foiled the scheme in one fell swoop just as everyone was seated and ready to begin voir dire. The bailiff was abruptly ordered to march the prospective jurors down the hall and to commandeer the pool from another judge's courtroom.[663] Determined to safeguard the sanctity of the trial, the judge also had the empaneled jurors sequestered and endeavored to keep the trial as short as possible.

Capone's trial on the tax charges commenced on October 5, 1931. In his defense, he claimed the entirety of his income was gambled away during each of the respective years it was earned.[664] Anyone marginally familiar with the Tax Code should cringe at this defense because gambling losses are only deductible to the extent of gambling *winnings*.[665] However, a closer look at the Tax Code's statutory history reveals the current restriction on the deductibility of gambling losses was enacted in 1934—after the tax periods covered by the indictments![666]

---

662. The preliminary examination of a prospective juror by a judge or lawyer during the jury selection phase of a trial. *Voir Dire*, BLACK'S LAW DICTIONARY 1886.

663. Wilson Memo, *supra* note 639, at 55–56; WILSON & DAY, *supra* note 643, at 50–52.

664. HOFFMAN, *supra* note 632, at 163.

665. 26 U.S.C. § 165(d) (2018).

666. Revenue Act of 1934, ch. 277, § 22(g), 48 Stat. 680, 689 (codified as amended at 26 U.S.C. § 165(d)) ("In computing net income there shall be allowed as deductions . . . losses from wagering transactions . . . to the extent of the gains from such transactions . . . ."); Stephen A. Zorn, *The Federal Income Tax Treatment of Gambling: Fairness or Obsolete Moralism?*, 49 TAX LAW. 1, 20–21 (1995).

In the 1920s, gambling losses were deductible without regard to the amount of a taxpayer's gambling winnings for the year—provided certain conditions were met.[667] As an initial matter, only losses sustained from *legal* gambling activities were deductible, meaning illegal gambling losses were never deductible.[668] Even if all Capone's gambling activities were legal, any losses were deductible only if those gambling activities were *primarily* undertaken "for profit." If determining someone's primary, subjective motivation for gambling sounds like a difficult task, you understand why the rule was changed to its present iteration. Unfortunately for Capone, relevant interpretations of the "primarily undertaken for profit" requirement generally concluded that wealthy individuals were not likely to gamble with a profit motive. Rather, because they were already rich, it was presumed they gambled primarily for the thrill associated with it.[669] Capone also appeared to have significantly more income than what he claimed to have lost gambling. So, while not as incomprehensible as it may initially seem, Capone's defense was clearly not a silver bullet.

Thanks to the testimony of several extremely nervous witnesses, the captured ledger from the Hawthorne Smoke Shop, and the expenditures evidence compiled in the course of Wilson's investigation, the verdict reached by the

---

667. Revenue Act of 1926, ch. 27, § 214(a)(5), 44 Stat. 9, 26–27 ("In computing net income there shall be allowed as deductions . . . losses sustained during the taxable year . . . if incurred in any transaction entered into for profit . . . ."); Zorn, *supra* note 666, at 20–21.

668. *In re* Frey, 1 B.T.A. 338, 341 (1925); Zorn, *supra* note 666, at 20–21.

669. Beaumont v. Commissioner, 25 B.T.A. 474, 482 (1932), *aff'd*, 73 F.2d 110 (D.C. Cir. 1934), *cert. denied*, 294 U.S. 715 (1935); Zorn, *supra* note 666, at 20–21.

jury on October 17, 1931, contained several convictions.[670] For all of the murder, bootlegging, prostitution, illegal gambling, and bribery Capone was (allegedly) responsible for, he was only ever convicted of three felony counts of tax evasion relating to tax years 1925, 1926, and 1927[671] and two misdemeanors for failing to file tax returns for the years 1928 and 1929.[672] On October 24, 1931, Judge Wilkerson sentenced Capone to 11 years in prison.[673] Capone was also fined $50,000 ($10,000 per conviction), assessed the costs of his prosecution, and received a tax bill

---

670. *Capone Convicted of Dodging Taxes; May Get 17 Years*, N.Y. TIMES, Oct. 18, 1931, at 1, 19, https://lexspirit.link/JRYA. Capone's defense attorneys made costly errors that greatly prejudiced their client. For example, the so-called "Mattingly Letter" (written by his attorneys and presented to the Bureau of Internal Revenue for settlement discussions) contained damning admissions and was ruled as admissible at the trial. Wilson Memo, *supra* note 639, at 25.

671. *See* Revenue Act of 1926 § 1114(b), 44 Stat. at 116. Prosecutors were shocked Capone's trial attorneys never attempted to quash portions of the indictment (in particular, the charges relating to the years 1924 and 1925) by arguing the statute of limitations had run. *See* Wilson Memo, *supra* note 639, at 57. The statute of limitations issue was (unsuccessfully) raised by Capone's attorneys for the first time on appeal. *Capone May Move for Cut in Sentence*, N.Y. TIMES, May 1, 1932, at 7, https://lexspirit.link/CT4H. The statute of limitations is not an element of a crime, neither is it jurisdictional. Rather, it is an affirmative defense and is waived if not raised at trial by a defendant. A district court's failure to enforce an unraised statute of limitations defense also does not constitute "plain error" under Federal Rule of Criminal Procedure 52(b). Musacchio v. United States, 577 U.S. 237, 245–48 (2016); FED. RS. CRIM. P. 51, 52(b). The Supreme Court has consistently recognized this "raise it or waive it" concept since 1872 and summarily denied certiorari to Capone's appeal on May 2, 1932. United States v. Cook, 84 U.S. (17 Wall.) 168 (1872); Capone v. United States, 56 F.2d 927 (7th Cir. 1932), *cert. denied*, 286 U.S. 553 (1932).

672. Revenue Act of 1928, ch. 852, § 146(a), 45 Stat. 791, 835; Verdict, United States v. Capone, Nos. 22852, 23232 (N.D. Ill. Oct. 17, 1931).

673. *Capone Sentenced to an 11-Year Term; Jailed till Appeal*, N.Y. TIMES, Oct. 25, 1931, at 1, 22, https://lexspirit.link/5S35. Federal juries are never involved in the sentencing phase of a criminal case. FED. R. CRIM. P. 32(i), (k).

from Uncle Sam for $215,000, plus interest.[674] At the time it was the stiffest punishment ever handed down for tax-related offenses.

Incidentally, Capone only remained incarcerated until November 1939. His early release was the combined result of good behavior and compassion for his serious medical ailments.[675] The gangster suffered from undiagnosed, untreated syphilis since the early 1920s, and the condition ravaged his brain during his incarceration at Alcatraz. Once free, he continued to deteriorate until his death in early 1947.

Hablot K. "Phiz" Browne, *Sir, I'm Not the Lunatic: That Is the Lunatic* (etching) *in* JAMES GRANT, SKETCHES IN LONDON pl. 16 (London, Wm. Tegg 1838).

---

674. *Liens Filed at Miami*, N.Y. TIMES, Oct. 25, 1931, at 22, https://lexspirit.link/3KYH.

675. *Al Capone is Freed from Prison*, N.Y. TIMES, Nov. 17, 1939, at 1, 3, https://lexspirit.link/ERXW.

§ 19

Irish Coffee
and Coffey

I rish Coffee was made famous by the Buena Vista Café®
in San Francisco, where it has been on the menu since
November 1952.[676] However, despite its strong
association with San Francisco, Irish Coffee was not
invented in the United States. The cocktail was "imported"
by the travel and food writer Stanton H. Delaplane, who
told the Buena Vista's owner, Jack Koeppler, about a
beverage he was served at the Shannon Airport in
Ireland.[677] The two men tried to reverse engineer the
cocktail but were unable to prevent the cream from sinking
into the piping hot liquid—as opposed to remaining on top
of it.[678] Koeppler's frustration with the sinking cream and
curiosity regarding other culinary aspects of the recipe
inspired him to make a pilgrimage to the Emerald Isle.

When Koeppler arrived at the Shannon Airport, he met
the man credited with inventing Irish Coffee: Chef Joe

---

676. SIMONSON, *supra* note 211, at 22, 51.
677. *Meet Chef Joe Sheridan, Inventor of Irish Coffee*,
FOYNES FLYING BOAT & MAR. MUSEUM, https://lexspirit.link/EM2O.
678. Koeppler and Delaplane also spent several evenings agonizing
over which Irish Whiskey produced the desired flavor.
The Irish Coffee Story, BUENA VISTA CAFÉ, https://lexspirit.link/RPEJ.

Sheridan. Sheridan was not the first person to pour Irish Whiskey into a cup of coffee (not by a long shot), but he *was* responsible for the formulation of the beverage that became famous. Sheridan came up with Irish Coffee on a stormy night in winter 1943 for some weary travelers whose flight to New York was forced to return to the Foynes Flying-Boat Station (like an airport, but for seaplanes). When one of the travelers asked Sheridan if he made the beverage using Brazilian coffee, he jokingly responded, "No, it was Irish Coffee."[679] The beverage was a hit, and after Foynes closed down in 1946 "Gaelic Coffee" (the original name) became the Shannon Airport's traditional welcome drink.

Koeppler explained how the cream sank into the cocktail whenever he attempted to make an Irish Coffee and asked Sheridan if he would share his method of creating the concoction. As it turned out, the cream had to be lightly whipped to a frothy consistency (not overwhipped) before being poured very gently over a warm, overturned spoon to remain afloat. Impressed, Koeppler offered Sheridan a job, and the Irishman emigrated to San Francisco in 1952.

Sheridan passed away in 1962, but his cocktail remains alive and well today. The Buena Vista serves around 2,000 Irish Coffees per day and is the largest consumer of Irish Whiskey in the United States. For several decades it used an Irish Whiskey produced by the Cooley® Distillery, but it has used Tullamore® D.E.W. since 2006—so that is the authentic choice.[680]

---

679. *The Origin of Irish Coffee*, FOYNES FLYING BOAT & MAR. MUSEUM, https://lexspirit.link/VO63.

680. Carl Nolte, *Coffee, Cream, Sugar and Irish Whiskey . . . But Buena Vista Changed Brands*, SFGATE (Nov. 22, 2006), https://lexspirit.link/A4R9.

Hablot K. "Phiz" Browne, *Mr. Cudmore Filling the Teapot*
(etching) *in* CHARLES J. LEVER, THE CONFESSIONS OF HARRY
LORREQUER pl. 9 (Dublin, Wm. Curry, Jun. & Co. 1839).

Irish Coffee[681]

1. Warm up a small glass[682] using hot water.
2. Once the glass is warm, discard the water and replace with the following:
    a. 3 oz. freshly brewed coffee
    b. 1-1/2 oz. Irish Whiskey
    c. 2 tsp. 2:1 brown sugar syrup (recipe follows)
3. Gently stir the contents of the glass.
4. Top with lightly whipped cream[683] by gently pouring the cream over the back of a warm spoon.
5. *Sláinte!*

2:1 Brown Sugar Syrup

This is sometimes called a "rich" simple syrup because it has double the sugar normally found in simple syrup. Combine brown sugar and water at a 2:1 ratio in a saucepan over low heat and stir until the sugar is fully dissolved. Optionally, you can add a few cinnamon sticks to the saucepan to infuse the syrup with some additional flavor. Bottle the mixture, but be certain to label it so you do not accidentally reach for the wrong bottle and positively annihilate a different cocktail with sweetness. If refrigerated, it should keep for several weeks.

---

681. MORGENTHALER ET AL., *supra* note 162, at 150.

682. For an authentic experience, use a 7 oz. Libbey® Georgian Irish Coffee Glass (model #8054). *Id.* You can also use a wine glass, but you run a higher risk of it shattering if the vessel is not sufficiently prewarmed before hot coffee is poured into it.

683. Mixologist Jeffrey Morgenthaler suggests a great no-fuss technique for making whipped cream with the perfect consistency for this cocktail: "Take a canning jar, fill it halfway with heavy cream, seal, and shake hard for fifteen seconds." *Id.* at 148. By the way, do not fret if the whipped cream sinks into your Irish Coffee because it is a great excuse to have another!

Coffey: The Decline of Irish Whiskey in Four Acts[684]

Irish Whiskey once constituted around 60% of the world whiskey market, but by 1980 it accounted for a mere 1% of it.[685] Another source estimates that in the early 1900s nearly 12,000,000 cases of Irish Whiskey cleared the market annually, but by the 1970s that figure was down to just 500,000 cases—1/24th of its former glory![686] Over the same period, Ireland (including Northern Ireland) went from having some 30 whiskey distillers to only 1.[687] The diminution of Irish Whiskey is a dramatic tale in which politics, pride, and regulation converged to nearly eradicate the spirit. As a trip down a few aisles at the liquor store will demonstrate, Scottish and American distillers probably benefited the most from Irish Whiskey's precipitous decline.

An authority on Irish Whiskey once wrote: "The spirit trade [in Ireland] survived only because . . . public demand could not be suppressed and because governments could not afford to lose the revenue derived from it," and "[i]f heavy taxes, enforced by severe fiscal regulations, could

---

684. At least in this chapter, the words "Great Britain" and "British" refer to the combined countries of England, Scotland, Wales, and Northern Ireland. If either of these terms are used in reference to a date preceding 1922, that list of countries also includes the whole of Ireland. The word "Commonwealth" refers to Great Britain and all of its former colonies (but not the United States, of course).

685. M. Carrie Allan, *Irish Whiskey Was Once on the Verge of Collapse. Now, It's Booming*, WASH. POST (Mar. 8, 2018, 7:00 AM), https://lexspirit.link/8NKV.

686. Barry O'Halloran, *Distillers in High Spirits as the Whiskey Sector Enters Golden Era*, IRISH TIMES (Nov. 8, 2013, 1:00 AM), https://lexspirit.link/L4CJ.

687. E.B. MCGUIRE, IRISH WHISKEY: A HISTORY OF DISTILLING, THE SPIRIT TRADE AND EXCISE CONTROLS IN IRELAND 246, 369–87 (Gill & MacMillan 1973).

make a people sober and industrious, the Irish would be the most so of any upon the face of the earth."[688] But if demand shifts and taxation do not deserve the lion's share of the blame, what does? Surprisingly, the demise of Irish Whiskey's dominance began with an Irishman's invention.

Act I: The Beginning of the End

In the year 1830, an Irish senior excise tax agent named Aeneas Coffey invented a new design of distilling apparatus shaped like a column, rather than a pot (the "Coffey Still").[689] Compared to the traditional pot still design, the Coffey Still used less fuel and yielded a much higher alcohol content.[690] In other words, it seemed to be an improvement over the pot still in every way. But was it really?

Coffey Stills excel at producing ethyl alcohol, which *is* the ultimate end goal of the fermenting and distilling process. What the Coffey Still fails to produce are the smaller quantities of extraneous alcohols and ethers found in traditional pot still whiskey. Those byproducts would be regarded as "impurities" if the aim was to *exclusively* distill ethyl alcohol, but those impurities happen to be what gives a spirit flavor.[691] In fact, the output of a Coffey Still can be so pure that it does not taste like much of anything at all.[692] This characteristic earned the grain-based liquor produced by a Coffey Still the nickname "silent spirit."[693]

---

688. *Id.* at xi–xii.

689. Coffey's Improvements in Apparatus for Brewing and Distilling, Gr. Brit. Patent No. 5974 (granted Feb. 5, 1831). *Of course* a tax collector was to blame!

690. McGuire, *supra* note 687, at 19, 39.

691. *Id.* at 1.

692. *Id.* at 319.

693. A Coffey Still produces something akin to Everclear® Grain Alcohol or vodka (ethanol diluted with water).

Reputable Irish distillers viewed their countryman's new invention with disdain and continued using the traditional pot still. In fact, most did not even regard silent spirit as being whiskey at all. They did not know what to label the end product of Coffey's invention, aside from "inferior."

Other distillers, on the other hand, thought the Coffey Still was a fantastic invention.[694] By blending Coffey's cheap silent spirit with the more flavorful pot still whiskey, they could multiply their whiskey output without diluting its alcohol content.[695] Blending whiskey with silent spirit also reduced some of the heaviness associated with pot still whiskey and achieved a consistent, uniform flavor between batches. Irish distillers thought this blending of spirits was sacrilege, and they bitterly complained that blended whiskey would undermine Irish Whiskey's stellar reputation.[696] But, as it turned out, consumers enjoyed the lighter blended whiskey. In particular, Blended Scotch became prevalent by the 1860s.[697]

The year 1860 was a dark one for the British distilling industry because Great Britain signed a treaty with

---

694. Scottish distillers make some fine Scotch Whisky I really enjoy. Unfortunately, in this story, the Scotch distillers might be the villain. Actually, they *could* be the hero if you are a hardcore free market capitalist devoid of any appreciation for tradition.

695. MCGUIRE, *supra* note 687, at 318 ("The process had everything in its favour. The harsh and heavier pot still whisky was reduced without loss of spirit strength and large quantities could be marketed with a brand name associated with a particular flavour."). "Blended" whiskey can also refer to several batches of pot still whiskey that have been mixed together, but mixing pot still whiskies was not found to be particularly objectionable—at least by comparison. As such, the use of the term "blending" or "blended" in this chapter *exclusively* refers to the mixing of pot still whiskey with silent spirit.

696. *Id.* at 260.

697. *Id.* at 3, 316–19, 440.

France that dispensed with a longstanding protectionist import tariff on foreign alcohol (the "1860 Treaty").[698] The import tax regime was altered as follows:

> Her Britannic Majesty undertakes to recommend to Parliament the admission into the United Kingdom of brandies and spirits imported from France, at a duty exactly equal to the excise duty levied upon home-made spirits, with the addition of a surtax of 2d. [2 pence] a gallon, which will make the actual duty payable on French brandies and spirits 8s. 2d. [8 shillings, 2 pence] the gallon.[699]

Compare that 2 pence (worth about £0.49/$0.66 in 2021) surtax with the astronomical *15 shilling* (worth about £44/$60 in 2021) tariff that was applicable to foreign imports before 1860.[700] A mere 2 pence tariff hardly discouraged consumers from purchasing French Cognac

---

698. *See* origin of the import tariff *supra* p. 166.

699. Treaty of Commerce Between Great Britain and France, Jan. 23, 1860, Gr. Brit.-Fr., arts. VI, VIII, 50 B.S.P. 13, 19, 21 (1867); McGuire, *supra* note 687, at 277.

700. *Currency Converter, 1270–2017*, Nat'l Archives (UK), https://lexspirit.link/61GV; *GBP/USD Historical Data*, Yahoo! Fin., https://lexspirit.link/TQEH (quoting the GBP/USD conversion rate as being 1.3498 on 12/31/2021); McGuire, *supra* note 687, at 277. In 1860, the British pound was subdivided into 20 shillings or 240 pence. To give you some idea of just how heavily spirits were taxed in Great Britain at the time, the purchasing power of 8 shillings, 2 pence in 1860 translates to about £24.14/$32.58 in 2021.[701]

701. A footnote for a footnote! How quaintly meta is that? If you have ever wondered why the symbol for the British pound sterling (£) is a stylized letter *L*, the symbol stands for the Latin phrase *libra pondo*, which was the standard unit of weight in the Roman Empire. The value of the British pound was originally tied to what one pound of sterling silver was worth. Of course, Great Britain is no longer the Roman province of Britannia, but there is clearly a lasting influence.

over domestically produced liquors. Fortunately for British distillers, an invasive North American aphid killed most of France's grapevines shortly after the 1860 Treaty was signed, and it was several decades before French Cognac was plentifully available again.[702]

Even so, the year 1860 proved especially detrimental for traditional Irish distillers because, in passing the 1860 Spirits Act, British Parliament effectively recognized the Coffey Still *did* produce whiskey.[703] Even worse, the legislation effectively *encouraged* the blending of liquor with silent spirit because it allowed for blending to be undertaken "in bond," meaning no tax was due until the final product was removed from the tax assessor's warehouse.[704] Formerly, blenders had to pay the tax due on barrels of pot still whiskey and silent spirit prior to blending the two products in the tax assessor's warehouse. Now, the blenders had less capital tied up while their whiskey blends were maturing because they deferred any associated tax payments for several years. Significantly, any whiskey that evaporated out of a barrel or was spilled was no longer subject to taxation.[705]

The resulting surge in whiskey blending eventually prompted four Dublin distillers to publish a book called *Truths About Whisky* in 1878. The work was the equivalent of a scathing blog post ranting about the evils of whiskey blending, and it began by stating its purpose:

---

702. *See* Clark, *supra* note 460.

703. An Act to Reduce into One Act and to Amend the Excise Regulations Relating to the Distilling, Rectifying, and Dealing in Spirits 1860, 23 & 24 Vict., 2d sess., c. 114, §§ 8, 119 (UK).

704. McGuire, *supra* note 687, at 243, 320.

705. *Id.* at 22, 257. Up to 10% of a barrel's contents can evaporate over the course of two years. Not having to pay a tax on the "angel's share" was a major benefit for all distillers—not just blenders.

The four firms of Whisky distillers by whom this book is published . . . who have for the last two years been engaged in an endeavor to place some check upon the practices of the fraudulent traders by whom silent spirit . . . is sold under the name of Whisky, have come to the conclusion that their efforts in this direction are more likely to be successful if their own position . . . is exactly known.[706]

And it got even more spiteful:

Silent spirit . . . is made in what are called "patent" [Coffey] stills from any vegetable matter which contains the materials necessary for fermentation . . . . Hence, damaged grain or potatoes, molasses refuse, and various other waste products are cast into the all-devouring maw of the patent still . . . . [T]hese things no more yield Whisky than they yield wine or beer.

. . . .

It is much more costly to produce Whisky than to produce silent spirit; . . . the silent spirit lowered the price of Whisky until the latter could scarcely be sold at a price to pay for its manufacture.

. . . .

[G]enuine Whisky derives a flavour from the substances from which it is distilled, and it is plain that patent still or silent spirit, which is not thus flavoured, cannot fulfil the terms of the definition, and is not Whisky.[707]

---

706. JOHN JAMESON & SON ET AL., TRUTHS ABOUT WHISKY 1 (London, Sutton Sharpe & Co. 1878).

707. *Id.* at 2, 11–12, 14.

Of the 28 distilleries in Ireland in 1887, only 5 owned a Coffey Still—and 4 of those were in the "English" part of the island that now constitutes Northern Ireland. Further, all 5 distilleries with a Coffey Still exclusively produced silent spirit for the *export* market.[708] The Coffey Still may have revolutionized the distilling industry, but none of the whiskey produced by it was being sold in Ireland. Unfortunately, the rest of the world continued purchasing blended whiskey because they really enjoyed it. Plus, it was cheaper.

As sales of straight Irish Whiskey continued declining, Irish distillers lobbied Parliament to legally define what *exactly* constituted whiskey—clearly hoping silent spirit and silent spirit blends would not make the cut.[709] In 1908, those efforts culminated in the formation of the Royal Commission on Whiskey and Other Potable Spirits to investigate the subject further. After gathering evidence on the matter, the Commission refused to declare that either silent spirit or blends with therewith were something other than whiskey.[710] On the contrary, the

---

708. *See* OXFORD COMPANION, *supra* note 6, at 775; *see also* ALFRED BARNARD, THE WHISKY DISTILLERIES OF THE UNITED KINGDOM (London, Harper's Wkly. Gaz. 1887) (cataloging the equipment and produce of the 28 distilleries in Ireland in 1887).

709. MCGUIRE, *supra* note 687, at 321–23.

710. A similar examination was simultaneously underway in the United States, where by 1905 blended whiskey accounted for an estimated 50–75% of the market. E.H. Taylor, Jr., & Sons v. Taylor, 85 S.W. 1085, 1086 (Ky. 1905). The Pure Food and Drug Act of 1906 prohibited the adulteration or misbranding of drugs or articles of food entering interstate commerce. Pure Food and Drug Act of 1906, ch. 3915, 34 Stat. 768. As you might expect, a question soon arose as to whether labeling silent spirit or silent spirit blends as "whiskey" constituted misbranding.

President Taft—who rarely drank but loved an interesting legal question—took it upon himself to define "whiskey." BRIAN F. HAARA, BOURBON JUSTICE: HOW WHISKEY LAW SHAPED AMERICA 105–06 (Potomac Books 2018). After hearing six months of evidence and,

Commission determined blends *were* whiskey. Many of their conclusions were influenced by the popularity of blended whiskey in the marketplace:

> The market for blended whiskeys is greater than that for the individual [unblended] whiskeys; so much so, that it would probably be safe to say that the majority of Englishmen who drink whiskey seldom drink anything but a blend. We are bound, therefore, to take into consideration the fact that any undue interference with the practice would not only destroy a flourishing industry, but would also prejudicially affect large numbers of the public.[711]

At this point Irish distillers should have recognized the public's taste had changed—both in Great Britain and abroad—over the previous 50 years and adapted accordingly. But they refused to entertain any such notion and continued to champion traditional distilling practices. English, Scottish, and American distillers, on the other hand, continued expanding their blending operations with enormous success.[712]

---

incidentally, considering the Royal Commission's conclusions, President Taft made his ruling: Whiskey was a potable liquor made from distilled grains. The term encompassed traditional pot still whiskey, neutral spirits, and blends of those two substances. William Howard Taft, *Decision by President Taft: What Is the Meaning of the Term "Whisky" Under the Pure Food Act, and the Proper Regulations for Branding Various Kinds of Whisky Under the Internal Revenue Act?, in* A COMPILATION OF THE MESSAGES AND PAPERS OF THE PRESIDENTS, VOL. 10, at 7837, 7842–44 (James D. Richardson ed., 1910). The Taft Decision, as it became known, largely persists to this day. *See* Standards of Identity for Distilled Spirits, 27 C.F.R. § 5.88 (2022).

711. ROYAL COMMISSION ON WHISKEY AND OTHER POTABLE SPIRITS, FINAL REPORT, 1909, Cd. 4796, at 21 (UK).

712. MCGUIRE, *supra* note 687, at 300–01, 325.

Act II: Trouble in Paradise

If the combined effect of each of the developments in Act I were not enough, the political and economic turmoil of the early 20th century could have singlehandedly killed off the Irish distilling industry—and very nearly did. To begin with, World War One (1914–1918) stifled trade, and wartime shortages brought restrictions on the distilling of valuable grains.[713] Then, in the middle of the Great War the Irish struggle for independence violently resumed with The Easter Rising (1916). This led to the creation of the Irish Free State in 1922. While it remained a part of the Commonwealth as a British Dominion, Ireland gained some autonomy.[714] Unfortunately, the Irish Civil War (1922–1923) followed, further hampering the economic activities of the Irish Free State.[715]

Stateside, the enactment of Prohibition (1920–1933) meant one of the largest consumers of Irish Whiskey—the United States—was no longer importing the spirit.[716] Not legitimately, anyway. Making matters worse, the spirit's reputation suffered because bootleggers realized they could sell gut-rot spirit at a premium by fraudulently labelling the substance as being Irish Whiskey.

Prohibition's repeal in late 1933 was not exactly the boon it could have been. The United States immediately imposed quota restrictions on imported spirits. Fortunately, those restrictions were short-lived and were

---

713. *Id.* at 306–07.

714. Articles of Agreement for a Treaty Between Great Britain and Ireland, Dec. 6, 1921, Gr. Brit-Ir., 114 B.S.P. 161 [hereinafter 1921 Treaty].

715. MCGUIRE, *supra* note 687, at 301. I feel compelled to apologize for not relating these events in the level of detail they truly deserve.

716. *See* U.S. CONST. amend. XVIII, *repealed by* U.S. CONST. amend. XXI.

largely abandoned by May 1934.[717] While a large export market reopening was great news for the distilling industry, the Great Depression (1929–1939) severely suppressed demand. Price-sensitive Americans were not interested in purchasing the more expensive, imported whiskey when there were cheaper alternatives. Then, the Anglo–Irish Trade War (1933–1938) erupted. This conflict amplified the effects of the Great Depression because products imported into Great Britain from Ireland (e.g., Irish Whiskey) were nearly taxed into nonexistence.[718] The situation was enough to drive a man to drink!

Hablot K. "Phiz" Browne, *Political Economists* (etching)
in CHARLES J. LEVER, NUTS AND NUTCRACKERS 179
(London, Bradbury & Evans 1845).

---

717. MCGUIRE, *supra* note 687, at 347. The Irish quota restriction was originally established at 15,000 gallons (later increased to 50,000 gallons). That allotment paled in comparison to Great Britain's 600,000 gallons. Letter from Michael MacWhite, Irish Minister to the United States, to Cordell Hull, U.S. Secretary of State (Nov. 25, 1933), *in* FOREIGN RELATIONS OF THE UNITED STATES 1933, VOL. 2, at 107, 107–09 (1949).

718. The 1921 Treaty included a provision where Ireland agreed to pay a "land annuity" to Great Britain as compensation for real estate loans brokered to Irish tenant farmers. When Ireland defaulted on the land annuity, a trade war erupted. *See* Aoife O'Donoghue, *Neutrality and Multilateralism After the First World War*, 15 J. CONFLICT & SEC. L. 169, 189 n.117 (2010); *see also* 1921 Treaty, *supra* note 714, at 162; Agreements between the Government of Ireland and the Government of the United Kingdom, I.T.S. No. 1/1938 (Ir.) (ending the Anglo–Irish Trade War).

Act III: Aging Whiskey Puts Distillers Over a Barrel

One of the wonderful hallmarks of whiskey is it improves with age. New whiskey is harsh, but it mellows considerably after maturing in oak barrels for several years.[719] In fact, whiskey aging was recognized as being so beneficial that a law passed by British Parliament in 1915 required "British or foreign spirits . . . [to be] warehoused for a period of at least three years."[720]

Interestingly, the silent spirit used in the production of blended whiskey, if it improved at all, practically ceased maturing after three years.[721] That was great news in the eyes of Irish distillers because straight pot still whiskey continued to improve when aged for an even longer period. Determined to capitalize upon this disparity, the Irish Free State enacted legislation in 1926 to extend the mandatory aging period for spirits to *five* years.[722] Aside from pot still whiskey benefiting from an additional two years of maturation, it also meant anyone cheeky enough to attempt to sell blended whiskey in Ireland (the nerve!) had capital tied up for a further two years despite their product not improving over that period.

In an ironic twist, the enhanced aging requirement hamstrung Irish distillers when Prohibition was repealed in 1933. While Scottish and English distillers could ramp up production to satiate the renewed demand overseas (with a three-year delay, anyway), it took Irish distillers

---

719. McGuire, *supra* note 687, at 20–21. No further maturation occurs after a spirit is bottled because the magic only happens when the liquor is in contact with wood.

720. Immature Spirits (Restriction) Act 1915, 5 & 6 Geo. 5 c. 46, § 1 (UK).

721. McGuire, *supra* note 687, at 309.

722. Immature Spirits (Restriction) Bill 1926 (Act No. 18a/1926) § 1(a) (Ir.).

nearly twice as long to bring increased quantities of Irish Whiskey to market.[723] Even if the Irish government tried bailing out the distillers by allowing them to export "immature" whiskey, it would not have helped.[724] A contemporary regulation in the United States required that all imported spirits meet or exceed the legal requirements (including any aging requirements) of their country of origin.[725] Market forces took over, and five years after Repeal a glut of Irish Whiskey flooded the market. This depressed whiskey prices, and Irish distillers could barely turn a profit.[726]

Hablot K. "Phiz" Browne, *An Irish Encore* (etching)
in CHARLES J. LEVER, NUTS AND NUTCRACKERS 99
(London, Bradbury & Evans 1845).

---

723. Oddly enough, in 1969 the *Dáil Éireann* (Assembly of Ireland) reverted the required aging period for spirits back to three years, where it remains today. It was a belated solution to an antiquated problem. Immature Spirits (Restriction) Bill 1969 (Act. No. 29/1969) (Ir.), https://lexspirit.link/TY43.

724. MCGUIRE, *supra* note 687, at 308–09.

725. Labeling and Advertising of Distilled Spirits, 1 Fed. Reg. 92, 100 (Apr. 2, 1936). Section 46 of the Regulation required a certification that imported spirits conformed "to requirements of the Immature Spirits Act of such foreign government for spirits intended for home consumption." *Id.*

726. MCGUIRE, *supra* note 687, at 347.

Act IV: Irish Independence and the Dominance of Scotch

Despite whatever impressions Acts II and III may have given you, the 1930s were not *all* bad in Ireland. In 1931, the Statute of Westminster granted British Dominions (including the Irish Free State) the right to self-govern.[727] This paved the way for Ireland to eventually terminate its status as a dominion in 1949, when the state became an independent republic.[728] This represented both a victory for Ireland and a setback for Irish distillers because Irish Whiskey sold in the Commonwealth was now subject to import tariffs. This was yet another advantage for Scottish distillers, whose product was duty-free.

Ireland's autonomy from Great Britain allowed it to escape the brunt of the *Luftwaffe*'s bombing campaigns during World War Two (1939–1945) because the country remained neutral throughout the conflict.[729] That is not to

---

727. Statute of Westminster 1931, 22 Geo. 5 c. 4, § 4 (UK) ("No act of Parliament of the United Kingdom passed after the commencement of this Act shall extend or be deemed to extend, to a Dominion as part of the law of that Dominion, unless it is expressly declared in that Act that that Dominion has requested, and consented to, the enactment thereof.").

728. The Republic of Ireland Act 1948 (Act No. 19/1948) § 2 (Ir.), https://lexspirit.link/S8E8. Contrary to common parlance, the name of the sovereign nation was *not* changed to the "Republic of Ireland" by this act. Rather, the legislation merely clarified "the description of the State shall be the Republic of Ireland." *Id.* The Constitution of Ireland, on the other hand, specifies the country's official name is *Éire* or, in English, Ireland. CONSTITUTION OF IRELAND 1937 art. 4, https://lexspirit.link/7GIT. Oftentimes "Republic of" is used as a descriptor to differentiate the sovereign state from the entire island.

729. Despite remaining neutral, Ireland permitted Allied planes to fly through their airspace and provided weather reports. Unfortunately, German bombers sometimes mistook Ireland for England and bombed the neutral country. To combat this problem, bright white stones, sand, and paint were used to spell out "*Éire*" along the coast in large letters to show aviators they were above Ireland. Even without any restoration,

say Ireland had an easy time during the war because shortages and trade disruptions wreaked havoc on an economy still reeling from the economic challenges of the 1930s. Even so, it was a welcome respite.

Once Ireland became fully independent of Great Britain in 1949, the Irish distilling industry seized the opportunity to once again lobby for a piece of legislation very near and dear to their heart: a *revised* legal definition of what constituted whiskey. In 1950, the *Dáil Éireann* adopted a new definition of the term, but it surprisingly reflected a more tolerant attitude toward blended whiskey. The Irish Whiskey Act of 1950 defined Irish Whiskey as a spirit "obtained by distillation in [Ireland] from a mash of malt and cereals."[730] Noticeably absent from the definition was any restriction on blending or an exclusion of silent spirit. Perhaps attitudes had finally changed, or maybe Irish distillers accepted they were fighting a losing battle. It was probably a combination of the two.

The old guard received some consolation in the form of a special class of whiskey called "Irish Pot Still Whiskey," which was defined as a straight whiskey distilled "solely in pot stills in [Ireland] from a mash of cereal grains such as are ordinarily grown in [Ireland] saccharified by the diastase of malted barley."[731] Unfortunately, there were hardly any distilleries left that produced a whiskey fitting that description. The public's preference for blended whiskeys, the lower prices of blended products, and masterful marketing by Scotch producers practically

---

many of those signs remain visible from the air today. *EIRE Signs of WWII*, EIRE MARKINGS, https://lexspirit.link/1DSC.

730. Irish Whiskey Act 1950 (Act No. 2/1950) § 1(a) (Ir.), https://lexspirit.link/VAZQ.

731. *Id.* § 1(b).

eradicated Irish Whiskey from the shelves.[732] Not even the rising popularity of Irish Coffee could stem the tide.

And then things got *really* ironic. Historically, the Scotch industry experienced enormous success by employing blending practices, but a new strategy emerged during the early 1960s. In 1963, the Glenfiddich Distillery® (owned by William Grant & Sons) became the first distiller to market and export a special product outside of Great Britain: Single Malt Scotch Whisky.[733] The term denotes a straight Scotch Whisky produced exclusively with pot stills (no blending allowed) by a single distillery.[734] If that sounds suspiciously familiar, it is because Single Malt is effectively the Scottish version of Irish Pot Still Whiskey. After driving the Irish distilling industry into the ground through the use of relatively unconventional distilling practices, Scottish distillers had come full circle to produce a traditional whiskey product! Today, Single Malt Scotch Whisky accounts for only 10% of the Scotch Whisky produced each year, but the product sells at a significant premium to its blended counterpart.[735]

In 1966, the last three distillers in Ireland—Cork Distilleries Company, John Jameson & Son, and John Power & Son—merged to form Irish Distillers Limited ("IDL"), and the company purchased the only remaining distillery in Northern Ireland, Bushmills, in 1972.[736] IDL was the last producer of Irish Whiskey left standing.

---

732. MCGUIRE, *supra* note 687, at 440.

733. Tim McKirdy, The Surprisingly Short History of Single-Malt Scotch, VINEPAIR (Apr. 30, 2019), https://lexspirit.link/XYWQ; OXFORD COMPANION, *supra* note 6, at 325.

734. The Scotch Whisky Regulations 2009, SI 2009/2890, art. 3, ¶ 2 (UK), https://lexspirit.link/EYXJ.

735. *FAQs*, SCOTCH WHISKY ASSOC., https://lexspirit.link/0TDT.

736. MCGUIRE, *supra* note 687, at 327, 369; OXFORD COMPANION, *supra* note 6, at 383. The entity formed in 1966 was named United

Epilogue

Fortunately, the outlook for Irish Whiskey has improved considerably. During the 1970s and 1980s IDL consolidated its operations and expanded sales. In fact, one of IDL's products, Jameson® Irish Whiskey, is probably what most people think of when they hear the words "Irish Whiskey." Legally, it *is* Irish Whiskey, but it is a *blended* whiskey—which almost seems antithetical to the tradition associated with the spirit.[737] Still, the Jameson brand served as a proverbial lifeboat for Irish Whiskey when the spirit was in danger of disappearing altogether, and there is no denying its significance.

As of the date of publication, IDL is owned by the French beverage conglomerate Pernod-Ricard S.A., which acquired the company for $442 million in a friendly takeover bid in 1988.[738] While foreign ownership of IDL is not ideal, it certainly beats throwing in the towel! Under the stewardship of Pernod-Ricard, sales of IDL's products have experienced significant growth.

Outside of IDL's sphere of influence, during the 21st century new distilleries have emerged as torchbearers for traditional Irish Whiskey. A major milestone of this resurgence occurred in 2015 when the Teeling Whiskey Company opened Dublin's first new distillery in over 125

Distillers of Ireland Limited, but the name was soon changed to Irish Distillers Limited.

737. *Our Jameson Whiskey Family: Jameson Irish Whiskey*, JAMESON WHISKEY, https://lexspirit.link/L3V2.

738. *Pernod-Ricard Bid Prevails in Battle for Irish Distillers*, N.Y. TIMES, Nov. 25, 1988, at D1, https://lexspirit.link/NCYG. A competing bidder offered a higher amount but intended to break-up the company. In more ways than one, Pernod-Ricard was IDL's white knight.

years.[739] Teeling is also notable for being one of several Irish distillers that produces a straight, unblended pot still whiskey.[740]

As of 2021, conservative estimates of the number of whiskey distilleries in Ireland indicate there are at least 25, which evidences a bountiful proliferation since the 1970s.[741] Still, Irish Whiskey may never enjoy the prevalence and reputation it once had. For that, the spirit deserves its very own Irish wake.

---

739. Stephanie Bailey, *The Irish Whiskey Revival Is Mixing Tradition with Modernity*, CNN (Sept. 26, 2019, 5:58 AM), https://lexspirit.link/QV7X.

740. *Teeling Single Pot Still*, TEELING WHISKEY, https://lexspirit.link/PNJK. I have a confession to make: I do not find straight Irish Whiskey to be vastly superior to its blended counterpart. But I do favor it for the tradition associated with the spirit. Today, "Pot Still Irish Whiskey" is the official term used to describe a straight, unblended Irish Whiskey. It denotes a double- or triple-distilled whiskey aged for a minimum of three years in wooden barrels on the island of Ireland (including Northern Ireland). FOOD INDUS. DEV. DIV. DEPT. AGRIC., FOOD & MARINE, TECHNICAL FILE SETTING OUT THE SPECIFICATIONS WITH WHICH IRISH WHISKEY/UISCE BEATHA EIREANNACH/IRISH WHISKY MUST COMPLY § 4.2.1 (2014), https://lexspirit.link/3PLT.

741. OXFORD COMPANION, *supra* note 6, at 775.

Hablot K. "Phiz" Browne, *An Irish Wake* (etching) *in*
CAMDEN PELHAM, THE CHRONICLES OF CRIME; OR,
THE NEWGATE CALENDAR, VOL. I, pl. 2 (London, Thomas Tegg 1841).

§ 20

The Mint Julep and Riding Under the Influence

The Mint Julep is a distant descendant of a Persian tonic called *gûlab*/julab, a medicinal combination of sweet water and macerated rose petals.[742] Julab was probably introduced to Europeans through the Muslim occupation of the Iberian Peninsula from the 8th to 15th centuries. Once the English got ahold of the "julep," they began incorporating other ingredients into the medicine. At some point (really, it was inevitable) someone experimented by adding liquor to it.[743]

It is thought that the julep made the voyage across the Atlantic Ocean during the late 17th or early 18th century. By that time, it may have consisted of sugar, rose water, the occasional sprig of mint, camphor, and liquor (either rum or brandy). Bourbon, an aged whiskey made from at least 51% corn (maize) mash, is a uniquely American spirit

---

742. Mark Will-Weber, *A Complete History of the Mint Julep*, TOWN & COUNTRY MAG. (Apr. 10, 2017), https://lexspirit.link/WD0J.

743. WONDRICH, *supra* note 4, at 189–93. Perhaps "adding even more liquor" is a more accurate phrase.

that was not invented until the mid-18th century.[744] Needless to say, the ice we take for granted in the drink today was also only seasonally available.

Americans are credited with adding mint to the julep (in a permanent, distinctive fashion, anyway) sometime during the 18th century.[745] One of the first references to what may have been an early iteration of the Mint Julep is found in issue 20 of *The New-England Courant* (1721), a Boston newspaper founded by Benjamin Franklin's older brother, James. The passing remark read, "And if the bare Reading of thoſe[746] Papers will not ſatisfy them, they may call at the Sloper Tavern, where they ſhall be treated with a Dram of Rum and Mint-Water (as a Premium) on Accompt of one that is."[747] However, David Wondrich discounts this early sighting by observing that the "mint-water" was likely a distilled liqueur.[748] It is far more likely that the Mint Julep originated in the Virginia Colony. This is supported by the following excerpt from a 1770 poem about foxhunting published in *The Virginia Gazette*:

---

744. Europeans had only recently been introduced to corn. Their first exposure to the cereal grain came when they "discovered" the Americas, where the indigenous inhabitants had been cultivating the crop for centuries. OXFORD COMPANION, *supra* note 6, at 769; MARIANI, *supra* note 97, at 167.

745. OXFORD COMPANION, *supra* note 6, at 398–99.

746. If you have not yet become acquainted with the letter ſ, the archaic letter denotes a long s sound. It was seldom used after the early 19th century—probably because it had some tricky rules associated with it. For instance, "[t]he long ſ muſt never be uſed at the End of a Word, or immediately after the ſhort or ſmall s." GEORGE FISHER, THE AMERICAN INSTRUCTOR, OR, YOUNG MAN'S BEſT COMPANION 10 (Philadelphia, B[enjamin] Franklin & D. Hall eds., 10th ed. 1758).

747. Unknown Hand, *To the Readers of the Courant in New Hampſhire*, NEW-ENG. COURANT, Dec. 18, 1721, at p. 3, col. 1, https://lexspirit.link/ZPO3. "Unknown Hand" is not the long-lost ancestor of famed jurist Learned Hand. This was how the 15-year-old printer's apprentice—Benjamin Franklin—denoted an anonymous author.

748. OXFORD COMPANION, *supra* note 6, at 398.

The ſportsmen ready, and the julep o'er,
which doctors ſtorm at, and which ſome adore;
we ſoon are mounted, and direct our way,
to bruſque the coverts where the foxes lay.[749]

A prominent post-Revolutionary War mention of the tipple appears in *Travels of Four Years and a Half in the United States of America* (1803) by John Davis, a British visitor to the United States. Evidently, Davis felt the need to footnote the word "julep" in his book because it had a different meaning in America than in the British Isles. "A dram of spirituous liquor that has mint steeped in it, taken by Virginians of a morning," is how he described the beverage.[750] Davis's description gives the impression that Americans seldom consumed a julep without mint, and they certainly were not incorporating rose petals into their spirited morning beverage!

It was the emergence of the American ice trade in the early 1800s that transformed the Mint Julep into something resembling the refreshing cocktail we know today.[751] Indeed, by the 1840s, the libation had become something of a stateside novelty to foreign visitors— potentially the first "American" cocktail.[752] Even so, the default spirit used in a Mint Julep at the time was brandy.[753]

---

749. S.X., *A ſhort Poem on Hunting*, VA. GAZ., Jan. 11, 1770, at p. 2, col. 2, https://lexspirit.link/KSFB. The title of this poem is incredibly inaccurate because the poem takes up one sixth of the issue!

750. JOHN DAVIS, TRAVELS OF FOUR YEARS AND A HALF IN THE UNITED STATES OF AMERICA; DURING 1798, 1799, 1800, 1801, AND 1802, at 379 (London, R. Edwards 1803).

751. WONDRICH, *supra* note 4, at 47, 192.

752. *See id.* at 9.

753. THOMAS, *supra* note 160, at 44–45. When "Professor" Jerry Thomas published his seminal book of cocktail recipes in 1862, he listed Cognac as the spirit to use in a "real" Mint Julep. He did, however, offer

Bourbon was not in vogue for this cocktail until two events occurred. The first was the Union blockade, which limited Cognac's availability in the South and forced residents to consider alternative spirits for a Mint Julep. The second was the Great French Wine Blight, which was caused by an invasive North American aphid accidentally imported into France in the course of trade. As noted earlier, the pest attacked the roots of French grapevines, killing the plant altogether.[754] Because Cognac is a French brandy derived from grapes, this meant the spirit became very scarce for several decades. Necessity being the mother of invention, the plentiful quantities of rye and corn whiskey being produced in the United States were quickly put to use. Bourbon was found to be preferable for a Mint Julep as a result of its sweeter, less spicy flavor profile. With that pairing made, the modern Mint Julep had finally arrived. The beverage reigned supreme as *the* summer drink for most of the 19th century.[755] Likewise, it remained highly regarded through Prohibition and garnered a prominent mention by F. Scott Fitzgerald in *The Great Gatsby* (1925).[756]

Today, this classic Southern cocktail is most commonly encountered at a certain annual event: the Kentucky

---

several variations on the cocktail featuring gin, whiskey, and even pineapple.

754. *See* Clark, *supra* note 460. The Sazerac® became associated with rye whiskey because of this same phenomenon. *See* discussion *supra* p. 140.

755. WONDRICH, *supra* note 4, at 193.

756. F. SCOTT FITZGERALD, THE GREAT GATSBY 126–29 (Scribner 2004) (1925) (depicting an outing to the Plaza Hotel® on a sweltering summer day, during which Daisy calls the front desk to request crushed ice and mint so the party can make themselves Mint Juleps). By the way, F. Scott Fitzgerald's full name was *Francis Scott Key* Fitzgerald. He was named for a certain attorney who was his second cousin thrice removed and is the third member of the Key family to appear in this book. *See* relatives *supra* pp. 116, 148.

Derby®. It was adopted as the official beverage of the Derby in 1938, but it was a mere formality because the two were already virtually inseparable.[757] Sadly, the cocktail has largely been relegated to that one weekend in May, but what a weekend it is! Approximately 120,000 Mint Juleps are served at Churchill Downs® every year, calling for 10,000 bottles of Bourbon, 60,000 pounds of ice, and 1,000 pounds of fresh spearmint.

While not especially complex on paper, the Mint Julep can be deceptively difficult to execute well. Pay close attention to the footnoted and parenthetical details in the recipe that follows (*infra* p. 242) because some of them *really* matter. A half-hearted endeavor might result in chilled and offensively sweetened whiskey with a bitter mint aftertaste. Basically—mouthwash. But do not get discouraged! This cocktail is worth the effort, and a well-executed Mint Julep is as refreshing as it looks.

Hablot K. "Phiz" Browne, *West Country Farmer After Two Glasses of Spirits* (etching) *in* CHARLES J. LEVER, NUTS AND NUTCRACKERS 186 (London, Bradbury & Evans 1845).

---

757. Will-Weber, *supra* note 742.

What's in a Name?[758]

Bonded Bourbon is an excellent choice of majority corn-derived whiskey to use in a Mint Julep. Bonded Bourbon is unique because it is bottled at a higher proof (100-proof/50 ABV) than most other Bourbon (typically around 90-proof/45 ABV). It is well suited for use in a Mint Julep because the cocktail is served with finely crushed ice, which melts quickly and can overdilute the beverage in short order. Large chunks of ice that melt slowly just will not do in a Mint Julep, and a high-proof Bourbon helps to offset the dilution.

As far as Bourbon is concerned, the term "Bonded" has nothing to do with the Eighth Amendment[759] or a surety. The term comes from the United States' first consumer protection law: the Bottled-in-Bond Act of 1897.[760] While most people would guess the United States' first consumer protection legislation was the Pure Food and Drug Act of 1906, the purity of liquor was apparently of a higher priority.[761]

In the 19th century, many unsavory distillers sought to increase their profits by diluting liquor with additives (sometimes hazardous ones, like sulphuric acid[762]) and/or

---

758. WILLIAM SHAKESPEARE, THE TRAGEDY OF ROMEO AND JULIET act 2, sc. 2, l. 46.

759. "Excessive bail shall not be required . . . ." U.S. CONST. amend. VIII.

760. An Act to Allow the Bottling of Distilled Spirits in Bond, ch. 379, § 2, 29 Stat. 626, 627 (1897). The Excise Tax Technical Changes Act of 1958 moved the Bottled-in-Bond Act's stamp provision to its final resting place in the Tax Code. *See* Pub. L. No. 85-859, sec. 201, § 5205, 72 Stat. 1275, 1358–59 (codified at 26 U.S.C. § 5205(a)(1) (1964)).

761. *See* Pure Food and Drug Act of 1906, 34 Stat. 768. In addition to what we commonly think of as food and drugs today, liquor was also covered by the act. *See* discussion *supra* note 710.

762. *See, e.g.*, United States v. Fifty Barrels of Whisky, 165 F. 966, 968 (D. Md. 1908) ("At the trial it was proved . . . that the spirits libeled had been distilled in New Orleans [from cheap molasses] . . . [and] to

fraudulently labeling bottles to imply they contained a premium spirit.[763] The Bottled-in-Bond Act of 1897 was passed to rectify this problem by providing an avenue for distillers to obtain a government certification attesting to a bottle's contents. This certification originally took the form of a green engraved strip stamp placed over the mouth of the bottle—an outward signal to consumers of quality. Although, technically, the green tax stamp was only a guarantee of a spirit's age, purity, and proof—and not of the overall quality of the spirit itself.[764]

To receive the "Bottled-in-Bond" or "Bonded" designation, the contents of a bottle needed to be (i) composed of the same kind of spirits produced from the same class of materials; (ii) produced in the same distilling season by the same distiller at the same distillery; (iii) stored for at least four years in wooden containers; (iv) unaltered from its original condition except for filtration; (v) reduced in proof only by the addition of pure water, and (vi) bottled at 100-proof (50 ABV).[765] If those requirements sound like they served the dual purpose of snubbing distillers who were blending liquor with silent

---

each 350 gallons of molasses was added about 1 gallon of sulphuric acid . . . ."). Despite the style of the case, the 50 barrels of "whisky" actually contained *rum* because their contents were manufactured from molasses. Regardless, the "burning" notes of liquor are *not* supposed to be derived from the presence of sulphuric acid (H_2SO_4).

763. HAARA, *supra* note 710, at 90–92.

764. W.A. Gaines & Co. v. Turner-Looker Co., 204 F. 533, 556–58 (6th Cir. 1913).

765. DEPT. TREAS., REGULATIONS AND INSTRUCTIONS CONCERNING BOTTLING OF DISTILLED SPIRITS IN BOND, May 22, 1897, arts. 10, 11, 13, *reprinted in* RULES AND REGULATIONS GOVERNING THE TREASURY DEPARTMENT IN ITS VARIOUS BRANCHES, VOL. 4, S. Doc. No. 59-399, at 913, 918–19 (2d Sess. 1907).

spirit (often called "rectifying" in the United States), that is not a coincidence.[766]

"Colonel" Edmund Haynes Taylor, Jr.,[767] was the driving force behind the Bottled-in-Bond Act of 1897. He distilled straight Bourbon whiskey in Kentucky and positively detested the charlatans who were blending inferior whiskeys and then marketing their products with names that mimicked his own brand's.[768] Producing a blended whiskey took little time and money—especially when compared to the cost of producing a quality Bourbon. Other distillers could not compete with the blenders on cost and found themselves under pressure.[769]

Fortunately, Taylor was remarkably astute and came up with a politically acceptable way to stifle the competition: legislation to protect "honest" distillers in the guise of a consumer protection law. With the assistance of Secretary of the Treasury John G. Carlisle (also from Kentucky), Taylor successfully lobbied for the passage of the Bottled-in-Bond Act of 1897.[770] Taylor's motives were not selfless, but the public *did* receive a legitimate benefit.

While consumer protection laws passed in the interim period diminished the usefulness of the Bonded designation, it took on a renewed importance in the 1930s. When Prohibition was repealed in December 1933 it took Congress just over a month to (re)enact federal legislation to derive revenue from the sale of alcohol.[771] Once the Liquor Taxing Act of 1934 became fully effective on

---

766. For a history of whiskey blending with silent spirit on the other side of the Atlantic Ocean see, discussion *supra* p. 213.

767. E.H. Taylor was a "Kentucky Colonel" who never actually served in the military. Instead of fried chicken, he used his commission to peddle whiskey.

768. *E.H. Taylor, Jr., & Sons*, 85 S.W. at 1086–88.

769. HAARA, *supra* note 710, at 90.

770. *Id.* at 91.

771. *See* Liquor Taxing Act of 1934, ch. 1, 48 Stat. 313.

February 10, 1934, every bottle of liquor sold to the public had to have a strip stamp over the mouth of the bottle to evidence payment of the applicable tax.[772] Any unmarked bottles were subject to seizure and could result in heavy penalties for the seller.[773] Spirits meeting the requirements for the Bottled-in-Bond designation continued to be marked with the green strip stamps, and all other "unbonded" liquor bottles were marked with a similar looking strip stamp that was red.[774] In a sea of red-stamped bottles, the green stamps stood out. They were different—and therefore had to be special, right? As it turned out, consumers came to regard the more expensive, green stamped bottles as containing a premium product.

Several decades later, the Distilled Spirits Tax Revision Act of 1979 threatened to erode Bonded liquor's status because it adopted the "all in bond" system of liquor tax administration. This had the effect of repealing the Bottled-in-Bond Act of 1897 because as of January 1, 1980, *all* liquor was technically being "bottled in bond."[775] However, the ATF recognized that Bonded whiskey, in particular, had transcended beyond a mere classification for revenue administration. The green stamps functioned as something akin to a government-issued trademark by serving as an indication of quality, and the decision was made to enshrine the Bottled-in-Bond Act of 1897's six

---

772. *Id.* §§ 201, 203, 48 Stat. at 316–17.

773. *Id.* §§ 203, 206, 207, 48 Stat. at 317.

774. Dept. Treas., Memorandum for the Press: February 7, 1934, *in* PRESS RELEASES OF THE UNITED STATES DEPARTMENT OF THE TREASURY, VOL. 11, at 139–40 (1934), https://lexspirit.link/QWTF. There were also blue strip stamps used to mark bottles for export.

775. Distilled Spirits Tax Revision Act of 1979, Pub. L. No. 96-39, sec. 807(a)(24)(A), § 5205(a)(1), 93 Stat. 273, 283 (1979).

requirements within the labeling regulations for distilled spirits.[776]

But with Bonded liquor divorced from the Tax Code after 1979, the distinctive green tax stamps no longer served a purpose. In 1980, tax stamps still had to be affixed to every bottle of liquor for sale to the public—Bonded or otherwise—but did that mean only the red stamps would continue to be issued? Despite no longer being *legally* required, the ATF announced it would continue issuing the green-colored stamps—at least for the time being.[777] Further deregulation efforts resulted in the demise of the green stamps on December 1, 1982, and effective July 1, 1985, *all* tax stamps—whatever their color—were discontinued.[778] Federal liquor tax stamps and the Bottled in Bond Act of 1897 are both officially defunct. However, thanks to federal distilled spirit labeling regulations, Bonded liquor persists to this day.

The Bottled-in-Bond tax strip stamp on the opposite page may have been placed by a United States Revenue Agent over the mouth of a 1-pint bottle of 100-proof (50 ABV) D.L. Moore Bourbon in fall 1902. I say "may have" because the stamp should have been torn apart if it was removed from a bottle. Someone either used steam to remove the stamp or it was a spare left over from the bottling process. Either way, saving the stamp without defacing it was probably illegal. It resembles a dollar bill in both design and color—which makes sense considering the Bureau of Engraving and Printing produced it!

---

776. Implementing the Distilled Spirits Tax Revision Act of 1979, 44 Fed. Reg. 71,612, 71,614 (Dec. 11, 1979) (codified at 27 C.F.R. § 5.88 (2022)).

777. *Id.* at 71,615.

778. Deficit Reduction Act of 1984, Pub. L. No. 98-369, § 454(a), 98 Stat. 494, 820 ("Section 5205 (relating to stamps) is hereby repealed.").

COMMISSIONER OF INTERNAL REVENUE, ENGRAVED BOTTLED-IN-BOND TAX STAMP (1902) (issued pursuant to the Bottled-in-Bond Act of 1897 § 2, 29 Stat. at 627) (Author's collection).

Mint Julep[779]

1. Put 5–6 fresh spearmint leaves and 3/4 oz. of simple syrup into a cocktail shaker.
2. *Gently*[780] bruise the mint leaves using a muddler.
3. Pour 2-1/2 oz. of Bonded Bourbon (or another high-proof Bourbon) into the shaker and pour (*do not* shake) the mixture between the lid and base of the shaker several times to gently mix the ingredients together.
4. Fill a glorious chalice called a "julep cup"[781] to the brim with finely crushed ice.[782]
5. Strain the contents of the stirring glass into the cup, thereby removing the muddled mint leaves.
6. Garnish with 2–3 attractive sprigs of mint, and serve with a straw.
7. Put on a gigantic hat (ladies) or a seersucker suit (gentlemen), take a sip, and begin your next sentence with the words, "I do declare . . . ."

---

779. DEGROFF, *supra* note 31, at 37.

780. If you muddle the leaves too aggressively, the mint flavor becomes quite bitter. Less really is more here.

781. These are traditionally made of silver or pewter. A highball glass will work in a pinch, but avoid sullying your good name by being seen in public with it!

782. The perfect crushed ice for this cocktail can be crafted by loading chunks of ice into a Lewis bag and then violently pulverizing it with a heavy mallet. Do this on top of a cutting board so you do not damage your kitchen counter. Also, be sure to use an ice scoop to transfer the crushed ice into the cup—the nerve endings in your hands will thank you. This wisdom comes from personal experience.

Riding Under the Influence

On April 7, 2002, Pennsylvania State Police Officers spotted two men riding horses down the middle of the highway. Whether or not this spectacle was out of the ordinary really depends on how far they were from the nearest Amish community. Still, something *was* unusual about the situation: Both were thoroughly inebriated. The men, of course—not the horses.[783] The pair were promptly pulled over, made to dismount, failed field sobriety tests, were taken into custody, and each man was charged with driving under the influence ("DUI").[784] Imagine the men's indignation at the charges after they responsibly chose *not* to operate a motor vehicle while drunk! In their defense, even though it may be dangerous to ride one on the highway while impaired, oftentimes a horse can safely find its own way home if its rider is three sheets to the wind.[785] They really are wonderful and majestic animals.[786]

---

783. *See* TOBY KEITH FEAT. WILLIE NELSON, *(Whiskey for My Men) Beer for My Horses*, *on* UNLEASHED (DreamWorks Records 2002). While I am not suggesting horses should consume alcohol, this song stands for the proposition that any equine drinking should be restricted to beverages with a lower alcohol content.

784. 75 PA. CONS. STAT. § 3731(a) (2002) (later moved to 75 PA. CONS. STAT. § 3802 (2020)). I wonder how/if the horses were impounded because calling a tow truck was out of the question. Hopefully they were well-tended in their owners' absence.

785. Or, as Long John Silver famously remarked to Captain Smollett, "Maybe you think we were all a sheet in the wind's eye. But I'll tell you I was sober; I was on'y dog tired . . . ." ROBERT LOUIS STEVENSON, TREASURE ISLAND 161 (London, Cassell & Co, Ltd. 1883). In a maritime context, rather than referencing a sail, the term "sheet" refers to the *rope* controlling the presentation of a sail to the wind. The more loose sheets, the less control a crew has over their vessel. A vessel with three loose sheets whipping in the wind would lurch about aimlessly—not unlike the manner in which a drunken sailor staggers about. *Sheet*, MERRIAM-WEBSTER'S COLLEGIATE DICTIONARY 1146.

786. "President Lincoln, when informed that Gen. Stoughton had been captured by the rebels at Fairfax, is reported to have said that he

The men lawyered up and filed habeas corpus petitions arguing they could not be charged under Pennsylvania's DUI statute because they were not operating a "vehicle," as the statute required. But one of the defendants (through his attorney) went a step further and also argued that section 3103(a) of the Pennsylvania Motor Vehicle Code (applying the code to animal-powered transportation) was unconstitutionally vague because it failed to provide reasonable notice of the conduct it proscribed. If this was the case, the provision would violate the Due Process Clause of the Fourteenth Amendment and be unenforceable.[787] Section 3103(a) read as follows:

> Every person riding an animal or driving any animal-drawn vehicle upon a roadway shall be granted all of the rights and shall be subject to all of the duties applicable to the driver of a vehicle by this part, except those provisions of this part *which by their very nature can have no application* or where specifically provided otherwise.[788]

You might be surprised to learn a judge found both arguments set forth in the habeas petitions to be compelling and dismissed the charges against both men. In so ordering, the judge found the DUI statute required a "vehicle" to be operated by the person charged with the crime, and horses did not qualify as vehicles under the

---

did not mind the loss of the Brigadier [General] as much as he did the loss of the horses. 'For,' said he, 'I can make a much better Brigadier in five minutes, but the horses cost a hundred and twenty-five dollars apiece.'" *News from Washington*, N.Y. TIMES, Mar. 11, 1863, at 4, https://lexspirit.link/SQC9. Considering Congressman Daniel Sickles made the cut, I am not sure this statement was spoken in jest. *See* incompetence *supra* p. 121.

787. Commonwealth v. Noel, 579 Pa. 546, 549–51 (2004).

788. 75 PA. CONS. STAT. § 3103(a) (emphasis added).

code. As for the constitutional argument pertaining to section 3103(a), the judge noted the provision was nearly identical to a Utah motoring statute found by the Utah Supreme Court to be unconstitutionally vague in 1986.[789] The judge agreed with much of the analysis espoused in that 1986 opinion and came to the same conclusion about the Pennsylvania statute. Prosecutors disagreed with the decision and appealed the dismissal.

The case eventually made its way to the Supreme Court of Pennsylvania, which reviewed the case *de novo*—meaning no deference would be given to the lower courts' decisions. This is because the applicability and constitutionality of a statute is a question of law.[790] The justices began their analysis of the constitutional issue by recognizing the old adage that statutes are presumed to be constitutional and are only invalidated if they "clearly, palpably, and plainly violate constitutional rights."[791] The defendants were tasked with the heavy burden of overturning this presumption, and the easiest way for them to prevail was to prove the statute did not provide reasonable notice of the conduct it was prohibiting.

The majority was unimpressed by section 3103(a)'s wording, which read like the state legislature's shorthand for, "You will just have to guess which provisions do not apply to animal traffic because we cannot be bothered to

---

789. *See Noel*, 579 Pa. at 550–51; *see also* State v. Blowers, 717 P.2d 1321 (Utah 1986).

790. United States v. May, 535 F.3d 912, 915 (8th Cir. 2008). Under certain circumstances, a court will defer to an agency's interpretation of a statute, but so-called "Chevron Deference" was not applicable in this situation. *See* Chevron U.S.A. Inc. v. Nat. Res. Def. Council, 467 U.S. 837 (1984).

791. *Noel*, 579 Pa. at 550 (citing Commonwealth v. MacPherson, 561 Pa. 571 (2000)).

enumerate them all here."[792] When the majority attempted to determine exactly which portions of the Motor Vehicle Code "by their very nature [could] have no application" to horse traffic, things did not improve.[793]

For instance, motorists in Pennsylvania are prohibited from driving over a deployed fire hose without first obtaining permission from the fire department.[794] This is because the hose could be damaged if it is run over by a car. Is a person riding a horse also subject to that restriction? A horse stands a fair chance of stepping over a fire hose entirely, leaving it unharmed.

For obvious reasons, it is also illegal to drive a car on the sidewalk in Pennsylvania.[795] Is a horseman also bound by this restriction? Unless a rider's goal is to joust with a motor vehicle, briefly riding a horse on the sidewalk to avoid a parked car is arguably preferable to crossing over the center line into oncoming traffic.

Another provision of the Pennsylvania Motor Vehicle Code states all accidents occurring on a public highway must be reported to the local police department.[796] But if a horse throws its rider while trotting down a public road, does that incident require a police report? Or is it akin to falling off of a bicycle, where no police report is necessary?

Finding too many of such questions unsatisfactorily resolved to justify the statute's presumption of constitutionality, a majority of the Supreme Court of Pennsylvania upheld the lower court's determination that the statute was unconstitutionally vague.[797]

---

792. Draftsmanship at its finest. Never mistake brevity for laziness—or sarcastically written footnotes for sincere statements.

793. 75 Pa. Cons. Stat. § 3103(a).

794. *Id.* § 3708.

795. *Id.* § 3703.

796. *Id.* § 3746(a)(1).

797. *Noel*, 579 Pa. at 554.

Hablot K. "Phiz" Browne, *Dr. Finucane and the Grey Mare* (etching)
in CHARLES J. LEVER, THE CONFESSIONS OF HARRY LORREQUER
pl. 10 (Dublin, Wm. Curry, Jun. & Co. 1839).

But hold your horses! Justice Michael Eakin disagreed and authored a dissenting opinion in which he told the majority—among other things—to get off their high horse and quit foaling around. I will let you read the best part of the dissenting opinion straight from the horse's mouth:

A horse is a horse, of course, of course,
and no one can talk to a horse, of course.
That is, of course, unless the horse is the famous Mr. Ed.

Go right to the source and ask the horse.
He'll give you the answer that you'll endorse.
He's always on a steady course. Talk to Mr. Ed.[798]

. . . .

A horse is a horse, of course, of course,
but the Vehicle Code does not divorce
its application from, perforce, a steed as my colleagues said.

"It's not vague" I'll say until I'm hoarse,
and whether a car, a truck, or horse,
this law applies with equal force, and I'd reverse instead.[799]

I think you will agree this dissenting opinion is already shaping up to be a horse of a different color.[800] It would

---

798. RAY EVANS & JAMES LIVINGSTON, *Mr. Ed Theme Song, appearing in* MR. ED (CBS 1961–1966). As the lyrics of the song suggest, Mister Edward is a horse who enjoys conversing in English.

799. *Noel*, 579 Pa. at 557, 559. Justice Eakin wrote several opinions in verse during his time on the bench and became somewhat infamous for the practice. *See, e.g.*, Busch v. Busch, 732 A.2d 1274, 1275, 1278 (Pa. Super. Ct. 1999); Liddle v. Scholze, 768 A.2d 1183, 1183 (Pa. Super. Ct. 2001).

800. *See* THE WIZARD OF OZ (Metro-Goldwyn-Mayer 1939) ("That's a horse of a different color."). *Contra* WILLIAM SHAKESPEARE, TWELFTH NIGHT, OR, WHAT YOU WILL act 2, sc. 3, l. 166 ("My purpose is indeed a horse of that colour.").

seem Justice Eakin[801] was champing at the bit[802] to reference the *Mr. Ed* theme song, and he quoted it right out of the gate. I guess it never hurts to give the reader a carrot to entice them into reading your dissent. In explaining why the majority had backed the wrong horse, the justice remarked, "Mr. Ed would know which sections of Part III [of the Pennsylvania Motor Vehicle Code] do not 'by their very nature' apply to his rider, and [attribute that] equivalent horse sense to the ordinary reasonable person."[803] He then accused the majority of riding "far afield wondering whether an equestrian could be cited for driving the horse over a fire hose or on a sidewalk," or whether a person thrown from a horse on a public highway needed to notify the police.[804] In his mind, the answer to each of those questions was "yes" (not *neigh*), and it all boiled down to common sense:

> It is the "rules of the road" that apply to the driver of the mustang and Mustang, alike. Here, an ordinary person of common intelligence would know that riding a horse while intoxicated would be a violation of [the DUI statute], just as the same person would recognize that the rider of a horse must stop at a stop sign, ride on the right side of the road, and signal before turning.[805]

---

801. "[H]e doth nothing but talk of his horse." WILLIAM SHAKESPEARE, THE MERCHANT OF VENICE act 1, sc. 2, ll. 40–41.

802. "Chomping at the bit" is the more commonly encountered version of this idiom today, but the original phrase was "champing at the bit." "Champing" describes the act of a horse repeatedly biting their bit because they are impatient or restless. *Champing*, MERRIAM-WEBSTER'S COLLEGIATE DICTIONARY 205.

803. *Noel*, 579 Pa. at 557.

804. *Id.* at 558.

805. *Id.* at 559. Horses do not have blinkers; a rider uses hand signals to indicate when they intend to change lanes or turn.

Justice Eakin had some sensible arguments, but his logic failed to put the majority's position out to pasture when they deliberated the case. As they say, "You can lead a horse to water, but you cannot make him drink." Still, even if it did not rein in the majority, his dark horse of a dissenting opinion is an enjoyable read.

However, the justices *did* unanimously agree on one point: Riding a horse while under the influence of alcohol is inadvisable, even if the legality of such horseplay is up for debate. So, if you ever gallop your noble steed over to your local watering hole and find yourself a little sluggish in the saddle at closing time, do yourself a favor and hitch a ride home with a sober companion.

Hablot K. "Phiz" Browne, *Installing a Comrade* (etching)
in JAMES GRANT, SKETCHES IN LONDON pl. 7
(London, Wm. Tegg 1838).

§ 21

The Last Word and Last Words

The Last Word appeared on the menu of the Detroit Athletic Club®[806] in 1916, where it was the bar's most expensive cocktail at a hefty 35 cents.[807] Around that same year, the Last Word also became—or already was—the beverage of choice for Frank "The Dublin Minstrel" Fogarty, a famous vaudeville entertainer. Confusingly, some accounts attribute the creation of this cocktail to him, while others indicate he merely adopted it from the Detroit Athletic Club.[808] While it is difficult to conclusively determine which party was responsible for creating it, the cocktail's name suggests Fogarty was involved in some capacity, as the performer was known for ending his shows on a poignant note.[809] Much like the last

---

806. At best, an equal emphasis was placed on athletics and socializing (drinking). In practice, it was probably entirely the latter.

807. Sam Dangremond, *How Three Classic Cocktails Got Their Names: The Untold History of the Harvey Wallbanger, Last Word, and Sazerac*, TOWN & COUNTRY MAG. (July 20, 2015), https://lexspirit.link/1LID.

808. WONDRICH, *supra* note 4, at 331; TED SAUCIER, BOTTOMS UP 151 (Greystone Press 1951).

809. BRETT PAGE, WRITING FOR VAUDEVILLE 70 n.1 (Home Correspondence School 1915) ("Frank Fogarty, 'The Dublin Minstrel,' one of the most successful monologists in vaudeville, often

word of the Dublin Minstrel's monologues, the Last Word is a sweet and entertaining beverage.

The Last Word faded into the background after World War Two (as did vaudeville) until the libation was "rediscovered" in 2004 by bartender Murray Stenson of the Zig Zag Café® in Seattle, Washington. Stenson found the cocktail recipe while digging through old cocktail books in the library and decided to put it on the menu.[810] Once reintroduced to the public, the libation spread like a wildfire, and the inferno rages to this day.

A few years after the Last Word's resurgence, Fort Defiance®, a bar in New York City, suffered extensive damage from Hurricane Sandy. Management creatively decided to fund repairs by selling "junk bonds." Despite the name of the promotion, securities law was not implicated because the "junk bonds" were really gift certificates worth half the amount they were purchased for.

As he was processing payments for those gift certificates one day, bartender St. John Frizell noticed one of the purchasers had an interesting name: *Frank Fogarty*. Frizell thought the name looked familiar and eventually connected it with the entertainer who popularized the Last Word. He reached out to the purchaser to see if the name on the form was some kind of joke, but soon learned that Fogarty (a New York attorney) was none other than the grandson of the Dublin Minstrel himself![811] The attorney had never heard of the cocktail or its association with his

---

opens with a song and usually ends his offering with a serious heart-throb recitation.").

810. Tan Vinh, *The Last Word, a Cocktail Reborn in Seattle, Is on Everyone's Lips*, SEATTLE TIMES (Mar. 11, 2009), https://lexspirit.link/RG61; SIMONSON, *supra* note 211, at 70. This is not the first time a cocktail-hunting expedition in a library has borne distilled fruit. *See* sleuthing *supra* p. 130.

811. Dangremond, *supra* note 807.

grandfather, so Frizell invited him to come over and try the Last Word for himself. Fogarty accepted the invitation, enjoyed a cocktail, and learned something new about his grandfather. One of the things I hope this book has illustrated is how full of serendipity history can be. The history of the Last Word is a prime example of how pure happenstance (and a little alcohol) can lead to meaningful connections. Even without considering the name of the cocktail, I can think of no better elixir to close this book with than the Last Word.

Like the Corpse Reviver No. 2,[812] the Last Word is a refreshing cocktail incorporating equal measures of four ingredients. However, it is a bit stronger than its zombifying brother.[813] The Green Chartreuse® Liqueur[814] gives this cocktail an interesting herbal and floral quality that complements the tartness of the lime juice. Those two ingredients also make the Last Word an excellent palate cleanser.

---

812. *See* Corpse Reviver No. 2 recipe *supra* p. 3.

813. Or, as attorney Frank Fogarty replied when I asked him about the cocktail: "If you haven't tried [the Last Word], be advised it packs a bit of a punch, so I'd recommend having just one."

814. Not to be confused with the slightly milder version of the spirit, Yellow Chartreuse® Liqueur, which is used in the Widow's Kiss *supra* p. 46.

The Last Word[815]

1. Combine the following ingredients in a cocktail shaker with ice:
   a. 1 oz. gin
   b. 1 oz. fresh-squeezed lime juice
   c. 1 oz. Luxardo® Maraschino Liqueur
   d. 1 oz. Green Chartreuse® Liqueur
2. Cap the cocktail shaker and shake vigorously for 20–30 seconds.
3. Garnish a coupe glass with a lime peel spiral.
4. Double strain the contents of the shaker into the coupe glass and serve "up."

---

815. SAUCIER, *supra* note 808, at 151.

Last Words

Shakespeare was not a barrister, but he certainly had a thing or two to say about the veracity of testimony. Through the prologue to John of Gaunt's famous soliloquy in *King Richard the Second,* Shakespeare summed up societal opinions (circa 1595) about a person's dying words thusly:

O, but they say the tongues of dying men
Enforce attention like deep harmony:
Where words are scarce, they are seldom spent in vain,
For they breathe truth that breathe their words in pain.[816]

A person's final moments on this earth have always been regarded as having special significance—particularly if they had something to say. Under the common law, the trustworthiness of someone's dying words was largely predicated on the idea that someone would not dare to tell a lie when they were about to meet their Maker:

> [W]hen the party is at the point of death, and when every hope of this world is gone, when every motive to falsehood is silenced, and when the mind is induced by the most powerful considerations to speak the truth, a situation so solemn, and so awful, is considered by the law as creating an obligation equal to that which is imposed by a positive oath administered in a Court of Justice.[817]

---

816. WILLIAM SHAKESPEARE, THE LIFE AND DEATH OF KING RICHARD THE SECOND act 2, sc. 1, ll. 5–10. Shakespeare may have made a decent trial attorney—he certainly had a way with words and possessed a theatrical flair that would resonate with a jury.

817. The King v. Woodcock (1789) 168 Eng. Rep. 352 (KB) 353; 1 Leach 500, 502.

While dying declarations were originally admissible at common law under a religious justification, modern proponents point to a late victim's decreased motivations to lie as being the present justification for admitting such statements. Whether someone who is about to die suddenly lacks an incentive to spout falsehoods is debatable, and some skepticism is probably justified.

However, there is a problem with admitting someone's dying declaration into evidence: Such statements are invariably hearsay. Hearsay is an out-of-court statement offered (in court) to prove the truth of the matter asserted.[818] In other words, if a witness is testifying utters the words, "and that's when the dying man said, 'It was—,'" opposing counsel will probably interrupt with, "Objection, your honor! Hearsay." Fortunately for the party whose witness is testifying—so long as the case involves either a civil matter or criminal homicide[819]—the objection is easily overruled, provided their attorney offers the correct justification to the judge.

One exception to the rule against hearsay permits the admission of a dying declaration if the unavailable declarant[820] made the statement while believing their death was imminent, and the statement concerned the cause or circumstances surrounding their impending death.[821] This makes some sense. For instance, if someone has been shot and wants to use their dying breath to say who did—or did not—shoot them, that would be a *very* useful piece of information for a judge or jury to know.

Critics of the admissibility of dying declarations often point to the hearsay exception running afoul of the Sixth

---

818. FED. R. EVID. 801(c).
819. I do not mean to imply that homicide is ever fortunate.
820. Death tends to make people unavailable to testify at trial.
821. FED. R. EVID. 804(b)(2).

Amendment's Confrontation Clause, which states: "In all criminal prosecutions, the accused shall enjoy the right . . . to be confronted with the witnesses against him . . . ."[822] This right essentially guarantees the accused is afforded the opportunity to look their accuser in the eye during their testimony. It is meant to provide an additional safeguard around the reliability of witness testimony in a criminal trial by ensuring a witness is available for cross examination.[823]

The Supreme Court takes the right to confrontation quite seriously and has commented that, "Dispensing with confrontation because testimony is obviously reliable is akin to dispensing with jury trial because a defendant is obviously guilty."[824] Even so, dying declarations remain admissible as a glaring exception to the right to confrontation and the rule against hearsay. Whether right or wrong, it certainly underscores the emphasis we continue to place on someone's last words today.

---

822. U.S. CONST. amend. VI.

823. FED. R. CRIM. P. 26 (codifying the preference for live witness testimony in open court, unless otherwise specified).

824. Crawford v. Washington, 541 U.S. 36, 62 (2004).

Justice Jackson's Cocktail

With that treatise on the rules of evidence out of the way, here is a more lighthearted observation with which I will close: If Supreme Court Justice Robert H. Jackson had a favorite cocktail, it might have been the Last Word.[825] Truthfully, this particular cocktail fell out of fashion during his time on the bench (1941–1954), but my suspicions arise from his concurrence in *Brown v. Allen*. In that opinion he declared, "[The Supreme Court is] not final because we are infallible, but we are infallible only because we are final."[826] In other words, the Supreme Court has the Last Word. See what I did there?

Justice Jackson once threw a clerk a small cocktail reception to mark the end of his clerkship. When an attendee commented he had never heard of a Justice hosting a farewell happy hour for a clerk, Justice Jackson is said to have remarked, "If you had worked with the fellow every day for two years and then he finally decided to go back to Philadelphia, don't you think that you would have some sort of celebration, too?"[827] He was always known for his wit, but I would expect nothing less from a justice famous for writing concurring and dissenting opinions that often overshadowed the majority opinions they followed.[828] He would have been a great conversationalist at any happy hour. And now, having read this book, I bet you would be too!

---

825. Thanks to Steven Lien for associating Justice Jackson with this cocktail.

826. Brown v. Allen, 344 U.S. 443, 540 (1953) (Jackson, J., concurring).

827. James M. Marsh, *The Genial Justice: Robert H. Jackson*, 60 A.B.A.J. 306, 306 (1974).

828. *See, e.g.*, Youngstown Sheet & Tube Co. v. Sawyer, 343 U.S. 579, 634–55 (1952) (Jackson, J., concurring); Korematsu v. United States, 323 U.S. 214, 242–48 (1944) (Jackson, J., dissenting).

Hablot K. "Phiz" Browne, *The Man of Genius* (etching)
in CHARLES J. LEVER, NUTS AND NUTCRACKERS pl. 2
(London, Bradbury & Evans 1845).

This book stands adjourned. Cheers!

Index

Further Cocktail Education

1. JEFF BERRY, BEACH BUM BERRY'S REMIXED: A GALLERY OF TIKI DRINKS (Club Tiki Press 2014).

2. HARRY CRADDOCK, THE SAVOY COCKTAIL BOOK (Richard R. Smith 1930).

3. DALE DEGROFF, THE ESSENTIAL COCKTAIL: THE ART OF MIXING PERFECT DRINKS (Clarkson Potter 2008).

4. DAVID EMBURY, THE FINE ART OF MIXING DRINKS (Doubleday & Co., 3d ed. 1958).

5. HUGO ENSSLIN, RECIPES FOR MIXED DRINKS (Fox Printing House 1916).

6. JEFFREY MORGENTHALER, MARTHA HOLMBERG & ALANNA HALE, THE BAR BOOK: ELEMENTS OF COCKTAIL TECHNIQUE (Chronicle Books 2014).

7. THE OXFORD COMPANION TO SPIRITS AND COCKTAILS (David Wondrich et al. eds., Oxford Univ. Press 2021).

8. SASHA PETRASKE, REGARDING COCKTAILS (Phaidon Press 2016).

9. TED SAUCIER, BOTTOMS UP (Greystone Press 1951).

10. ROBERT SIMONSON, A PROPER DRINK: THE UNTOLD STORY OF HOW A BAND OF BARTENDERS SAVED THE CIVILIZED DRINKING WORLD (Ten Speed Press 2016).

11. JERRY THOMAS, BAR-TENDER'S GUIDE, OR HOW TO MIX DRINKS, OR THE BON VIVANT'S COMPANION (New York, Dick & Fitzgerald 1862).

12. DAVID WONDRICH, IMBIBE! UPDATED AND REVISED EDITION: FROM ABSINTHE COCKTAIL TO WHISKEY SMASH, A SALUTE IN STORIES AND DRINKS TO "PROFESSOR" JERRY THOMAS, PIONEER OF THE AMERICAN BAR (Perigee Books 2015).

Acknowledgments

This book almost never came into being. When everything locked down because of the COVID-19 pandemic in early 2020, my sudden inability to order a cocktail motivated me to try my hand at mixing my own. My oldest and dearest friend insisted I resist the temptation to begin that adventure by purchasing a gigantic book of cocktail recipes. Instead, he suggested I start by learning about techniques and the *why* behind good cocktail recipes. It was great advice—as usual. Once I began learning about individual cocktails, curiosity drove me to delve into their histories. After a cocktail (or two) one evening, I began typing. A small ember of an idea resembling a scaled-down version of the Manhattan chapter was kindled into a raging inferno through the encouragement of my wife, my stepfather, a former classmate, and the Editor-in-Chief from my days at the *Houston Law Review*. As time passed and the book progressed, my personal bar at home went from having a grand total of 4 bottles to an almost respectable 40. Over that same period, I amassed an expanded collection of books about history, areas of the law outside my typical practice, and (of course) cocktails.

Then there were the people I met along the way— virtually, anyway. Researching this book connected me with several attorneys in other jurisdictions as well as the authors of several fine books. It also reconnected me with a few professors and classmates I lost touch with through the years. I owe all of these people (and so many more that are not mentioned here) a great deal of gratitude. Researching and writing this book was a whole lot of fun, but having old and new friends to share a cocktail with is perhaps the greatest outcome of this venture. *Prost!*

About the Author

Michael is an attorney in Houston, Texas. When he is not trying out new cocktails or reading books about history, he enjoys woodworking with hand tools, driving standard transmission automobiles, watching bad movies, making sure dogs (especially golden retrievers) know how special they are, and spending time with his wife and daughters. He firmly believes sparkling wine is not a substitute for Champagne, the book is usually better than the movie, and *Die Hard* (20th Century Fox 1988) is a Christmas movie.

This is his first (and perhaps only) book. He has no website, blog, or podcast to his name. He is neither a bestselling author nor has he ever been the keynote speaker at a major function. But he does believe if Nicholas Cage can win an Academy Award® for Best Actor, you can accomplish anything you set your mind to . . . within reason.

APPENDIX A:
GARNISHES FOR THE PAPER PLANE

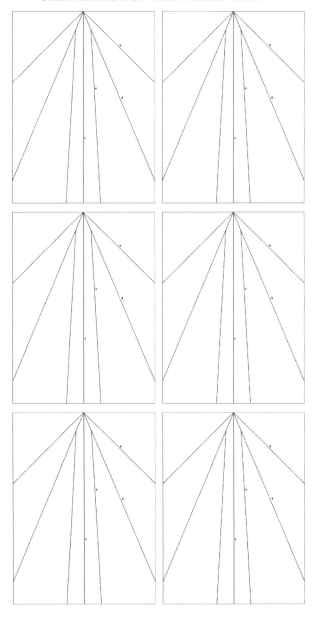

Made in the USA
Monee, IL
02 August 2022

ce88c94a-e222-43c1-a35b-16879a989fa3R02